COMMON CORE
English Language Arts

in a PLC at Work™

GRADES 6-8

DOUGLAS FISHER
NANCY FREY
Foreword by Rick Wormeli

A Joint Publication With

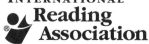
INTERNATIONAL
Reading
Association

555 North Morton Street
Bloomington, IN 47404
800.733.6786 (toll free) / 812.336.7700
FAX: 812.336.7790

email: info@solution-tree.com
solution-tree.com

Visit **go.solution-tree.com/commoncore** to download the reproducibles in this book.

Printed in the United States of America

16 15 14 13   2 3 4 5

IRA Stock No. 9248

Library of Congress Cataloging-in-Publication Data

Fisher, Douglas, 1965- author.

   Common core English language arts in a PLC at work, grades 6-8 / Douglas Fisher, Nancy Frey ; foreword by Rick Wormeli.

          pages cm

   "A joint publication with IRA."

   Includes bibliographical references and index.

   ISBN 978-1-936764-22-8 (perfect bound) 1. Language arts (Middle school)--Standards--United States. 2. Language arts (Middle school)--Curricula--United States. 3. Professional learning communities--United States. I. Frey, Nancy, 1959- author. II. Title.

   LB1631.F566 2013

   428.0071'2--dc23

                         2012038341

Solution Tree

Jeffrey C. Jones, CEO
Edmund M. Ackerman, President

Solution Tree Press
President: Douglas M. Rife
Publisher: Robert D. Clouse
Editorial Director: Lesley Bolton
Managing Production Editor: Caroline Wise
Senior Production Editors: Joan Irwin and Suzanne Kraszewski
Copy Editor: Sarah Payne-Mills
Proofreader: Ashante Thomas
Cover and Text Designer: Jenn Taylor
Text Compositor: Rian Anderson

ACKNOWLEDGMENTS

Solution Tree Press would like to thank the following reviewers:

Rene Barrow
Seventh-Grade English Language Arts Teacher
Tanglewood Middle School
Greenville, South Carolina

Kathy D'Amico
Sixth-Grade Teacher
Lordship Elementary School
Stratford, Connecticut

Naja Freeman
Seventh-Grade Language Arts Teacher
Bunche Middle School
Atlanta, Georgia

Jessica Monroe
Sixth-Grade Teacher
Fairview Elementary School
Bloomington, Indiana

Visit **go.solution-tree.com/commoncore** to download
the reproducibles in this book.

TABLE OF CONTENTS

About the Authors. vii

Foreword. ix

Introduction 1

    Professional Development and Professional Learning Communities 3

    Purpose of This Book 4

    Organization of This Book. 4

CHAPTER 1

Using Collaborative Teams for English Language Arts 7

    The Common Core State Standards 12

    Shift One: Focus on Reading and Writing to Inform, Persuade, and Convey
        Experiences. 13

    Shift Two: Focus on Increasing Text Complexity 14

    Shift Three: Focus on Speaking and Listening. 15

    Shift Four: Focus on Text-Based Evidence for Argumentation 17

    Shift Five: Focus on Academic Vocabulary and Language 18

    Purposes and Organization of the CCSS ELA. 20

    What Is Not Covered in the Standards 22

    Conclusion 24

CHAPTER 2

Implementing the Common Core State Standards for Reading 25

    A Collaborative Planning Team in Action 26

    Anchor Standards for Reading 29

    Reading Standards for Literature in Grades 6–8 36

Reading Standards for Informational Text in Grades 6–8 46

Conclusion 57

CHAPTER 3

Implementing the Common Core State Standards for Writing **59**

A Collaborative Planning Team in Action 60

Anchor Standards for Writing 60

Characteristics of Writers 66

Writing Standards for Grades 6–8 70

The Writing Process 87

Conclusion 94

CHAPTER 4

Implementing the Common Core State Standards for Speaking and Listening and for Language **97**

A Collaborative Planning Team in Action 98

Anchor Standards for Speaking and Listening 99

The Power of Peer Learning 104

Speaking and Listening Standards for Grades 6–8 104

Anchor Standards for Language 111

Language Standards for Grades 6–8 115

Conclusion 129

CHAPTER 5

Implementing Formative Assessments to Guide Instruction and Intervention **131**

A Collaborative Planning Team in Action 132

The Role of Assessment and the Common Core State Standards 132

Feed Up, Back, and Forward 135

Formative and Summative Assessments 142

What to Do When Students Struggle 146

Assessment, Intervention, and Instruction 149

Conclusion 152

References and Resources **155**

Index **165**

ABOUT THE AUTHORS

Douglas Fisher, PhD, is a professor of educational leadership at San Diego State University and a teacher leader at Health Sciences High and Middle College. He teaches courses in instructional improvement. As a classroom teacher, Fisher focuses on English language arts instruction. He also serves as the literacy instructional advisor to the Chula Vista Elementary School District.

Fisher received an International Reading Association Celebrate Literacy Award for his work on literacy leadership and was elected to the board of directors in 2012. For his work as codirector of the City Heights Professional Development Schools, Fisher received the Christa McAuliffe award. He was corecipient of the Farmer Award for excellence in writing from the National Council of Teachers of English for the article, "Using Graphic Novels, Anime, and the Internet in an Urban High School," published in the *English Journal*.

Fisher has written numerous articles on reading and literacy, differentiated instruction, and curriculum design. His books include *In a Reading State of Mind*, *Checking for Understanding*, *Better Learning Through Structured Teaching*, and *Text Complexity*.

He earned a bachelor's degree in communication, a master's degree in public health education, and a doctoral degree in multicultural education. Fisher completed postdoctoral study at the National Association of State Boards of Education focused on standards-based reforms.

Nancy Frey, PhD, is a professor of literacy in the School of Teacher Education at San Diego State University. Through the university's teacher-credentialing and reading specialist programs, she teaches courses on elementary and secondary reading instruction and literacy in content areas, classroom management, and supporting students with diverse learning needs. Frey also teaches at Health Sciences High and Middle College in San Diego. She was a board member of the California Reading Association and a credentialed special educator, reading specialist, and administrator in California.

Before joining the university faculty, Frey was a public school teacher in Florida. She worked at the state level for the Florida Inclusion Network helping districts design systems for supporting students with disabilities in general education classrooms.

She is the recipient of the 2008 Early Career Achievement Award from the National Reading Conference and the Christa McAuliffe Award for excellence in teacher education from the American Association of State Colleges and Universities. She was corecipient of the Farmer Award for excellence in writing from the National Council of Teachers of English for the article "Using Graphic Novels, Anime, and the Internet in an Urban High School."

Frey is author of *The Formative Assessment Action Plan*, *Productive Group Work*, *Teaching Students to Read Like Detectives*, and *Content-Area Conversations*. She has written articles for *The Reading Teacher*, *Journal of Adolescent and Adult Literacy*, *English Journal*, *Voices From the Middle*, *Middle School Journal*, *Remedial and Special Education*, and *Educational Leadership*.

To book Douglas Fisher or Nancy Frey for professional development, contact pd@solution-tree.com.

FOREWORD

Gathered in the conference room of a local school, English teachers discuss one of the new eighth-grade Common Core State Standards (CCSS) they have to teach: "Cite the textual evidence that most strongly supports an analysis of what the text says explicitly as well as inferences drawn from the text."

One teacher asks, "What are we going to accept as the proper way to cite textual evidence in a written analysis? And how much textual evidence will we require students to use to support their claims?"

Another teacher mulls over a common error her students make. She asks, "What if the student cites enough evidence but it's for an incorrect claim? Or, what if the student is novel or stylistic in some way—will that be acceptable as long as he or she fulfills the general criteria?"

The group agrees that these concerns need to be addressed, but then a new round of questions arises: "How specific does a student need to be in order to demonstrate being explicit? Is the analysis complete if he or she just makes the claim and cites evidence without a line or two to tie it all back to the theme? What does 'as well as inferences drawn from the text' mean? Does it mean students make inferences about the text and back them up with text references or outside-the-text references? Are students supposed to comment on the quality of inferences within the text? What if they can do it with one piece of text but not another or they can do it one week, but can't do it next month? What text formats will we require students to analyze in this manner?" Finally, looking at the school's 4.0 grading scale, one teacher asks, "What will constitute Exceeds the Standard on our scale?"

Reflecting on these questions, the department chair says, "This is going to take some time. Let's pour the coffee and get started."

The issues these teachers express represent the challenges involved in unwrapping the CCSS. But asking such questions doesn't address the concerns for how to breathe life into the CCSS in classrooms with real students—including students with special needs—in urban, rural, suburban, and distance-learning situations.

Within the hour, that department chair is going to wish she had an insightful book that could create a clear vision for her department as well as provide realistic procedures for implementing the Common Core that make the process and the standards compelling. Thank goodness Douglas Fisher and Nancy Frey spend considerable time, energy, and expertise doing just that in this book, *Common Core English Language Arts in a PLC at Work™, Grades 6–8.*

The Common Core State Standards are a response to simplistic views of learning evident in standardized testing, which has consumed millions of dollars, endless work hours, and political hype for improving student performance. Being good at taking standardized tests doesn't qualify students for creative contribution to society or successful citizenship as adults. These test structures have encouraged students to believe that academic success comes only by identifying one correct answer. The CCSS confront this dilemma with expectations that in the 21st century students will need to be able to pose important questions and follow through on their investigations of them. Students must understand complexity, nuance, and multiple perspectives. Test-score emphasis has narrowed the curriculum in many schools and elevated a one-size-fits-all approach as the only acceptable route to student learning.

In the 21st century, we know our students need more than basic recall skills to be college and career ready. They require mental dexterity and skill versatility to remain competitive. It's worth emphasizing, however, that the CCSS are basic competencies, not the full curriculum for a state or local district, nor are the CCSS the cure-all for all that ails our schools. Luckily, gifted thinkers, Douglas and Nancy, have not only made the CCSS compelling and useable but also given us the analytical mindset and strategic practices we can employ with any set of standards, Common Core or future version thereof. *Common Core English Language Arts in a PLC at Work™, Grades 6–8* is a welcome lifeline to teachers and schools drowning in Common Core mandates and wanting to do right by their students.

Importantly, Douglas and Nancy do not speak in abstractions. They use applicable classroom scenarios representing real needs of young adolescents in order for teachers and principals to see themselves using the tools in the book. These examples of classroom practice and teacher collaboration are fully connected to the tenets of *This We Believe* from the Association for Middle Level Education (www.amle.org). Furthermore, they provide a concise overview of up-to-date research in each chapter without losing momentum or becoming pedantic. Cogent in their incorporation of all things English (reading, writing, speaking, listening, viewing, media literacy, vocabulary acquisition, and critical and creative thinking), they wisely thread formative assessment, descriptive feedback, and collaboration.

Additionally, Douglas and Nancy are careful to note what the CCSS are and are not, and they provide specific insight in terms of what to expect and what to avoid when implementing the CCSS in an English language arts program. Their work here helps teachers and their leaders work smarter, not harder, helping us prioritize and save time. This book should be consulted when constructing teacher professional development for Common Core implementation and before reforming English language arts programs of study.

Three areas of particular expertise stand out. First, Douglas and Nancy make vivid connections between the Common Core and the requirements of response to intervention (RTI) programs that are sure to open many minds. Second, they tackle one of the biggest stumbling blocks of English language arts teachers and CCSS implementation: the need for steadily increasing text complexity. The authors' inspired approach to this aspect provides effectives vehicles for building students' proficiencies, and their examples demonstrate deep expertise in literacy and a widely read background—many of our favorite novels and poems are incorporated into their suggestions. Third, and perhaps most importantly, they ask their audience to be the reflective practitioners necessary to be highly accomplished teachers. They do this at every turn via their insights on the collaborative processes of professional learning communities (PLCs) and invitations to annotate text and incorporate technology. The classroom scenarios depict this essential collaboration and show how faculty thinking can be revised in light of new evidence. Just as impressive, the vignettes illustrate in real time the effective learning sequences and contemplative acts the authors recommend teachers use in their classrooms, showing that actions speak louder than words.

There's no question that the book is written with the teacher in mind. Truly, the most frequent comment teachers are likely to make while reading is, "I can really use this!" Douglas and Nancy have been there, done that, and improved our profession in the process. They acknowledge skills and perspectives that help teachers transcend current teaching algorithms yet are not taught often in schools of teacher preparation.

I've been a fan of Douglas and Nancy for years. Time spent with them at a conference or via their writings is time well spent. In this new endeavor of theirs, I invite you to do your part and elevate the playing field for all students by incorporating these ideas into your own classrooms. Well-fortified, let's begin.

—Rick Wormeli

INTRODUCTION

The investment of time and expertise by schools and districts to make the transformation into an effective Professional Learning Community (PLC) at Work™ is about to pay off once again. The adoption of the Common Core State Standards for English language arts (CCSS ELA) represents a significant change in how the education profession looks at curriculum, instruction, and assessment. In addition, the implications for implementation of the CCSS ELA will have ramifications for years to come. As new research on best practices related to the Common Core State Standards is conducted and disseminated, educators will need to interpret these results and determine how best to put them into practice. The PLC process offers an ideal foundational system for doing so. This process provides the necessary conditions and support to accomplish the work of ensuring continuous improvement. Ongoing professional development is embedded into the process, because teachers work as members of high-performing collaborative teams. Becoming a PLC is a process of reculturing a school; the concept is not just another meeting (DuFour, DuFour, & Eaker, 2008; Frey, Fisher, & Everlove, 2009). Effective districtwide or schoolwide PLCs have the following six characteristics (DuFour et al., 2008; DuFour, DuFour, Eaker, & Many, 2010).

1. **Shared mission, vision, values, and goals all focused on student learning:** The *mission* defines why the organization exists; the *vision* defines what the organization can become in the future; the *values* consist of demonstrated attitudes and behaviors that further the vision; and the *goals* are markers used to determine results and assess progress. A thriving PLC immerses itself in the behaviors necessary to the development of these concepts.

2. **A collaborative culture with a focus on learning:** *Collaboration*, an essential ingredient in the PLC process, enables people to work interdependently to improve teaching and learning.

3. **Collective inquiry into best practice and current reality:** *Collective inquiry* is the process through which PLC educators strive to build shared knowledge about research and what works in their classrooms.

4. **Action orientation:** An *action orientation* is characteristic of successful PLCs that learn by doing and recognize the significance and necessity of actions that engage their members in planning learning tasks, implementing them, and evaluating results.

5. **A commitment to continuous improvement:** *Continuous improvement* is a cyclical process that PLCs use to plan, implement, and check to determine the effectiveness of their efforts to improve teaching and learning.

6. **Results orientation:** *Results* are what count for PLCs; they are the measurable outcomes that reveal the success of the collaborative efforts to improve teaching and learning. Results outweigh intentions.

Visit **www.allthingsplc.info** for a glossary of PLC terms.

These six characteristics must be woven into the fabric of the school; they have to become part of the air that teachers, parents, students, and administrators breathe. In creating this culture, PLCs must reach agreement on fundamental issues, including (DuFour et al., 2008):

- What content students should learn

- What common and coherent assessments to develop and use to determine if students have learned the agreed-on curriculum

- How to respond when students do or don't learn the agreed-on curriculum

To accomplish these three tasks, teachers need adequate time to collaborate with their colleagues. We are not suggesting that scheduling time for teachers to collaborate is easy, but without dedicated time, teams will not develop the collaborative structures needed to support student learning, especially if teachers are going to address the Common Core State Standards in grades 6–8. As part of their collaborative team time, teachers in PLCs engage in inquiry into student learning. The following four critical questions of a PLC highlight and provide a foundation for the work of collaborative planning teams (DuFour et al., 2008).

1. What do we want our students to learn?

2. How will we know when they have learned it?

3. How will we respond when some students don't learn?

4. How will we extend and enrich the learning for students who are already proficient?

Professional Development and Professional Learning Communities

Linda Darling-Hammond (2010) summarizes the research on effective professional development as follows:

> Effective professional development is sustained, ongoing, content-focused, and embedded in professional learning communities where teachers work overtime on problems of practice with other teachers in their subject area or school. Furthermore, it focuses on concrete tasks of teaching, assessment, observation, and reflection, looking at how students learn specific content in particular contexts. . . . It is often useful for teachers to be put in the position of studying the very material that they intend to teach to their own students. (pp. 226–227)

In other words, effective professional development is often the opposite of what most teachers receive—it is sustained and embedded within the work of professional learning communities and focused on the actual tasks of teaching using the material teachers use with students. Professional development practices have moved beyond stand-alone workshops to ones that are tied to a school's chosen area of focus. Through the work of researchers like Bruce Joyce and Beverly Showers (1983) and others, educators began to understand that professional development could be linked to the change process. In particular, the value of an agreed-on focus, the need for continued support after the session, and a plan for measuring success have become expected elements of any school's professional development plan. To succeed as a high-performance school, professional development should be part of a teacher's overall involvement in a learning community.

The link between professional development and school change has been further strengthened through PLCs (Eaker, DuFour, & DuFour, 2002). PLCs recognize that teacher collaboration lies at the heart of learning and change. Collaborative planning teams within PLCs are able to bridge theory to practice as they convene regularly to examine student performance data, discuss student progress, develop and implement curricula, and coach one another through meaningful collaborative work between meetings.

The evidence of PLC effectiveness is mounting. A study of elementary teachers in PLCs identifies a strong statistical correlation between their participation in professional learning communities, their classroom cultures, and their use of formative assessments to advance learning (Birenbaum, Kimron, & Shilton, 2011). Robert Bullough and Steven Baugh (2008) find that the conditions created to foster a schoolwide PLC in turn deepened a school-university partnership. In an analysis of nearly four hundred schools as PLCs, Louise Stoll, Ray Bolam, Agnes McMahon, Mike Wallace, and Sally Thomas (2006) note a positive relationship between student achievement, adoption of innovative practices, and healthy learning communities. In fact, Robert Marzano notes that school and district-level PLCs are "probably the most influential movement with regards to actually changing practices in schools" (DuFour & Marzano, 2011, p. x).

Purpose of This Book

We hope we have made the case, however, briefly, that a PLC at the school or district level is vital to school change. Furthermore, collaborative planning teams functioning within the school's PLC provide embedded professional development that sustains change.

In fact, chances are good that you are interested in this book because it promises to link an important change—implementing the Common Core State Standards in English language arts—with a process you already know to be powerful: professional learning communities. The remainder of this book provides collaborative teacher teams with information about the *what* and the *how* of teaching students to master these standards, including how to develop effective formative assessment and respond when students fail to make progress. We expand the Common Core standards so that you and your team can examine them in detail. You will find that each chapter begins with questions for your team to consider, and we invite you to return to these after you examine the standards to discuss implications for instruction, curriculum, assessment, and intervention.

Organization of This Book

This book has been crafted with your collaborative team in mind. Use it as a workbook—mark it up, dog-ear the pages, highlight passages that resonate, underline the ones that raise a question. In the same way that the Common Core ELA standards focus our collective attention on the practices of close reading and argumentation, we hope to contribute to a similar process for your team. The conversation begins in chapter 1 with an overview of the CCSS and the major shifts in our practices as these relate to informational texts, the role of speaking and listening in learning, the development of academic language and vocabulary, and the importance of argumentation in writing. Later in chapter 1, we explain how the standards are organized, so that the thirty-three-page original document and its three appendices become a bit less bewildering. We also discuss what the standards don't say: about English learners, students with special needs, and those who struggle with literacy. The National Governors Association Center for Best Practices (NGA) and Council of Chief State School Officers (CCSSO), developers of the CCSS, provide some general guidelines for students learning English and those who struggle in school, but these are brief summaries and will likely generate a great deal of additional ideas for implementation (for more information, visit www.corestandards.org/the -standards for the documents "Application of Common Core State Standards for English Language Learners" and "Application to Students With Disabilities"). Importantly, these gaps highlight why PLCs are so important. In the words of the NGA and CCSSO (2010a):

> While the Standards focus on what is most essential, they do not describe all that can or should be taught. A great deal is left to the discretion of teachers and curriculum developers. The aim of the Standards is to articulate the fundamentals, not to set out an exhaustive list or a set of restrictions that limits what can be taught beyond what is specified herein. (p. 6)

Chapters 2, 3, and 4 form the heart of this book because they each focus on a specific *strand* addressed in the CCSS. Reading is the subject of chapter 2: each and every standard is examined as it applies to literary and informational texts, as well as the important reading foundational skills of phonics, word recognition, and fluency that are critical in the development of readers in grades 6–8. Chapter 3 turns the spotlight to the Writing standards and similarly reviews each standard as it applies to the major text types of student writing: opinion and persuasive, informative and explanatory, and narrative. In chapter 4, we discuss the two sets of Common Core standards that are integral to what we teach and how students learn—through speaking and listening and by understanding and producing academic language and vocabulary.

Chapter 5 returns to the subject of student consideration in the CCSS, including discussion on using formative assessment processes and summative assessment instruments informatively, and designing and implementing interventions for students who are not performing at expected levels.

Know that this book has been designed with you in mind. All of the research cited is specific to grades 6–8. In addition, we've designed scenarios written from the perspective of teachers and students in grades 6–8 to illuminate the standards.

These scenarios are fictionalized accounts of our personal teaching activities and our collective experience working with teachers across grade levels in schools with diverse populations. We have developed these scenarios as a way to make the ELA standards come alive for you. We want you to personalize this experience as you and your collaborative team plan for implementation of the Common Core for English language arts. To begin this process, we encourage you to reflect on and discuss with your colleagues the following questions.

1. What is the status of collaborative teams at your school? Acknowledging the reality of your school's commitment to an effective PLC process is a critical first step that can establish the future direction for collaborative professional growth. Recall the six characteristics of effective PLCs (pages 1–2) and consider the extent to which your PLC embodies these characteristics. If you want to delve deeper into your school's PLC status, you can explore where your school would place on the PLC continuum: preinitiating, initiating, implementing, developing, or sustaining (DuFour et al., 2010). Visit www.allthingsplc.info and search the Tools & Resources section for helpful PLC reproducibles, such as the PLC continuum reproducible "Laying the Foundation" from *Learning by Doing* (DuFour et al., 2010).

2. How are your students performing? Are there areas of need in terms of curriculum development? Are there areas of need in terms of instruction? Are there areas of need in terms of assessment? These questions address key topics for your PLC to consider as you focus on the current status of your school's language arts programs in relation to the expectations of the Common Core ELA standards. Discussions with your collaborative team will enable you

to gain insight into *where you are* and *where you need to go* to support and advance your students' language development.

We've designed this book to guide the conversations that are necessary to fully implement the Common Core State Standards. As such, it should serve as a resource that you return to regularly to consider the ways in which student learning can be improved. The anchor standards and the grade-level expectations are the outcomes expected of us as teachers. *Common Core English Language Arts in a PLC at Work, Grades 6–8* provides the process to get there.

CHAPTER 1

Using Collaborative Teams for English Language Arts

KEY QUESTIONS

- To what extent does your team understand the conceptual shifts represented in the Common Core State Standards for English language arts?

- How often are informational texts used in instruction across the day?

- To what extent do teachers at your school use complex texts?

- Do students routinely discuss and develop texts that feature arguments with supporting evidence?

- To what extent do teachers at your school focus on speaking and listening activities?

- In what ways do teachers at your school develop academic vocabulary and language?

A team of seventh-grade English teachers is meeting to discuss the results of a common formative assessment the team recently administered. The teachers had previously agreed on a pacing guide for their unit focused on informative text and had discussed the various ways that they would teach the unit. Unlike most previous state standards, the Common Core State Standards require an integrated approach to lesson development in which teachers build student competence in multiple standards simultaneously. As an example, the teachers' three-week unit had its primary focus on the Reading Standards for Literature (RL.7) and Reading Standards for Writing (W.7) at the seventh-grade level (NGA & CCSSO, 2010a):

- Cite several pieces of textual evidence to support analysis of what the text says explicitly as well as inferences drawn from the text. (RL.7.1)

- Determine the meaning of words and phrases as they are used in a text, including figurative, connotative, and technical meanings; analyze the impact of a specific word choice on meaning and tone. (RL.7.4)

- Write informative/explanatory texts to examine a topic and convey ideas, concepts, and information through the selection, organization, and analysis of relevant content. (W.7.2) (pp. 36, 42)

Of course, teachers always have to consider the complexity of the text and ensure that students are reading appropriate materials. As part of their common formative assessment, these teachers wanted to determine if students could summarize and inform readers using material explicitly stated in a text. As part of the assessment, the teachers asked students to read a selection from *Phineas Gage: A Gruesome but True Story About*

Brain Science (Fleischman, 2002), a text about a man in 1848 who survived an accident in which a large iron bar passed through his head, leaving him with brain damage that affected his personality. His alarming change in behavior after the accident led scientists to understand for the first time that specific regions of the brain govern personality and behavior. See figure 1.1.

The most unlucky and lucky moment in the life of Phineas Gage is only a minute or two away. It's almost four-thirty in the afternoon on September 13, 1848. Phineas is the fore-man of a track construction gang that is in the process of blasting a railroad right-of-way through Cavendish, Vermont. Phineas is twenty-six years old, unmarried, and five feet, six inches tall, short for our time but about average for his. He is good with his hands and good with his men, "possessing an iron will as well as an iron frame," according to his doctor. In a moment, Phineas will have a horrible accident. **STOP**

It will kill him, but it will take another eleven years, six months, and nineteen days to do so. In the short run, Phineas will make a full recovery, or so it will seem to those who didn't know him before. Old friends and family will know the truth. Phineas will never be his old self again. His character will change. Long after the accident, his doctor will make him world famous, but fame will do him little good. Yet for many others—psychologists, medical researchers, doctors, and especially those who suffer brain injuries—Phineas Gage will become someone worth knowing. **STOP**

That's why we know so much about Phineas. It's been 150 years since his accident, yet we are still learning more about him. There's also a lot about Phineas we don't know and probably never will. The biggest question is the simplest one and the hardest one to answer: Was Phineas lucky or unlucky? Once you hear his story, you can decide for yourself. But right now, Phineas is working on the railroad, and his time has nearly come. **STOP**

Building a railroad in 1848 is muscle work. There are no bulldozers or power shovels to open a way through Vermont's Green Mountains for the Rutledge & Burlington Railroad. Phineas's men work with picks, shovels, and rock drills. Phineas's special skill is blasting. With well-placed charges of black gunpowder, he shatters rock. To set those charges, he carries a special tool of the blasting trade, his "tamping iron." Some people confuse a tamping iron with a crowbar, but they are different tools for different jobs. **STOP**

A tamping iron is for the delicate job of setting explosives. Phineas had his tamping iron made to order by a neighborhood blacksmith. It's a tamping iron rod that is three feet, seven inches long and weighs thirteen and a half pounds. It looks like an iron spear. At the base, it's fat and round, an inch and three quarters in diameter. The fat end is for tamping—packing down—loose powder. The other end comes to a sharp, narrow point and is for poking holes through the gunpowder to set the fuse. Phineas's tamping iron is very smooth to the touch, smooth from the blacksmith's forge as well as constant use. **STOP**

Source: Adapted from Fleischman, 2002, pp. 1–2.

Figure 1.1: Excerpt from *Phineas Gage*.

Haylee Ostertag, a teacher on the seventh-grade team, starts by distributing the passage from the beginning of *Phineas Gage*. The students immediately notice that the passage has lines marked "STOP" appearing several times throughout the text.

"We'll be using a technique called GIST to write a summary of the reading," Ms. Ostertag says. "Writing a summary is important for comprehension. It's also a kind of writing you're often asked to do in school. Certain careers also require summary writing—a police officer writes reports, for instance," she continues. "I've marked this reading in several places. At each stopping point, we're going to write one summary sentence containing the important information in that section of the passage. When we're finished, we'll have a string of sentences to form a summary paragraph." She reminds students that summary writing should never be done during the first reading, but only after they have read and understood the entire text.

After the students read the first segment silently, Ms. Ostertag composes a summary sentence using a think-aloud strategy by stating her decisions as a writer verbally. She discusses how she uses a dependent clause to construct a complex sentence containing multiple ideas. She also points out that Phineas's age, height, and town are probably not important details in a summary. She writes the following sentence on a language chart: "Phineas Gage, a railroad worker in Vermont, is about to have a terrible accident."

She repeats the process for the next segment, this time composing the summary sentence with the students' assistance. They agree on the following: "He will survive for eleven years after the accident, and others will learn about how the brain works, but he will never be the same."

Satisfied that students have the hang of it, Ms. Ostertag turns the writing over to them. After adding the first two sentences to their journals, they continue reading and writing several more summary sentences. Ms. Ostertag observes one student, Edgar, as he writes, pausing to ask him questions about word choice and writing conventions when he gets stuck.

As students finish, Ms. Ostertag invites them to re-read their summary sentences as a single piece of text, making necessary edits as they go. Karanne's completed GIST summary reads:

> Phineas Gage, a railroad worker in Vermont, is about to have a terrible accident. He will survive for eleven years after the accident, and others will learn about how the brain works, but he will never be the same. Everyone wonders whether Gage was lucky or unlucky to survive. Phineas had the dangerous job of blasting rock to build the railroad. An important tool for his railroad work was the tamping rod, 3'7", 13.5-pound iron bar used to set explosives.

Following the assessment, the members of the collaborative planning team meet and focus their attention on answering two of the guiding questions of a PLC (DuFour et al., 2008): How will we respond when some students don't learn, and how will we extend and enrich the learning for students who have already demonstrated mastery?

Jim Davenport starts the conversation by saying, "They really did get this one. In about 80 percent of the cases, students were able to provide key information from the text. I'm also really impressed with their use of domain-specific vocabulary."

Haylee Ostertag chimes in, "I agree, they are getting the hang of summarizing, and now we have to get them to really move to more formal types of papers. How can we do this?"

Isabel Jorgensen responds, "I'd like to try modeling some more, specifically using examples. I'd be willing to find some texts and write some sample modeling lessons, if you think that would help." Ms. Ostertag enthusiastically agrees, adding, "I appreciate our time together and your offer to provide us with resources."

Mr. Davenport adds, "I agree. Thank you so much. I feel like we have a handle on that, or at least a plan. So what else do we see in this data? What about the 20 percent who still can't really summarize information? What do we do about them?"

Ms. Ostertag says, "I'll develop some reteaching lessons. What do you think about having them attend some of the after-school tutorials with some specific review content?"

The other teachers agree and decide that they should meet in a week to review the intervention plans and efforts.

Conversations like this are possible when teachers have had the opportunity to work together in collaborative planning teams. To teach the Common Core State Standards well, teachers need to collaborate with their colleagues. In doing so, they can ensure learning for *all* students. It is imperative that collaborative team members work to answer the four critical questions of a PLC as they devote attention to the CCSS (DuFour et al., 2008).

1. What do we want our students to learn?

2. How will we know when they have learned it?

3. How will we respond when some students don't learn?

4. How will we extend and enrich the learning for students who are already proficient?

In other words, teachers need to plan together, look at student work together, identify needs for reteaching together, trust one another, and ask for help when they need it. Figure 1.2 provides a tool we have found useful in helping collaborative teams work together. As part of their overall PLC work, collaborative teams focus on the four critical questions and begin to build the culture of the school in which student learning drives the discussions teachers and administrators have.

Over time, teams will modify and change the tool to suit their unique needs, but to start, it is likely useful to focus on each aspect of the tool. At the top of the form ("Collaborative Team Meeting Logistics"), teachers record the grade level, the date of the meeting, who was facilitating, and who was in attendance. Given that there are different phases that a collaborative team uses to complete the work, we ask that the team agree on its focus for each of its collaborative meeting times. Importantly, there may be two or more foci during a meeting, and we ask teams to complete different forms for each shift in focus. The reason for this is simple: the team learns to integrate the stages as a habit of interaction when it names each stage each time. It also provides a record that the team can use to review past efforts to improve student achievement. School systems are very good at documenting when things are going wrong and not so good at recording successes. Using a tool like the one in figure 1.2 provides a record of success that team members can review when they need to revisit a successful time in the past.

Collaborative Team Meeting Logistics	
Grade:	Date:
Lead teacher or facilitator:	
Teachers in attendance:	

Focus
 	
(Check one.)
    ☐ Curriculum pacing guide
    ☐ Strategy implementation
    ☐ Coaching practice
    ☐ Consensus scoring cycle
        + Common assessment development
        + Item analysis (See Item Analysis Summary.)	

Discussion points:	Questions raised:
Objective for the coming week:	Resources needed:
Implementation steps:	
Item Analysis Summary	
Assessment tool:	
Areas of strength in student work:	
Areas of weakness in student work:	
Teacher practice: What should be preserved?	
Teacher practice: Identify gaps between existing and desired practice.	
Teacher practice: What aspects of existing practice pose a barrier to implementing desired practice?	
Teacher practice: Identify interventions or unit modifications.	
Unanswered questions:	

Source: Adapted from Fisher & Frey, 2007a. Reprinted with permission. Learn more about ASCD at www.ascd.org.

Figure 1.2: Collaborative team meeting record.

Visit **go.solution-tree.com/commoncore** for a reproducible version of this figure.

The remainder of the logistics portion of the form focuses on the discussion that team members have, including the development of pacing guides, teaching strategy implementation, and peer advice and coaching. During some of the meetings, the team will develop common assessments or review the results of an assessment. We recommend that teams use the "Item Analysis Summary" portion when they are discussing assessment results since there are a number of specific decisions to be made in terms of intervention and changes in practice.

Teachers are able to hold these types of conversations because they understand the power of PLCs and the conceptual shifts in the Common Core State Standards for English language arts. They also know the specific standards for their grade level and how these are developed across grades 6–8. In this chapter, we will discuss these major shifts represented in the CCSS, especially their implications for teaching English language arts. In addition, we will highlight what is *not* included in the standards.

The Common Core State Standards

The adoption of the Common Core State Standards for English language arts extends a trend in U.S. education to collaborate across organizations in order to obtain better learning results. Standards-driven policies and practices have yielded notable results, especially in our collective efforts to articulate purposes and learning outcomes to our stakeholders (Gamoran, 2007). This in turn has led to improved alignment between curriculum, instruction, and assessment. But the years have also exposed weaknesses of this system, many of which are related to the disjointed efforts of individual states trying to put their own standards in motion. No matter how effective the process or product, states simply could not share them with other states, as no standards were held in common. Consequently, states like Arkansas and Arizona could not pool human and fiscal resources to develop common materials and assessments.

As standards-based assessments rose to prominence in the 2000s, a mosaic of testing results made it virtually impossible to fairly compare the effectiveness of reform efforts across states. The National Governors Association Center for Best Practices and Council of Chief State School Officers sought to rectify these shortcomings by sponsoring the development of a shared set of standards each state could agree on. Beginning in 2010, state boards of education began adopting these standards in English language arts and mathematics. In 2012, nearly all the states adopted them and began to determine timelines for implementation, as well as methods for assessment.

In an effort to capitalize on new opportunities for collaboration among states, two assessment consortia are developing standards-based assessments. Both the Partnership for Assessment of Readiness for College and Careers (PARCC) and the Smarter Balanced Assessment Consortium (SBAC) consist of representatives from states working to develop assessments of the standards. Some states belong to both and will eventually determine which instruments they will use. While these efforts are works in progress, common themes are emerging from both consortia. For one, it is likely that a significant part of the tests will be computer based. In addition, it is anticipated that benchmark assessments will play a prominent role in order for schools to be better able to identify students who are falling behind. But perhaps the biggest shift in these assessments has to do with the ELA standards themselves. (Visit www.parcconline.org or www.smarterbalanced.org for more information.) In the next section, we will outline five major shifts to how we view literacy teaching and learning.

Shift One: Focus on Reading and Writing to Inform, Persuade, and Convey Experiences

The Common Core ELA standards reflect a trend in elementary literacy that has been occurring since the 1990s: a deepening appreciation of the importance of informational and persuasive texts in a student's *reading diet*, or the range of reading genre and materials students encounter across the year. (For now, we will focus our discussion on informational texts, with further attention to persuasive texts featured later in this chapter in the section on argumentation.) The reasons for increasing informational text usage are often related to the need to improve content knowledge (Moss, 2005), to meet increased demand in digital environments (Schmar-Dobler, 2003), and even to address the so-called *fourth-grade slump* (Chall & Jacobs, 2003), which suggests that student achievement stagnates starting in fourth grade. Perhaps reflective of these efforts, access to and use of informational texts appears to be increasing in elementary school. Jongseong Jeong, Janet Gaffney, and Jin-Oh Choi's (2010) study of second-, third-, and fourth-grade classrooms' informational text usage finds that while use hovers at one minute per day in second-grade classrooms, it greatly accelerates to sixteen minutes per day in third and fourth grades. However, this is still well short of Barbara Moss's (2005) measure of informational text usage on standardized tests—50 percent at the fourth-grade level.

The National Assessment of Educational Progress (NAEP), sometimes called "the nation's report card," has steadily increased the use of informational text passages on its assessments of fourth-, eighth-, and twelfth-grade students across the United States. In keeping with this initiative, the CCSS ELA recommend an evenly divided diet of literary and informational texts by the fourth grade (see table 1.1, page 14), gradually increasing throughout middle and high school. Keep in mind that this doesn't mean that students in grades 6–8 should no longer be allowed to read narrative text; nothing could be further from the truth. Narrative remains essential as a means of conveying ideas and concepts through story. However, just as a diet limited to only one or two foods cannot provide sufficient nourishment, neither should we limit the types of texts used in the classroom. Furthermore, it is helpful to measure the use of informational text across the school day, not only in the reading and language arts block, in which teachers use a greater volume of literary texts.

Just as the reading diet of learners needs to be expanded, so does their writing repertoire. A key practice is to link the reading of expository texts with original writing in the same genre, as the link between reading and writing abilities is strong in students (Langer, 1986), and there is an especially strong positive longitudinal effect between

Table 1.1: Grade Distribution of Literary and Informational Passages in the 2009 NAEP Framework

Grade	Literary Texts	Informational Texts
4	50 percent	50 percent
8	45 percent	55 percent
12	30 percent	70 percent

Source: Adapted from NGA & CCSSO, 2010a, p. 5.

grades 2 and 6 (Abbott, Berninger, & Fayol, 2010). In other words, consistent exposure to and use of text genres is positively linked to children's growing ability to write within these same genres. In the same way that narrative texts are used as a springboard for young writers to convey their own experiences, informational texts should be used to teach how one explains and persuades. Students in grades 2 through 6 are not fully aware of audience, especially in recognizing what an unseen reader might need or expect from a text they have written (Bereiter & Scardamalia, 1987). When purposefully taught, these skills transfer to students' writing ability, and students' capacity to write grows with age and experience. Susan De La Paz and Steve Graham (2002) find this to be true in their study of the effects of intentional writing instruction on seventh- and eighth-grade students. In classrooms in which planning and writing strategies are taught several times a week, students improve in the areas of developing advanced plans and improving the quality of their expository writing.

The ELA standards for grades 6–8 call for a major investment in the time teachers spend instructing students to raise their ability to comprehend informational and persuasive texts. This may require an assessment of where and when students use these types of texts across the school day. Additionally, there is a renewed expectation that students can also write in these genres. Much of the research on expository writing for grades 6–8 students reinforces what many of us already knew: immersion in these texts, when coupled with explicit instruction, can lead to more sophisticated writing (Duke & Roberts, 2010; Moss, 2004).

Shift Two: Focus on Increasing Text Complexity

Closely related to an emphasis on informational texts is "steadily increasing text complexity" (NGA & CCSSO, 2010b, p. 2). This aspect has received considerable attention as educators figure out how to apply a three-part model for determining how complex a reading really is. In addition, U.S. school teams are working to design methods for accessing complex texts among students who struggle to read, English learners, and students with special needs. The CCSS ELA define text complexity as "the inherent difficulty of reading and comprehending a text combined with consideration of reader and task variables; in the Standards, a three-part assessment of text difficulty that pairs qualitative [factors] and quantitative measures with reader-task considerations" (NGA

& CCSSO, 2010b, p. 43). In other words, it is multidimensional, with attention given to (1) *quantitative measures*, such as readability formulae; (2) *qualitative factors*, such as complexity of ideas, organization, and cohesion; and (3) *reader and task considerations*, such as motivation and task difficulty.

The issue of text complexity raises the case for backward planning, with the outcome being that graduating high school students are sufficiently prepared to tackle the kinds of texts they will encounter as they enter college and careers. While this may initially seem to be a remote goal for teachers in grades 6–8, keeping it in mind is helpful in identifying what texts are useful for students in the intermediate grades.

Appendix B of the Common Core ELA (NGA & CCSSO, 2010c), a useful tool for teachers, includes an extensive list of text exemplars to illustrate this concept of text complexity. These text exemplars should not be misconstrued as a required reading list for a specific grade. To do so would be to ignore the third dimension of identifying complex texts: reader and task considerations. A necessary complication is that text exemplars are arranged somewhat differently across grade bands due to the developmental nature of reading in elementary school. Text exemplars for grades 6–8 are listed together, and there are examples of stories, drama, poetry, and informational texts appropriate for students in these grade levels to understand.

Referenced within the standards document is a *staircase* effect to systematically develop students' capacity for understanding more complex texts (NGA & CCSSO, 2010a). This should be considered at several levels of analysis: within a unit of instruction, throughout a school year, and across multiple grades. That is, the texts a student uses at the beginning of a unit to build background knowledge are more explicit, while those that occur later in a unit to deepen student knowledge are less so. Similarly, the texts students use early in a given school year are less complex than those that occur near the end. In addition, students' capacity and stamina for reading complex texts should build across grade-level bands. For this reason, work concerning text complexity should involve at least two collaborative planning team configurations as teachers work within and across grades 6–8 to articulate a cohesive plan. These horizontal and vertical team collaborations ensure that students experience a cohesive curriculum without gaps or redundancy.

Text complexity poses a major challenge for educators in grades 6–8 as students transition to classroom environments that increasingly rely on texts as a major source of learning. Defining what makes a text complex requires analyzing qualitative factors and quantitative measures, while also considering the characteristics of the reader and the demands of the related task. In addition, the CCSS encourage teachers to look across units, the school year, and grade bands to build a purposeful plan to staircase student capacity for complex texts.

Shift Three: Focus on Speaking and Listening

While oral language development is widely regarded as a key feature of early elementary education, in practice this is more often regarded as being of less importance in grades 6–8, except for students with identified language learning needs. Perhaps this is due to more text-based instruction or too-large class sizes. Whatever the specific reason, there is a noticeable decline in the amount of meaningful discussion that occurs in class-rooms after the primary grades. In observations of 2,500 elementary classrooms, Robert Pianta and colleagues (Pianta, Belsky, Houts, & Morrison, 2007) find that fifth-grade teachers spend less than 7 percent of the school day instructing students for analysis and inference, in contrast to nearly 32 percent devoted to basic skills, 18 percent reserved for managerial instructions, and 17 percent for transitions. Notably, these findings are statis-tically similar to those observed in third- and first-grade classrooms. It is difficult to see how students can develop critical speaking and listening skills when a large part of their school day involves listening to low-level directions. Importantly, this has implications for middle school educators, who need well-prepared students who are ready to engage in high levels of academic discourse.

The CCSS place a strong emphasis on speaking and listening in the primary grades. Furthermore, NGA and CCSSO (2010b) state:

> The importance of oral language extends well beyond the earliest grades. . . . Sticht and James found evidence strongly suggesting that children's listening comprehension outpaces reading comprehension until the middle school years (grades 6–8). (p. 26)

Speaking and listening skills have a concomitant relationship with reading and writ-ing development. To observe this effect, Virginia Berninger and Robert Abbott (2010) examine two cohorts of students from elementary into middle school, measuring their listening comprehension, speaking expression, reading comprehension, and writing com-prehension in grades 1, 3, 5, and 7. They note students' relative strengths and weaknesses vary considerably across the years, supporting the assertion that these language modali-ties are not fixed but rather are influenced considerably by experiences and education. The researchers note:

> Some [people] still believe that children learn oral language before they come to school and that the purpose of schooling is to teach written lan-guage. . . . When the four separate language systems are well integrated and synchronized, language may be experienced as a unitary construct, much as rain is experienced as unitary wetness rather than as isolated drops. (p. 649)

Berninger and Abbott (2010) advocate for a view of "comprehension and expression via language by ear, mouth, hand, and eye" (p. 635), weaving these language experiences into as many instructional events as possible.

The Common Core ELA standards for grades 6–8 call for teachers to nest speaking and listening within literacy instruction. Importantly, these performance-based standards include delivering and listening to the presentations of other students and exchanging information and ideas featured in those performance events. Speaking and listening also extend to a variety of instructional arrangements, especially small-group interactions across content areas. Students are encouraged to collaborate with one another and communicate in formal and informal settings; like shifts one and two, they should not be bound exclusively to the reading and language arts block and should be integrated across the school day.

Shift Four: Focus on Text-Based Evidence for Argumentation

A fourth shift concerns the development of argumentation skills, which are a predominant feature in the grades 6–12 standards. This shift is unfamiliar to many English teachers who may have only experienced rhetorical reading and writing as college students themselves. Perhaps they recall formal argumentation in writing, such as Stephen Toulmin's (1958) model of argumentation.

- **Claim:** The position being argued; for example, "Our family should get a dog."

- **Grounds:** The reasons given for the claim; answers the question, "What's the proof?" For example, "Dogs have been bred for thousands of years to be good companions and to provide security to their owners."

- **Warrant:** The more formal reasoning or principle that serves as the underpinning for the claim; this links the claim to the grounds, such as, "Many families choose a dog for a pet for these reasons."

- **Backing:** The justification for the warrant; for example, "The Humane Society of the United States says that there are seventy-eight million pet dogs in this country, and 39 percent of all households have at least one dog."

- **Rebuttal:** The counterclaim an opponent might assert, such as, "Some parents might worry that they will need to do all the care, but I promise to walk the dog every day."

- **Qualification:** The limits to the claim; for example, "I know I will need help in the beginning because I don't have a lot of experience with dogs. I know I will need to read more about pet care to get really good at it."

Toulmin's (1958) model of argumentation is meant to illustrate that grades 6–8 students are developmentally capable of laying out a simple argument and supporting it with evidence. While we don't advocate for teaching formal argumentation as Toulmin describes it, the foundations of rational thought are completely within the scope of what students in middle childhood can do. Scott Beers and William Nagy (2011) call this *discursive literacy* and consider this the second step for young adolescent writers after they have mastered the *linguistic literacy* taught in the elementary grades. Indeed, we regularly teach some aspects already: detecting the differences between fact and opinion, recognizing advertising techniques, and even examining propaganda, editorial cartoons, and letters to the editor. Two elements are often missing, however: students rarely engage in formal writing of persuasive essays, and they are seldom required to cite evidence from texts to support their claims (Bransford, Brown, & Cocking, 2000; Davidson, 2011; Leithwood, McAdie, Bascia, & Rodrigue, 2006).

Although persuasive writing has been featured in most states' content frameworks, it is rarely put into practice in a consistent way (Moore & MacArthur, 2012). A national survey of teachers in grades 4–6 finds that nearly 80 percent of participating teachers assign persuasive writing *never at all* (8.25 percent) or *several times a year, but less than monthly* (71.13 percent; Gilbert & Graham, 2010). The amount of writing alone is inadequate for students to become more skilled at writing persuasively. Additionally, this may have instructional implications as well. Writing is more than just assigning students to compose text; the skills of writing must be taught. Scott Beers and William Nagy (2011) note that the writing development of more than one hundred third graders for five years through seventh grade—in four genres (narrative, descriptive, compare and contrast, and persuasive)—progressed slowly over the course of the study, but was especially slow for persuasive writing. Noting that the syntactic demand of persuasive writing is challenging for young writers, Beers and Nagy (2011) state:

> Children face two steep learning curves in their attempts to develop as writers: they must acquire academic vocabulary and the ability to use increasingly complex syntactic forms, and they also must learn to use these newly-acquired linguistic tools correctly in a variety of different genres. (p. 185)

Persuasive writing requires students to use subordinate clauses (for example, "Because dogs make excellent watch dogs, families feel more protected"); those students inexperienced in using subordinate clauses are not able to adequately develop more sophisticated persuasive-writing abilities.

A second characteristic of persuasion and argumentation is the ability to cite evidence to support one's claims. The skills of argumentation, like those of persuasion, can be taught; however, they require purposeful instruction. Stuart Yeh (1998) uses a variant of Toulmin's (1958) model to teach middle school students to write argumentative essays with significant gains for all students, especially those from culturally and linguistically diverse backgrounds.

The CCSS ELA encourage the purposeful teaching of the elements of argumentation and persuasion to expand students' breadth and depth of formal writing. These rhetorical skills are essential as students progress through middle and high school. Students gain these rhetorical skills as they read and write texts and through small-group discussions and classroom discourse.

Shift Five: Focus on Academic Vocabulary and Language

A final shift in the Common Core standards concerns the development of academic vocabulary and language. As with the other major conceptual changes, this shift's intent is to foster disciplinary links in order to build learning. This approach acknowledges that vocabulary should not be seen as an isolated list of words but rather as labels that we use as a proxy for conceptual understandings. In fact, the language of the standards illuminates this idea. The CCSS note the use of *general* and *domain-specific words and phrases*, underscoring two key points: (1) academic vocabulary and language entails the use of a broad range of terms (*lexical dexterity*) and (2) vocabulary development extends beyond teaching decontextualized words (NGA & CCSSO, 2010b).

Much of the research underpinning this view of academic vocabulary and language comes from the work of Isabel Beck, Margaret McKeown, and Linda Kucan (2008), whose familiar three-tier model categorizes words and their instruction.

1. **Tier one:** These words are used in everyday speech, are in the vocabulary of most native speakers, and are taught only in the primary grades. However, students who need more language support, such as English learners, will need instruction beyond the first years of schooling. Examples of tier one words include *clock, happy,* and *baby* (Beck, McKeown, & Kucan, 2002).

2. **Tier two:** These words (called *general academic words and phrases* in the CCSS) appear more often in texts than in verbal exchanges. For instance, *inevitable, disinterested,* and *entrenched* are examples of tier two words for eighth-grade students (Beck et al., 2002). In addition, tier two words are used in many kinds of texts, not just those that are found within a specific discipline. These need to be explicitly taught throughout the school years.

3. **Tier three:** These words (called *domain-specific words and phrases* in the CCSS) are closely associated with a specific content and also require specific instruction. Examples of such words and phrases in seventh-grade English include *personification, argumentation,* and *superlative adjective.*

While teachers often give tier three words and phrases quite a bit of attention, tier two words are more often overlooked. After all, domain-specific words and phrases are closely tied to a discipline and a unit of instruction, and attention is therefore focused on knowing both the definition of the word and its associated concepts. But by overlooking tier two words, students can face more difficulty reading complex texts (NGA & CCSSO, 2010b). Knowing that a character is *disinterested* alerts the reader to his or her mood and intent. An *inevitable* decision foreshadows the conclusion for the reader before the characters have confronted the issue. Unless attention is also provided for these words, readers of complex texts are not able to comprehend at a deeper level. Similarly, they will not use sophisticated terms in their expressive language.

Therefore, an important shift in the Common Core standards concerns the importance of using academic language and vocabulary throughout the school day. Special attention should be given to the types of academic language students require in order to express themselves and to understand the writings of others. Furthermore, the rush to profile domain-specific words and phrases can overshadow the importance of general academic vocabulary that students encounter in many kinds of texts. The investment in academic vocabulary and language is well worth it, as vocabulary knowledge is a robust predictor of reading comprehension through eighth grade (Yovanoff, Duesbery, & Alonzo, 2005).

Purposes and Organization of the CCSS ELA

In the previous section, we highlighted five major shifts in the way we look at the literacy development of grades 6–8 students across the school day. As noted previously, a primary purpose of the CCSS is to prepare students for their eventual college and career choices. All schools aspire to successfully prepare students for the future; however, some argue that starting this in high school is too late for some students (National Education Goals Panel, 1998). However, this doesn't mean that middle school students must start making plans for their adult lives. But insufficient literacy skills do limit one's choices in employment, careers, and postsecondary education. By shining a spotlight on the importance of literacy development across grades K–12, we hope to collectively consider how our 21st century instruction factors into students' lives long after they have left our classrooms.

The CCSS spotlight college and career readiness with *anchor standards*. Anchor standards are the threads that tie the grade-level standards together, for kindergarteners through graduating seniors. Anchor standards frame each language arts strand: Reading, Writing, Speaking and Listening, and Language. Figure 1.3 explains the different elements of the Common Core State Standards for English language arts.

In the next three chapters, we utilize the anchor standards as a means for fostering the work of collaborative planning teams. The following principles for college and career readiness shape these anchor standards and describe the growing capabilities of learners as they progress through school. To be college and career ready, students must do the following.

- **Demonstrate independence:** Students must comprehend complex texts in all content areas, participate as speakers and listeners in academic discussions and presentations, direct their own learning, and utilize resources.

- **Build strong content knowledge across all subjects and disciplines:** Cross-discipline knowledge is important for students' writing and discussions. In addition, students should engage in the research and study skills needed to build their content knowledge.

- **Respond to the varying demands of audience, task, purpose, and discipline:** College- and career-ready students communicate in speaking and writing with a range of audiences and are knowledgeable about the variances of discipline-specific evidence.

- **Comprehend as well as critique:** Students learn this skill as they read and listen to others. They are able to ask questions, evaluate information, and discern reasonableness.

Strands are the categories for English language arts in K–5 and 6–12: Reading, Writing, Speaking and Listening, and Language. Additionally, literacy in history and social studies, science, and technical subjects in grades 6–12 focuses on two strands—Reading and Writing.

College and career readiness (CCR) anchor standards define general, cross-disciplinary expectations for reading, writing, speaking and listening, and language. These anchor standards are designated by strand and standard number; for example, R.CCR.6 signifies reading strand (R), anchor standard (CCR), and standard number (six). This standard is from the domain Craft and Structure, which has three standards numbered four, five, and six. The anchor standards are numbered consecutively, one through ten, in the domains.

Domains define categories of CCR anchor standards for each of the strands in the CCSS ELA—Reading, Writing, Speaking and Listening, and Language. For example, four domains are defined for the Writing strand: Text Types and Purposes (standards one, two, and three), Production and Distribution of Writing (standards four, five, and six), Research to Build and Present Knowledge (standards seven, eight, and nine), and Range of Writing (standard ten).

Grade-specific standards define what students should understand and be able to do. The grade-specific standards parallel the CCR anchor standards by translating the broader CCR statements into grade-appropriate end-of-year expectations.

Grade-specific standards are designated by strand, anchor standard, grade level, and standard number; for example, RL.6.1 signifies Reading Standards for Literature (RL), sixth-grade level (6), standard one in the domain Key Ideas and Details.

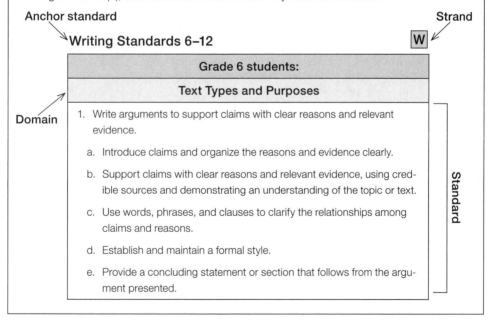

Source: Adapted from NGA & CCSSO, 2010a, p. 42.

Figure 1.3: How to read the CCSS ELA.

- **Value evidence:** Students should provide evidence in their own oral and written discourse and expect others to furnish evidence.

- **Use technology and digital media strategically and capably:** As they integrate online and offline resources, students should use critical-thinking and communication skills within their digital lives.

- **Understand other perspectives and cultures:** In order to better communicate with and learn from and alongside people, students should understand a wide range of cultural and experiential backgrounds.

The principles and assumptions that guided development of the anchor standards provide a framework for understanding them and their function in girding the grade-level standards. While the CCSS map the territory for literacy development, they do not pretend to describe every aspect of teaching and learning.

What Is Not Covered in the Standards

Keep in mind that the standards themselves are end-point results. It has been left to educators, instructional leaders, collaborative planning teams, and curriculum developers to design the ways to get there. The CCSS state, "The Standards define what all students are expected to know and be able to do, not how teachers should teach" (NGA & CCSSO, 2010a, p. 6). This is intentional, as it is essential for educators at the local, state, and national levels to engage in dialogue about essential topics related to content and scope, intervention materials and methods, and supports and expectations for English learners, students with special needs, and students who struggle.

The Content and Scope

The Common Core ELA standards describe essential outcomes but do not address all aspects of learning, or even disciplines, that are important for learners. Even within the scope of English language arts, not all aspects are featured. Consequently, some states have supplemented the standards with additional content. For example, California added 15 percent of content to the CCSS, such as *career development documents* to the domain Text Types and Purposes in W.8.2 (California Department of Education, n.d.; Sacramento County Office of Education, 2012). The Common Core State Standards are intended to guide the development of formative and summative assessments. It is important for states to cap their additions to ensure they do not undermine this design and make it impossible to develop meaningful assessments that can be used across states. This process will ensure that assessment results based on the CCSS will allow for comparisons of student performance across states. PARCC and SBAC, the two consortia developing standards-based assessments, consist of representatives from states that provide additional opportunities for collaboration among states. Teachers should check their state's department of education website to determine any content that's been added to the CCSS.

Intervention Methods and Materials

The standards should be viewed as end-of-grade expectations, but they do not in any way describe either the approaches for intervention or the materials that accompany them. In every school, some students are performing well below grade-level expectations, and others are currently benefitting from a response to intervention (RTI) approach to learning. RTI involves identifying whether, and to what extent, a struggling student is responding positively to specific instruction that has been designed to meet individual learner's needs. His or her responsiveness (or unresponsiveness) to intervention is determined through dynamic, ongoing assessment that monitors student progress and shapes modifications to the assessment plan. The CCSS ELA do not discuss RTI; however, we will explore this topic in chapter 5.

Supports and Expectations for English Learners

The NGA and CCSSO include people knowledgeable about issues related to English learners. NGA and CCSSO acknowledge that students acquiring English require supports and that these supports should be carefully designed to meet the needs of these students (see "Application of Common Core State Standards for English Language Learners," www.corestandards.org/assets/application-for-english-learners.pdf). They caution, however, that accommodations should not result in a reduction of expectations, which could severely affect students' educational progress. The limited information about supports and expectations for ELs in the CCSS implies that meeting the needs of these students is a local responsibility.

Supports and Expectations for Students With Special Needs

Similarly, the CCSS do not define supports for students with special needs beyond assistive technologies such as Braille, screen-reader technologies, sign language, and so on. Use of such devices is determined through an individual education program (IEP) and supersedes educational standards. These devices and approaches are more commonly used for students with sensory or motor disabilities, or in some cases, for those with mild disabilities that involve reading and learning (see "Application to Students With Disabilities," www.corestandards.org/assets/application-to-students-with-disabilities.pdf). What has not been determined is how these supports and expectations might be adapted for students with more significant cognitive and intellectual delays and disabilities. It is likely that development of these systems will continue as general and special educators collaborate. Participation and access are priorities, and the CCSS language mirrors that used in the Individuals With Disabilities Education Improvement Act of 2004: "The Standards should also be read as allowing for the widest possible range of students to participate fully from the outset and as permitting appropriate accommodations to ensure maximum participation of students with special education needs" (NGA & CCSSO, 2010a, p. 6).

Supports and Expectations for Students Who Struggle

The Common Core State Standards do not provide specific advice about supporting students who struggle with school. Instead, there is recognition among educators that reduced expectations often cause students to fail to reach high levels of achievement. Support for students who struggle with school should be part of the ongoing conversations within collaborative planning teams. As Richard DuFour, Rebecca DuFour, and Robert Eaker (2008) note, collaborative teams should discuss what to do when students fail to achieve the expected learning targets. During discussions, team members can identify additional instructional interventions to close the gap between students who mastered the content and those who did not. This may involve reteaching content through guided instruction or targeting students for RTI efforts (Fisher & Frey, 2010). A pyramid of RTI that provides teams with systems for intervention can be helpful (Buffum, Mattos, & Weber, 2009). In this book, we focus on quality teaching for all students and encourage the development of collaborative planning teams to monitor and adapt instruction to ensure learning for all. This systematic approach to students who struggle in school has a better potential to result in positive outcomes than reducing expectations or preventing students from accessing high-quality instruction aligned with the Common Core State Standards. That's not to say that teachers should avoid scaffolding or support. As we illustrate with the teaching scenarios in this book, teaching Common Core ELA well requires a deep understanding of the content as well as skills in responding to students' understanding and misunderstanding.

Conclusion

The Common Core State Standards in the English language arts present grades 6–8 educators with challenges as well as opportunities. The shifts in our ways of thinking about literacy development are considerable and require us to collectively look at our own practices and plan collaboratively with our colleagues. These expectations can pose a major roadblock for schools that do not have a forum for conducting this important work. It is not the kind of work that can be accomplished in a few workshops and some follow-up meetings. Determining how to implement these changes, as well as identifying effective practices that have already proven to be successful, will require focused and sustained attention as educators develop curriculum, design formative assessments, and interpret results. Collaborative teams within a professional learning community are an ideal forum for accomplishing this work. Indeed, the major shifts described in this chapter parallel the characteristics of successful PLCs: they emphasize collaboration and communication across disciplines and grade levels, and they reward those who seek to deepen their understanding of their professional practice.

CHAPTER 2

Implementing the Common Core State Standards for Reading

KEY QUESTIONS

- To what extent does your team understand the Reading standards: What is familiar? What is new? What may be challenging for students? What may be challenging for teachers?

- Examine current texts being used in grades 6–8 and assess them quantitatively and qualitatively and for reader and task demands. Which ones work? Which ones should be used in another grade, or eliminated altogether?

- How do teachers in grades 6–8 at your school extend the foundational skills of reading from grades 3–5? How will middle school students be prepared for high school reading demands?

The eighth-grade students in Oscar Cruz's English class have been studying open-verse poetry as part of a unit of instruction on poetic forms. Today they are reading and performing Carl Sandburg's poem "Chicago" (1916/1994). They begin by examining the content, looking especially at the tone. Mr. Cruz draws the students' attention to the differences in the three stanzas.

"You'll recall that an open-verse poem doesn't play by the rules," he says. "It can have a different rhythm and rhyme in each stanza and use a different meter. In this case, Sandburg is talking to that teenager named Chicago," he continues. "I know that because of the colon at the end of the last line in the first stanza. It makes me think about how I get someone's attention."

After reading the stanza aloud as if calling to someone, Mr. Cruz says, "Now I want you to try it. Everyone stand up and move around the room. Read that first stanza aloud as if you're calling out to someone across a crowded and noisy room."

> Hog Butcher for the World
>
> Tool Maker, Stacker of Wheat . . .

The students choral read with enthusiasm. They cup their hands around their mouths as they continue:

> Stormy, husky, brawling
>
> City of the Big Shoulders. (p. 86)

Mr. Cruz then instructs the class, "OK, Sandburg has gotten your attention, and you walk over to him because it seems like he wants to tell you something. That's the second verse. So you cross the room so you can continue the conversation. Go ahead; meet up with your partners."

The students move into pairs as Mr. Cruz draws their attention back to the poem projected on the interactive whiteboard. "Read it to yourself again so you can notice how the message changes," he tells them. After re-reading silently, his students begin to murmur. "Tell me what you're thinking, Deon," Mr. Cruz asks.

"Now [Sandburg] is telling Chicago about all the bad stuff it did," says Deon.

"Tell me more. How do you know that?" asks Mr. Cruz.

For the next several minutes, Deon and other students note that the second stanza is a list of evils: *painted women*, *gunmen*, and *wanton hunger*. Marta comments, "It's like when my dad calls me in from outside, and I go back to the house, and I'm happy to see him because he just got home from work, and then I get there, and he's just yelling at me."

"That's a great observation, Marta," Mr. Cruz says. "Let's use that image. One partner is the scolding dad, and the other is the kid who was happy at first and then found out she's in trouble."

After the students have taken turns reading the second stanza, they discuss how the tone shifts by the end of that stanza, as Sandburg admits some admiration for this rough and tough place:

"Here is a tall bold slugger set vivid against the soft little cities."

The class examines the final stanza, observing that the poet uses nominalizations of *laugh* times and references *youth* twice. "Marta, let's go back to the image you created for all of us in the second stanza. Can you build on that and give us another image?" asks Mr. Cruz. She thinks for a moment, and then says, "Sometimes my parents might start out kinda yelling at us, but then they start sorta laughing at us, too. Like when my brother messes up but then he's funny, too, and they can't help themselves."

Mr. Cruz throws his head back and laughs at Marta's story. He says, "Perfect! Let's go with that. Partners, read the third stanza to each other like that parent who knows you're going to get in a bit of trouble from time to time, but also knows that you can take care of yourself." He encourages them to pat each other on the back to show their approval, and to tousle each other's hair as a parental gesture of affection. "Now you've got it. Go ahead back to your seats, and we're going to look at how Sandburg uses these three stanzas to change the tone from seeing Chicago as a troublesome teenager, to seeing it as a place that is strong."

A Collaborative Planning Team in Action

Before delving into the main purpose of this chapter, which is to examine the Common Core State Standards for reading in grades 6–8, we want to comment on Mr.

Cruz's curricular decisions and the contributions of his collaborative planning team—composed of the English faculty in all three grades—toward those decisions.

Working together, Mr. Cruz and his colleagues developed a consistent and coherent approach for planning the instructional unit by taking the following actions.

- Examining the text exemplars list in appendix B of the CCSS (NGA & CCSSO, 2010c) to gain a sense of the text complexity appropriate for middle school students

- Identifying texts they currently use in their classrooms, redistributing across the grade levels as needed

- Creating a list identifying a range of informational texts and literature readings that represent a progression of complexity throughout the school year

- Matching identified texts to concepts and content to be taught in English across the three grade levels

- Developing lessons to be delivered and common formative assessments to be administered

- Discussing findings with one another during their weekly meetings to plan interventions for students in need of extra supports, including those who struggle to read and comprehend grade-level texts

- Developing a classroom observation schedule to use within one another's classrooms

In other words, Mr. Cruz didn't develop and teach this poetry unit alone. He relied on the collective strengths of his collaborative team to plan the unit and analyze student outcomes. However, before the team could engage in these actions, members had to analyze the Common Core ELA standards and compare them to their existing curriculum and instruction. They used four questions to guide their analysis.

1. What is familiar in the CCSS at each grade level?

2. What appears to be new based on prior standards?

3. What may be challenging for students?

4. What may be challenging for teachers?

This initial conversation allowed the teacher team to begin an analysis of its current status in curriculum and instruction. Importantly, the teachers situated student learning at the heart of their planning. "After all, I don't teach Sandburg," Mr. Cruz notes, "I teach students." Based on its initial work, the team was able to identify areas of need regarding professional development and materials acquisition and set the stage for later decisions regarding curriculum development, data analysis, intervention, and collaborative observations. A copy of this initial tool Mr. Cruz's collaborative team used appears in figure 2.1 (page 28). Visit **go.solution-tree.com/commoncore** for an

Reading anchor standard four (R.CCR.4): Interpret words and phrases as they are used in a text, including determining technical, connotative, and figurative meanings, and analyze how specific word choices shape meaning or tone.

CCSS grade band: Grades 6–8

CCSS strand: Reading Standards for Literature (RL)

Anchor standard domain: Craft and Structure

Grade-Level Standard	What Is Familiar?	What Is New?	What May Be Challenging for Students?	What May Be Challenging for Teachers?
Grade 6 **RL.6.4:** Determine the meaning of words and phrases as they are used in a text, including figurative and connotative meanings; analyze the impact of a specific word choice on meaning and tone.				
Grade 7 **RL.7.4:** Determine the meaning of words and phrases as they are used in a text, including figurative and connotative meanings; analyze the impact of rhymes and other repetitions of sounds (for example, alliteration) on a specific verse or stanza of a poem or section of a story or drama.				
Grade 8 **RL.8.4:** Determine the meaning of words and phrases as they are used in a text, including figurative and connotative meanings; analyze the impact of specific word choices on meaning and tone, including analogies or allusions to other texts.				

Source: Adapted from NGA & CCSSO, 2010a, p. 36.

Figure 2.1: Guiding questions for grade-by-grade analysis of the Reading standards.

Visit **go.solution-tree.com/commoncore** for a reproducible version of this figure.

online-only reproducible of figure 2.1 that your collaborative team can use to analyze other reading standards.

Anchor Standards for Reading

The Common Core English language arts standards are organized across four *strands:* Reading, Writing, Speaking and Listening, and Language. As discussed in chapter 1, a set of K–12 anchor standards for college and career readiness frames each strand. These anchor standards articulate the overarching goals that shape the grade-specific standards and are designed to create commonality across elementary, middle, and high school. As the CCSS note, "Students advancing through the grades are expected to meet each year's grade-specific standards and retain or further develop skills and understandings mastered in preceding grades" (NGA & CCSSO, 2010a, p. 11). This structure can reduce the *silo effect* that can creep into education in which teachers work in isolation from their peers and curriculum is not coordinated. By viewing education across grade bands and buildings, we can begin to mirror more closely the experiences of our students and their families. The anchor standards are an attempt to foster communication across educational systems.

There are ten 6–8 anchor standards for reading organized into the following four domains (NGA & CCSSO, 2010a, p. 10).

1. Key Ideas and Details

2. Craft and Structure

3. Integration of Knowledge and Ideas

4. Range of Reading and Level of Text Complexity

These anchor standards are directly tied to two parts in the Reading strand at grades K–12: Literature and Informational Text. In addition, a second set of standards address literacy in history and social studies, science, and the technical subjects. The anchor standards remain the same as those articulated for English language arts, but the grade-level standards reflect the discipline-specific applications of reading in content area instruction. In this book, we confine our review of the standards for English language arts, as English teachers implement them. We will examine each of the parts—Literature and Informational Text—in this chapter, after first discussing the anchor standards in more detail.

Key Ideas and Details

The first three anchor standards describe the explicit and implicit comprehension of readers as they glean the purposes and main points of the text. In addition, the domain emphasizes the importance of being able to follow plot, character development, and themes, all necessary for literary analysis.

1. Read closely to determine what the text says explicitly and to make logical inferences from it; cite specific textual evidence when writing or speaking to support conclusions drawn from the text. (R.CCR.1)

2. Determine central ideas or themes of a text and analyze their development; summarize the key supporting details and ideas. (R.CCR.2)

3. Analyze how and why individuals, events, and ideas develop and interact over the course of a text. (R.CCR.3) (NGA & CCSSO, 2010a, p. 35)

Craft and Structure

The three anchor standards in this domain discuss the reader's ability to analyze texts at the micro and macro levels. Readers should attend to the author's craft in how he or she purposefully uses word choice, literary techniques, and organizational structures to shape the text; a character's voice and experiences; or the interaction between the choice of genre and the information shared.

4. Interpret words and phrases as they are used in a text, including determining technical, connotative, and figurative meanings, and analyze how specific word choices shape meaning or tone. (R.CCR.4)

5. Analyze the structure of texts, including how specific sentences, paragraphs, and larger portions of the text (such as a section, chapter, scene, or stanza) relate to each other and the whole. (R.CCR.5)

6. Assess how point of view or purpose shapes the content and style of a text. (R.CCR.6) (NGA & CCSSO, 2010a, p. 35)

Integration of Knowledge and Ideas

In this domain, anchor standards seven through nine are dedicated to the content within and across texts, in print, and in digital environments. Anchor standard seven (R.CCR.7) is also closely tied to the Writing anchor standard domain, Research to Build and Present Knowledge (see NGA & CCSSO, 2010a, p. 41), as well as the Speaking and Listening anchor standard domain, Comprehension and Collaboration (see NGA & CCSSO, 2010a, p. 48). Anchor standard eight (R.CCR.8) on argumentation is not addressed in the Literature part as it is not applicable to these text types.

7. Integrate and evaluate content presented in diverse media and formats, including visually and quantitatively, as well as in words. (R.CCR.7)

8. Delineate and evaluate the argument and specific claims in a text, including the validity of the reasoning as well as the relevance and sufficiency of the evidence. (R.CCR.8)

9. Analyze how two or more texts address similar themes or topics in order to build knowledge or to compare the approaches the authors take. (R.CCR.9) (NGA & CCSSO, 2010a, p. 35)

Range of Reading and Level of Text Complexity

This domain with the tenth and final anchor standard for reading has arguably been the predominant topic of discussion about the CCSS ELA.

> 10. Read and comprehend complex literary and informational texts independently and proficiently. (R.CCR.10) (NGA & CCSSO, 2010a, p. 35)

The Common Core ELA and its appendices devote a considerable amount of space to this standard, noting that K–12 students' use of complex texts has diminished since the 1970s, while texts used in college and the workplace have not (Chall, Conard, & Harris, 1977; Hayes, Wolfer, & Wolfe, 1996; as cited in NGA & CCSSO, 2010b). The CCSS advocate for a staircase approach to systematically raising reading comprehension and critical thinking through the purposeful use of complex texts that require students to stretch their cognitive and metacognitive abilities (NGA & CCSSO, 2010a). For students who struggle with reading, this means that they must be taught with complex texts and asked to read increasingly complex texts across the year. However, it is important to note that the text alone should not be the only scaffold; instruction is critical for these students to progress and accelerate.

Text complexity is defined across three dimensions: (1) quantitative measures, (2) qualitative factors, and (3) reader and task considerations. Quantitative measures, using a mixture of word length, sentence length, and syllables, are familiar to middle school educators. In addition, many readability formulae calculate the number of difficult words that appear in a text by comparing these to grade-level lists. Examples of quantitative measures include the Fry Readability Formula, Dale-Chall Readability Formula, and Flesch-Kincaid Grade-Level Index (see Fisher, Frey, & Lapp, 2012), as well as commercial ones such as ATOS (used by Accelerated Reader), Source Rater (Educational Testing Service), Pearson Reading Maturity Scale (Pearson Education), Degrees of Reading Power (Questar), and Lexile (MetaMetrics). Table 2.1 compares these readability scales. Published quantitative reading scores can provide a platform for collaborative teams to begin to examine which texts to use with their students.

Table 2.1: Text Complexity Ranges Within Grade Bands

Grade Band	Revised CCSS 2011	Accelerated Reader	Degrees of Reading Power	Flesch-Kincaid	Source Rater	Reading Maturity Scale
K–1	n/a	n/a	n/a	n/a	n/a	n/a
2–3	420–820	2.75–5.14	42–54	1.98–5.34	0.05–2.48	3.53–6.13
4–5	740–1010	4.97–7.03	52–60	4.51–7.73	0.84–5.75	5.42–7.92
6–8	925–1185	7.00–9.98	57–67	6.51–10.34	4.11–10.66	7.04–9.57
9–10	1050–1335	9.67–12.01	62–72	8.32–12.12	9.02–13.93	8.41–10.81
11–CCR	1185–1385	11.20–14.10	67–74	10.34–14.20	12.30–14.50	9.57–12.00

Source: CCSSO, 2012.

The Lexile measures used in the CCSS have been revised; consequently, the measures in table 2.1 differ from those provided in appendix A of Common Core for ELA (NGA & CCSSO, 2010b, p. 8). For example, the original range for the grades 6–8 band was

955–1155L compared to the revised range of 925–1185L. Lexile measures are based on word frequency (semantic difficulty) and sentence length (syntactic complexity), both of which have been shown to be effective predictors of text difficulty (Lennon & Burdick, 2004).

While quantitative reading formulae are calculated by machine, qualitative factors require a human reader. Computers use mathematical formulae to estimate difficulty. Teachers and parents focus on ideas that will confuse the reader or be inappropriate for students at a given age. Furthermore, teachers use their knowledge of text structures to identify areas of difficulty which will require instruction.

Qualitative factors of texts include the following (Fisher et al., 2012; NGA & CCSSO, 2010b).

- **Levels of meaning and purpose:** Such as the density and complexity of the information, use of figurative language, and stated and implied purposes

- **Structure:** Including the text's genre, organization, narration, and use of text features and graphics

- **Language conventionality and clarity:** Especially in its use of English language variations and registers

- **Knowledge demands:** Including the assumed background knowledge, prior knowledge, cultural knowledge, and vocabulary knowledge

Qualitative factors can make a text more or less complex, and they cannot be measured quantitatively. For example, *Out of the Dust* (Hesse, 1997), a book often used in the middle grades, does not have a Lexile score because of its extensive use of poetic verse, rendering it unsuitable for quantitative measures. However, its recounting of a young girl's life in the Dust Bowl, her struggles with the physical scars from the fire that claimed her mother's life, and her sense of guilt, shame, and loss, make it a complex read for young adolescents. Assessment of text complexity using these factors is an excellent task for collaborative team members who are experienced with using a text and are familiar with a specific text's structure.

Using the rubric in table 2.2, an eighth-grade English team meets to discuss informational texts for use in class. The team members turn their attention to *Travels With Charley* (Steinbeck, 2002), an informational text with a Lexile score of 1010L. The team identifies several aspects of the book that will make it more or less difficult. It notes that the story has a conversational tone, with lots of short dialogue-driven scenes that will draw on students' knowledge of narrative structures. However, team members soon agree that the levels of meaning ultimately make the book more complex. The team recognizes that the author probably knew he was dying when he wrote the book and that it represented a last attempt to see America and relive his youthful travels. Students will not immediately recognize the challenges facing a man near the end of his life.

Table 2.2: Qualitative Factors of Text Complexity

	3 Points (Stretch) Texts That Stretch a Reader or Require Instruction	2 Points (Grade Level) Texts That Require Grade-Appropriate Skills	1 Point (Comfortable) Texts That Are Comfortable or Build Background, Fluency, and Skills
	Levels of Meaning and Purpose		
Density and Complexity	Text has significant density and complexity, with multiple levels of meaning; meanings may be more ambiguous.	Text has a single, but more complex or abstract level of meaning; some meanings are stated, while others are left to the reader to identify.	Text has single and literal levels of meaning; meaning is explicitly stated.
Figurative Language	Figurative language plays a significant role in identifying the meaning of the text; more sophisticated figurative language is used (irony and satire, allusions, archaic or less familiar symbolism); the reader is left to interpret these meanings.	Figurative language such as imagery, metaphors, symbolism, and personification are used to make connections within the text to more explicit information, and readers are supported in understanding these language devices through examples and explanations.	There is a limited use of symbolism, metaphors, and poetic language that allude to other unstated concepts; language is explicit and relies on literal interpretations.
Purpose	The purpose is deliberately withheld from the reader, who must use other interpretative skills to identify it.	The purpose is implied but is easily identified based on title or context.	The purpose or main idea is directly and explicitly stated at the beginning of the reading.
	Structure		
Genre	Genre is unfamiliar or bends and expands the rules for the genre.	Genre is either unfamiliar but is a reasonable example or it is a familiar genre that bends and expands the rules for the genre.	Genre is familiar and the text is consistent with the elements of that genre.

continued →

	3 Points (Stretch) — Texts That Stretch a Reader or Require Instruction	2 Points (Grade Level) — Texts That Require Grade-Appropriate Skills	1 Point (Comfortable) — Texts That Are Comfortable or Build Background, Fluency, and Skills
Structure			
Organization	The organization distorts time or sequence in a deliberate effort to delay the reader's full understanding of the plot, process, or set of concepts; may include significant flashbacks, foreshadowing, or shifting perspectives.	The organization adheres to most conventions, but digresses on occasion to temporarily shift the reader's focus to another point of view, event, time, or place, before returning to the main idea or topic.	The organization is conventional, sequential, or chronological, with clear signals and transitions to lead the reader through a story, process, or set of concepts.
Narration	An unreliable narrator provides a distorted or limited view to the reader; the reader must use other clues to deduce the truth; multiple narrators provide conflicting information; shifting points of view keep the reader guessing.	Third-person limited or first-person narration provides accurate, but limited perspectives or viewpoints.	Third-person omniscient narration or an authoritative and credible voice provides an appropriate level of detail and keeps little hidden from the view of the reader.
Text Features and Graphics	There is limited use of text features to organize information and guide the reader. Information in the graphics is not repeated in the main part of the text but is essential for understanding the text.	Has a wider array of text features including margin notes, diagrams, graphs, font changes, and other devices that compete for the reader's attention; graphics and visuals are used to augment and illustrate information in the main part of the text.	Text features (such as bold and italicized words, headings, and subheadings) organize information explicitly and guide the reader; graphics or illustrations may be present but are not necessary to understand the main part of the text.
Language Conventionality and Clarity			
Standard English and Variations	The text includes significant and multiple styles of English and its variations, and these are unfamiliar to the reader.	Some distance exists between the reader's linguistic base and the language conventions used in the text; the vernacular used is unfamiliar to the reader.	The language closely adheres to the reader's linguistic base.

	Knowledge Demands		
Register	The register is archaic, formal, domain specific, or scholarly.	The register is consultative or formal, and may be academic but acknowledges the developmental level of the reader.	The register is casual and familiar.
Background Knowledge	The text places demands on the reader that extend far beyond his or her experiences, and provides little in the way of explanation of these divergent experiences.	There is distance between the reader's experiences and those in the text, but there is acknowledgement of these divergent experiences, and sufficient explanation to bridge the gaps.	The text contains content that closely matches the reader's life experiences.
Prior Knowledge	Presumes specialized or technical content knowledge and little in the way of review or explanation of these concepts is present in the text.	Requires subject-specific knowledge, but the text augments this with review or summary of this information.	The prior knowledge needed to understand the text is familiar, and it draws on a solid foundation of practical, general, and academic learning.
Cultural Knowledge	The text relies on extensive or unfamiliar intertextuality and uses artifacts and symbols that reference archaic or historical cultures.	The text primarily references contemporary and popular culture to anchor explanations for new knowledge; intertextuality is used more extensively but is mostly familiar to the reader.	The reader uses familiar cultural templates to understand the text with limited or familiar intertextuality.
Vocabulary Knowledge	Vocabulary demand is extensive, domain specific, and representative of complex ideas; the text offers little in the way of context clues to support the reader.	Vocabulary draws on domain specific, general academic, and multiple meaning words, with text supports to guide the reader's correct interpretations of meanings; the vocabulary represents familiar concepts and ideas.	Vocabulary is controlled and uses the most commonly held meanings; multiple meaning words are used in a limited fashion.

Source: Adapted from Fisher, Frey, & Lapp, 2012.

Visit **go.solution-tree.com/commoncore** for a reproducible version of this table.

In addition, John Steinbeck's references to contemporary events in 1960, such as Soviet leader Nikita Khrushchev, open racism and discrimination in the South, and references to the Works Progress Administration, might tax their background knowledge. By identifying what makes the text more complex, teachers are able to design their instruction around reading informational text written more than fifty years earlier, identifying multiple levels of meaning and establishing the author's stated and unstated purposes.

The third dimension for determining text complexity concerns the match between the reader and the task (NGA & CCSSO, 2010b). Factors that are internal to the reader include his or her cognitive capabilities, motivation, knowledge, and experiences. The task demand also influences the relative difficulty of the text. Teacher-led tasks, such as an interactive read-aloud, provide a high degree of scaffolding and make an otherwise difficult text much more comprehensible. Peer-led tasks, such as a small-group literature circle discussion, provide a moderate level of scaffolding as students collaborate to understand the task. Individual tasks, such as independent reading, provide the least amount of scaffolding and place most of the responsibility on the reader. In order for students to progress toward increasingly more complex texts, they need a mixture of all of these tasks (Fisher, Frey, & Lapp, 2012). An over-reliance on one level of task difficulty occurs at the expense of others and can stymie a student's progress. This is perhaps the ongoing discussion collaborative teams should have as they design instruction with specific students in mind.

The anchor standards, and the grade-level standards that follow them, are far too complex to teach in a single lesson, or to teach in isolation. Keeping this concept in mind is important as collaborative team members examine these standards for in-depth reading. It is the interaction of these standards within and across domains that makes them powerful. To divide and then reassemble them as isolated lessons will undermine the enduring understandings the standards articulate. The overarching goals should be to teach the habits of effective communicators and to avoid isolated strategy instruction (Frey, Fisher, & Berkin, 2008).

In the following sections, we will examine the two parts in the Reading strand—Literature and Informational Text—across grades 6–8. The grade band is an essential vantage point for viewing and discussing the CCSS, precisely because it prevents the silo effect that can occur when grade levels operate independently from one another. While grade-level planning must occur, the work of a professional learning community at the school level should first and foremost foster communication and collaboration across grades in order to maximize the potential of the anchor standards. This horizontal collaboration ensures that all grade-level teams understand their role in relationship to teaching toward the anchor standards.

Reading Standards for Literature in Grades 6–8

This part is linked directly to narrative text types—poems, drama, and stories, including folktales, fantasy, and realistic fiction. Although nonfiction biographies and autobiographies often use a narrative structure, they are situated as a type of informational text. Students in middle school are traditionally exposed to a high volume of literature, although genres like poetry and drama are often reserved for specific genre studies units and used more rarely across the school year. Table 2.3 contains sample titles from the text exemplars in appendix B of the Common Core State Standards (NGA & CCSSO, 2010c).

Table 2.3: Exemplars for Literature Texts in Grades 6–8

Genre	Grade 6	Grade 7	Grade 8
Stories	Yep (1975): *Dragonwings*	Cooper (1973): *Dark Is Rising*	Alcott (2012): *Little Women*
Drama	Fletcher (1948a, 1980): "Sorry, Wrong Number"		
	Goodrich and Hackett (2009): *The Diary of Anne Frank*		
Poetry	Dickinson (1997): "The Railway Train"	Soto (1995): "Oranges"	Longfellow (2012): "Paul Revere's Ride"

Source: Adapted from NGA & CCSSO, 2010c.

The standards for literature for each grade level are drawn directly from the anchor standards and are organized in the same manner: Key Ideas and Details, Craft and Structure, Integration of Knowledge and Ideas, and Range of Reading and Level of Text Complexity. We invite you and your collaborative team to discuss the standards using the four-part protocol described in figure 2.1 (page 28): (1) What is familiar? (2) What is new? (3) What may be challenging for students? (4) What may be challenging for teachers? (Visit **go.solution-tree.com/commoncore** for a reproducible version of figure 2.1.) We will share observations of our own to seed your discussions.

Key Ideas and Details in Literature

Table 2.4 (page 38) lists the grades 6–8 standards for this domain. The standards contain many expected elements, as well as some more challenging demands that have implications for instruction. Anchor standard one (R.CCR.1) emphasizes the importance of citing evidence directly from the text in order to support explicit and inferential levels of meaning. This is a significant leap for middle school students, who have learned about opinion, but not the more formal elements of argumentation. An important skill in rhetorical writing and speaking is the ability to link textual evidence to claims. Anchor standard two (R.CCR.2) challenges students to look more broadly across the text to locate central themes and connect them to details, and to further summarize. These expectations are expanded in anchor standard three (R.CCR.3), in which character, plot, and dialogue are examined as well.

This domain represents a shift in practice, which can be a challenge for students who have become accustomed to stating their thoughts and opinions without referring back to the text. Building the habit of referring to the text requires a shift in instruction, especially in our questioning habits. Regularly using text-dependent questions can drive

Table 2.4: Literature Standards for Domain Key Ideas and Details, Grades 6–8

Anchor Standards	Grade 6 Standards	Grade 7 Standards	Grade 8 Standards
R.CCR.1: Read closely to determine what the text says explicitly and to make logical inferences from it; cite specific textual evidence when writing or speaking to support conclusions drawn from the text.	**RL.6.1:** Cite textual evidence to support analysis of what the text says explicitly as well as inferences drawn from the text.	**RL.7.1:** Cite several pieces of textual evidence to support analysis of what the text says explicitly as well as inferences drawn from the text.	**RL.8.1:** Cite the textual evidence that most strongly supports an analysis of what the text says explicitly as well as inferences drawn from the text.
R.CCR.2: Determine central ideas or themes of a text and analyze their development; summarize the key supporting details and ideas.	**RL.6.2:** Determine a theme or central idea of a text and how it is conveyed through particular details; provide a summary of the text distinct from personal opinions or judgments.	**RL.7.2:** Determine a theme or central idea of a text and analyze its development over the course of the text; provide an objective summary of the text.	**RL.8.2:** Determine a theme or central idea of a text and analyze its development over the course of the text, including its relationship to the characters, setting, and plot; provide an objective summary of the text.
R.CCR.3: Analyze how and why individuals, events, and ideas develop and interact over the course of a text.	**RL.6.3:** Describe how a particular story's or drama's plot unfolds in a series of episodes as well as how the characters respond or change as the plot moves toward a resolution.	**RL.7.3:** Analyze how particular elements of a story or drama interact (such as how setting shapes the characters or plot).	**RL.8.3:** Analyze how particular lines of dialogue or incidents in a story or drama propel the action, reveal aspects of a character, or provoke a decision.

Source: Adapted from NGA & CCSSO, 2010a, pp. 35 and 36.

young readers back to the text, and it reinforces selective re-reading and look-backs as methods of supporting deeper comprehension (Bossert & Schwantes, 1996).

Remembering to ask text-dependent questions requires preparation. After all, it is much easier to ask more general questions about a reading, especially the kind that allow students to make personal connections. However, these don't advance student knowledge of the reading itself, and they can derail classroom discussions about a text. As depicted in figure 2.2, there are six types of questions that require students use evidence from the text in their responses.

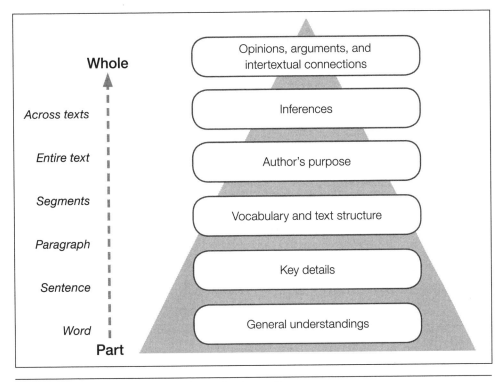

Figure 2.2: Progression of text-dependent questions.

These questions represent a progression of increasingly more complex understandings, with literal-level knowledge forming the foundation as students move toward inferential meaning and critical analysis.

1. **General understanding questions:** Teachers post these questions to determine whether students grasp the overall meaning of the text. While they may appear more global in nature, they are crafted so that students are required to *explain* as well as *describe*. For example, in Mr. Cruz's lesson in which his eighth-grade students read Sandburg's poem "Chicago" (1916/1994), Mr. Cruz asks a general understanding question: "What are the qualities Sandburg admires in the people of this city?" A student, Iman, replies, "He sees them as tough, but they laugh off the stuff that's hard for them and they just keep going."

2. **Key detail questions:** These questions build on the foundational knowledge needed for general understanding by drawing attention to critical details that relate to the whole. For example, in his lesson, Mr. Cruz asks, "Give me an example of that, Iman. In what line of the poem do you see that idea playing out?" Iman replies, "Under the smoke, dust all over his mouth, laughing with white teeth."

3. **Vocabulary and text structure questions:** These questions bridge the literal-level meanings of a text to move toward inferential interpretations. Questions

regarding word choice, use of figurative language, and organization of information further build students' understanding of the author's craft. Mr. Cruz's earliest questions about the shifts in conversational tone from one stanza to the next invited students to consider the organizational structure of the poem.

4. **Author's purpose questions:** Invite students to step back from the text in order to examine the reading's effect on an audience and to look closely for clues that illuminate the author's intentions. These questions may focus on genre and narration, or require students to engage in critical analysis in determining whether another viewpoint is missing. The text itself shapes the author's purpose questions. Mr. Cruz asks, "Why would Sandburg write such a poem? How does he feel about the city?" The students discuss the poet's acknowledgment of its crime, but settle on an image of a "City of the Big Shoulders," recognizing that such a place could carry a heavy burden without falling.

5. **Inferencing questions:** These questions further the progression toward deeper understanding by requiring students to locate the nuances of a literary text, examine the arguments contained in a persuasive piece, or probe the details of major ideas in an informational text passage. As the students began to settle on strength as a central theme of the poem, Mr. Cruz encourages them to identify the images that evoke ruggedness. They note the lifting and carrying required by a "Stacker of Wheat" and the use of words like *toil, bold, husky, battle,* and *savage.* A student offers an example of a boxer in a fight standing over his defeated opponent in the third stanza, and the use of the word *slugger* earlier in the poem.

6. **Opinions, arguments, and intertextual connection questions:** These questions advance students' thinking about the broader meanings of a text by foregrounding it against a backdrop of personal experiences and inviting comparisons across texts. When these questions are delayed until after students have had a chance read and re-read a text, the discussions themselves are richer and more complex. Mr. Cruz encourages his students to develop a question they still have after reading the poem. Abriana's group states that it wants to find out if Sandburg wrote about other places and what his relationship to Chicago might have been.

Although these examples come from reading a literary work, text-dependent questions are just as important when reading informational text. Sixth-grade English teacher Viola Preston uses readings from *Unlikely Friendships: Forty-Seven Remarkable Stories from the Animal Kingdom* (Holland, 2011) as part of a unit exploring the use of the theme of unlikely friendships. Students read about well-known accounts of cross-species animal friendships, such as the baby hippo Owen and a 130-year-old giant tortoise named Mzee.

One literature circle group reads *Rules* (Lord, 2008), a realistic fictional story of a twelve-year-old girl who has a younger sibling with autism and strikes up an unexpected friendship with an older boy who is nonverbal. At 780L, the book is quantitatively slightly below the sixth-grade band, but the collaborative planning team's qualitative analysis determines the book's subject matter to be slightly more difficult. In addition, the team feels that the context of the unit also elevates the task complexity. It determines that the goals of the unit are for students to examine how the device (the unexpected alliance) is used in fiction and to look at nonfiction accounts that parallel these occurrences. Ms. Preston chooses *Rules* as informational reading for the literature circle because it also addresses issues of communication. She joins the group of four students who are discussing "The Tortoise and the Hippo" (Holland, 2011).

"I know you've been talking about this reading, so I'll add some questions for all of you to consider," says Ms. Preston. "I'd like to remind you to use the text, so you can answer with specific examples. You don't have to hold all this information in your head. So, here's my first question. The title of the book is *Unlikely Friendships*. How does this passage uphold this concept?"

Oliver responds, "It's not normal for a hippopotamus and a tortoise to be friends." Ms. Preston replies, "Keep digging, Oliver. Where's the evidence for that?" Oliver continues, "In the first sentences on page 191: 'It has fast become one of the most famous examples of interspecies friendship ever told. Reptiles aren't typically known for their warm, fuzzy natures. Nor are hippos.'"

Amy then states, "On page 192, it says that hippos don't really bond socially except for their mothers, and Mzee was annoyed when the hippo snuggled with him." Ms. Preston responds, "I'd be annoyed, too, if a hippo was snuggling up with me! Now let's dig deeper, because I'd like us to focus on the last paragraph, about their communication. It says on page 193, 'The two animals developed their own physical and verbal language.' What are some examples?"

For the next few minutes, the students list examples from the article, such as gentle nips to guide each other, and rumbling sounds not characteristic of either species. Ms. Preston then turns their focus to an animal behaviorist's comments about the role of the animals shaping each other's communication. Ms. Preston asks the students questions about the vocabulary used in the passage from *Unlikely Friendships*, concentrating on *instinct*, *shaping*, and *preset program*. Eventually, she begins to ask students to connect these ideas to the story *Rules* (Lord, 2008).

Ms. Preston says, "So let's shift our attention to *Rules*. You'll need your books for this. Your task today will be to write about the communication processes that Catherine and Jason use, and how those are similar to and different from the ones Owen and Mzee use. And let me stop you before you even go there: I know the two characters aren't biting each other. But you've got the animal behaviorist's insights about the role of shaping. Do you see similar examples in *Rules*?"

Ms. Preston first helps the group locate examples in the book, and soon the students are listing others. As she excuses herself from the literature circle, she says, "It's easy to just think about one reading at a time and not make any connections between them. What you're doing is relating real-life examples to a common literary theme. I'm going to be interested to learn about what you've noticed."

Craft and Structure in Literature

The language of structure in literature dominates this domain (see table 2.5). In anchor standard four (RL.CCR.4) of this grade band, students are analyzing the effects of words and phrases on tone and meaning, especially as it relates to connotative meaning and figurative language. Anchor standard five (RL.CCR.5) builds on this concept, especially in relating part (sentence, paragraph, or stanza) to the whole text. In standard six, students consider the author's point of view, as well as opposing points of view.

Eighth-grade English teacher Mattie Dunlap uses the short story "Salvador, Late or Early" (Cisneros, 1991) with her class, which engages in an author study of the writer's works. After a short introduction, she asks her students to read it silently, and she reminds them to circle words or phrases they found difficult or puzzling within the context of the story. After they read it, she leads them in a discussion of what they noticed.

Amelia says, "Well, it's not like the words are hard. I mean, I get them. But I'm not sure I know what the author means." Ms. Dunlap asks her for some examples. "Like, I don't know what she means by 'eyes the color of caterpillars' or that he has 'limbs stuffed with feathers and rags.' Wouldn't that be a scarecrow?" Amelia asks.

"Ah, she writes like a poet, doesn't she?" Ms. Dunlap replies. "Cisneros doesn't make it really easy for us to just read her stuff once and then move on," she continues. "We're going to have to figure out her language to know what she really wants us to understand about this boy. Let's start with our general understanding: what do we know for sure about Salvador?"

As Ms. Dunlap acts as the class scribe, the students collectively note that the character is a boy who takes care of his little brothers, but he is quiet at school. The students are particularly disturbed that "the teacher cannot remember his name" and that "he is no one's friend." Ms. Dunlap then invites students to follow along in their text while she reads aloud; they then hear the poetic language come to life. She asks text-based questions, such as "How does the author use color words?" that cause students to read passages again. After some discussion, another student, Dan, comments, "The drab color words are outside of school, and the bright ones are all about in-school stuff."

But soon, the students are confronted with a contrast: they realize the school-based words are associated with injury: a *geography of scars* and *a history of hurt*. Roman, another student, has some insight: "It's like when you get punched or something, and you see all bright colors for a few seconds." Finally, Mariana notices the boy's name. "It's Salvador. That means *savior* in Spanish. He's the family's savior, even if he doesn't get noticed at school. Maybe he is like a scarecrow, in a good way, because he guards his little brothers and keeps them safe." Ms. Dunlap smiles with satisfaction.

Table 2.5: Literature Standards for Domain Craft and Structure, Grades 6–8

Anchor Standards	Grade 6 Standards	Grade 7 Standards	Grade 8 Standards
RL.CCR.4: Interpret words and phrases as they are used in a text, including determining technical, connotative, and figurative meanings, and analyze how specific word choices shape meaning or tone.	**RL.6.4:** Determine the meaning of words and phrases as they are used in a text, including figurative and connotative meanings; analyze the impact of a specific word choice on meaning and tone.	**RL.7.4:** Determine the meaning of words and phrases as they are used in a text, including figurative and connotative meanings; analyze the impact of rhymes and other repetitions of sounds (like alliteration) on a specific verse or stanza of a poem or section of a story or drama.	**RL.8.4:** Determine the meaning of words and phrases as they are used in a text, including figurative and connotative meanings; analyze the impact of specific word choices on meaning and tone, including analogies or allusions to other texts.
R.CCR.5: Analyze structure of text, including how specific sentence, paragraphs, and larger portions of the text (like a section, chapter, scene, or stanza) relate to each other and the whole.	**RL.6.5:** Analyze how a particular sentence, chapter, scene, or stanza fits into the overall structure of a text and contributes to the development of the theme, setting, or plot.	**RL.7.5:** Analyze how a drama's or poem's form or structure (such as in a soliloquy or sonnet) contributes to its meaning.	**RL.8.5:** Compare and contrast the structure of two or more texts and analyze how the differing structure of each text contributes to its meaning and style.
R.CCR.6: Assess how point of view or purpose shapes the content and style of a text.	**RL.6.6:** Explain how an author develops the point of view of the narrator or speaker in a text.	**RL.7.6:** Analyze how an author develops and contrasts the points of view of different characters or narrators in a text.	**RL.8.6:** Analyze how differences in the points of view of the characters and the audience or reader (like those created through the use of dramatic irony) create such effects as suspense or humor.

Source: Adapted from NGA & CCSSO, 2010a, pp. 35 and 36.

While the reading is only three paragraphs long, the students have explored the deeper meaning of the text that reveals the inner life of Salvador.

Integration of Knowledge and Ideas in Literature

Only two of the three anchor standards for this domain appear in the Literature part, as anchor standard eight (R.CCR.8) on argumentation is not commonly utilized in fiction (see table 2.6). There are familiar elements in this domain, especially the emphasis in anchor standard nine (R.CCR.9) on comparing and contrasting multiple forms of a text, which by eighth grade has become an analysis of archetypes and myths that have been reinterpreted in contemporary literature—for example, the links between Celtic and Greek mythology and Neil Gaiman's (2008) *Stardust*. The language in anchor standard seven (R.CCR.7) about comparing and contrasting print and audio or visual interpretations of a text may also feel familiar.

Table 2.6: Literature Standards for Domain Integration of Knowledge and Ideas, Grades 6–8

Anchor Standards	Grade 6	Grade 7	Grade 8
R.CCR.7: Integrate and evaluate content presented in diverse media and formats, including visually and quantitatively, as well as words.	**RL.6.7:** Compare and contrast the experience of reading a story, drama, or poem to listening to or viewing an audio, video, or live version of the text, including contrasting what they *see* and *hear* when reading the text to what they perceive when they listen or watch.	**RL.7.7:** Compare and contrast a written story, drama, or poem to its audio, filmed, staged, or multimedia version, analyzing the effects of techniques unique to each medium (for example, lighting, sound, color, or camera focus and angles in a film).	**RL.8.7:** Analyze the extent to which a filmed or live production of a story or drama stays faithful to or departs from the text or script, evaluating the choices the director or actors make.
R.CCR.8: Delineate and evaluate the argument and specific claims in a text, including the validity of the reasoning as well as the relevance and sufficiency of the evidence.	n/a	n/a	n/a
R.CCR.9: Analyze how two or more texts address similar themes or topics in order to build knowledge or to compare the approaches the authors take.	**RL.6.9:** Compare and contrast texts in different forms or genres (such as in stories and poems, historical novels, and fantasy stories) in terms of their approaches to similar themes and topics.	**RL.7.9:** Compare and contrast a fictional portrayal of a time, place, or character and a historical account of the same period as a means of understanding how authors of fiction use or alter history.	**RL.8.9:** Analyze how a modern work of fiction draws on themes, patterns of events, or character types from myths, traditional stories, or religious works such as the bible, including describing how the material is rendered new.

Source: Adapted from NGA & CCSSO, 2010a, pp. 35 and 37.

The use of film has a long history in English education, but it is important to keep in mind that the use of audio and video should not devolve into a passive experience for students. The challenge is to ensure that true analysis is happening, and not to tell students, "First we read the book, and now we're going to watch the movie." Instead, consider the ways in which you can disrupt the video through discussion, writing, and vocabulary instruction. When possible, consider how students might create their own original versions.

The focus on visual literacy in anchor standard seven (R.CCR.7) is likely to represent a genuine departure from what most middle school educators teach. In sixth grade, multi-literacies take a front seat: movement, light, sound, and images are prominent (Frey, Fisher, & Gonzalez, 2010).

Sixth-grade English teacher Omar Ali uses the radio play "Sorry, Wrong Number" (Fletcher, 1948a, 1980) to work toward the standard seven concepts. He says, "I came by this play when I first saw it in the text exemplars list in the CCSS document. To be honest, I really wasn't familiar with it. But I got my hands on the radio script version of the play, and I was hooked. I could really see how I could use it to teach about dramatic form, and use a bit of modern technology to do so."

Using the Dramatists Play Service version (Fletcher, 1948a), Mr. Ali leads his class in analyzing the playwright's introduction and discusses with students the evolution of the play from radio drama, to live stage play, to film. He also builds some background knowledge about the context, knowing that his students will be unfamiliar with a telephone operating system that includes an operator and a switchboard. "I needed them to get into the context of the 1940s and its state of technology," he says, "so they could understand the suspense that builds."

During multiple readings of the short play, the class discusses the vocabulary of the stage directions. "The stage directions were more difficult than the scripted lines," Mr. Ali comments. "It says on the first page that the main character is a 'querulous, self-centered neurotic' so we had to spend some time on what that meant. We also looked for actions and words that reaffirmed those characteristics."

After reading the play, the class listens to the original radio version with Agnes Moorehead (Fletcher, 1948b). Mr. Ali notes, "It really challenged them to listen to the sound design, and to understand how the sounds were an integral part of the suspense. They wouldn't have gotten that by just reading it." His students then produce their own version as a podcast, using sound effects to move the plot forward. "I have to say I was a little skeptical about this suspense unit, because my first impression was that it would just be horror stories. But now we're hooked. The kids found an episode from the *Twilight Zone* on YouTube, and now they are asking when we're going to do 'The Hitchhiker'!" (the other script in the book).

Range of Reading and Level of Text Complexity in Literature

Anchor standard ten (R.CCR.10) in this domain is brief but heavily influences much of the instruction across all the domains and other standards. Viewed across the grades 6–8 band, one can see how text complexity and scaffolded instruction intersect (see table 2.7). The grade-level standards reference the grades 6–8 text exemplars and further note that by the end of eighth grade, students should be able to read similar stories, dramas, and poems independently and proficiently (NGA & CCSSO, 2010a). The grades 6–8 band is further defined with a 925–1185L (Lexile range). This range is broader range than that MetaMetrics previously defined for the grades 6–8 band (860–1010L) (NGA & CCSSO, 2010b).

Table 2.7: Literature Standards for Domain Range of Reading and Level of Text Complexity, Grades 6–8

Anchor Standard	Grade 6 Standard	Grade 7 Standard	Grade 8 Standard
	Lexile Range: 925–1185L*		
R.CCR.10: Read and comprehend complex literary and informational texts independently and proficiently.	**RL.6.10:** By the end of the year, read and comprehend literature, including stories, dramas, and poems, in the grades 6–8 text complexity band proficiently, with scaffolding as needed at the high end of the range.	**RL.7.10:** By the end of the year, read and comprehend literature, including stories, dramas, and poems, in the grades 6–8 text complexity band proficiently, with scaffolding as needed at the high end of the range.	**RL.8.10:** By the end of the year, read and comprehend literature, including stories, dramas, and poems, at the high end of grades 6–8 text complexity band independently and proficiently.

* This is a quantitative measure only. Full assessment of text complexity must also include qualitative factors, and reader and task considerations.

Source: Adapted from NGA & CCSSO, 2010a, pp. 35 and 37.

These text-complexity levels are likely to be challenging for many students, but keep in mind that these are end-of-year expectations. Furthermore, merely giving students difficult texts and then expecting them to somehow read them is a sure recipe for failure (Allington, 2002). In order for students to be able to read and comprehend more difficult texts, they require purposeful instruction that relies on a gradual release of responsibility model of instruction (Fisher, Frey, & Nelson, 2010; Pearson & Gallagher, 1983).

Reading Standards for Informational Text in Grades 6–8

The Reading Standards for Informational Text parallel the Reading Standards for Literature. These standards describe the uses of content-rich literary nonfiction that focus on a concept or topic, biographies and autobiographies, photographic essays, procedural texts, and texts that draw from primary source documents (Moss, 2003). Informational texts can and should be used across disciplines, not only in the English classroom, as they are equally as valuable for building content knowledge as they are as materials for reading instruction. The CCSS recommend that by eighth grade, students should have a reading diet comprised of 45 percent literary text and 55 percent informational text (NGA & CCSSO, 2010a). However, this percentage should take into account all of the texts a student reads across the school day. This goal is easy to attain in middle school where students use complex informational texts in history and social studies, science, mathematics, and technical subjects. In the English classroom, literature dominates, but students should also encounter informational text there—not only in their content classes. Like the literature exemplars in appendix B of the CCSS (NGA & CCSSO, 2010c), informational text exemplars are organized as a 6–8 grade band. Table 2.8 lists example texts.

Table 2.8: Exemplars for Informational Texts in Grades 6–8

Genre	Grade 6	Grade 7	Grade 8
Informational Texts	Petry (1996): *Harriet Tubman: Conductor on the Underground Railroad*	Douglass (2005): *Narrative of the Life of Frederick Douglass, an American Slave*	Churchill (1940): "Blood, Toil, Tears and Sweat"

Source: Adapted from NGA & CCSSO, 2010c.

As with the ELA standards for literature, the Informational Text standards emanate from the same set of anchor standards. One noticeable difference is that anchor standard eight (R.CCR.8), which concerns argumentation, is represented in the Informational Text part. In the same fashion that your collaborative team analyzed the standards for literature, we invite you to do the same in this section using the four-part protocol described in figure 2.1 (page 28): (1) What is familiar? (2) What is new? (3) What is likely to be challenging for students? (4) What is likely to be challenging for teachers? (Visit **go.solution-tree.com/commoncore** for an online-only reproducible version of figure 2.1 that you can use for this analysis with your collaborative team.)

Key Ideas and Details in Informational Texts

The grade-level standards for informational texts are similar to those for literature in the sense that they require students to cite textual evidence (see table 2.9, page 48). In fact, standards one and two for informational texts are duplicates of those for literature. As a reminder, using text-based questions is especially valuable in encouraging students to engage in multiple readings. This is particularly important when students are reading conceptually dense informational texts. Anchor standard three (R.CCR.3) is somewhat different because it describes the progression of key individuals, events, and ideas across a text, rather than story elements such as plot. In addition, understanding

Table 2.9: Informational Text Standards for Domain Key Ideas and Details, Grades 6–8

Anchor Standards	Grade 6 Standards	Grade 7 Standards	Grade 8 Standards
R.CCR.1: Read closely to determine what the text says explicitly and to make logical inferences from it; cite specific textual evidence when writing or speaking to support conclusions drawn from the text.	**RI.6.1:** Cite textual evidence to support analysis of what the text says explicitly as well as inferences drawn from the text.	**RI.7.1:** Cite several pieces of textual evidence to support analysis of what the text says explicitly as well as inferences drawn from the text.	**RI.8.1:** Cite the textual evidence that most strongly supports an analysis of what the text says explicitly as well as inferences drawn from the text.
R.CCR.2: Determine central ideas or themes of a text and analyze their development; summarize the key supporting details and ideas.	**RI.6.2:** Determine a central idea of a text and how it is conveyed through particular details; provide a summary of the text distinct from personal opinions or judgments.	**RI.7.2:** Determine two or more central ideas in a text and analyze their development over the course of the text; provide an objective summary of the text.	**RI.8.2:** Determine a central idea of a text and analyze its development over the course of the text, including its relationship to supporting ideas; provide an objective summary of the text.
R.CCR.3: Analyze how and why individuals, events, and ideas develop and interact over the course of the text.	**RI.6.3:** Analyze in detail how a key individual, event, or idea is introduced, illustrated, and elaborated in a text (such as through examples or anecdotes).	**RI.7.3:** Analyze the interactions between individuals, events, and ideas in a text (such as how ideas influence individuals or events or how individuals influence ideas or events).	**RI.8.3:** Analyze how a text makes connections among and distinctions between individuals, ideas, or events (such as through comparisons, analogies, or categories).

Source: Adapted from NGA & CCSSO, 2010a, pp. 35 and 39.

the relationships between ideas, concepts, or events also grows across the three grades, with students examining the internal construction of the content knowledge, eventually drawing distinctions through the use of comparisons and analogies.

In one sixth-grade English classroom, four students gather around a table to discuss their latest reading, *Roll of Thunder, Hear My Cry* (Taylor, 1976), which has raised debate regarding race. Their teacher, Ben Hansen, selects a brief reading from the PBS documentary *Race—The Power of an Illusion* (California Newsreel, 2003). Mr. Hansen chose a section of the discussion guide (California Newsreel, 2003), which proved to be an ideal tool for *reciprocal teaching*, a small-group reading routine that increases comprehension through consolidation of information (Palincsar & Brown, 1986). In reciprocal teaching, students read short passages of a longer text together, then briefly summarize the main points, ask text-based questions, clarify difficult words or concepts, and make predictions about what information they expect to encounter in subsequent passages.

Students read "Ten Things Everyone Should Know About Race," a one-page expository text that presents ten facts in an annotated list format (California Newsreel, 2003). Students Leah, Charles, Francisco, and Zena have used reciprocal teaching a number of times and quickly begin chunking the text. Zena says, "It seems to me that it makes sense to read a couple of items at a time. They probably have a lot to do with each other." The other students agree and draw lines under the third, sixth, and tenth items, and then they read the title and opening statement silently.

"The writer for this really made our job easy!" remarks Francisco. "The questions are all right there for us. Listen: 'Our eyes tell us that people look different. But what do those differences mean? Are they biological? Has race always been with us? How does race affect people today?' So there's my prediction—the list will answer the questions at the beginning of this reading. Let's read the first set of facts."

After reading the first statement about race as a modern concept, the conversation picks up. Leah observes, "I'm really surprised that the word *race* didn't exist before the year 1500. How can that be?"

"I guess it's because of what it says in the third fact: 'Human subspecies don't exist.' I never thought of it exactly that way before, but it's not like we can be divided up like the plants we're studying about in science," says Charles.

"I wonder why it got changed around all of a sudden," speculates Francisco. "What happened to make people think about race?"

"We've still got to summarize," Zena reminds the group. "How about this? '*Race* is an idea that started in 1500, even though there's no genetic reason for it.' How does that sound?"

"That's good! Write it down on the list for us. Let's read the next three so we can get finished," Leah responds.

The group continues until each student finishes the text. By the end, the students have created some summary sentences that Mr. Hansen will use when he leads the entire class in a discussion of the article.

Craft and Structure in Informational Texts

Anchor standard four (R.CCR.4) in this domain is on the importance of general and domain-specific words and phrases within a larger piece of text, especially as it applies to the author's word choice and purposeful use of connotative and figurative language to express ideas (see table 2.10, page 50). Anchor standard five (R.CCR.5) deserves special attention, as it highlights how the organizational structures and features tie these words and phrases to conceptual knowledge. Anchor standard six (R.CCR.6) requires students to understand both the author's point of view and how it contrasts with the viewpoints of others.

Table 2.10: Informational Text Standards for Domain Craft and Structure, Grades 6–8

Anchor Standards	Grade 6 Standards	Grade 7 Standards	Grade 8 Standards
R.CCR.4: Interpret words and phrases as they are used in a text, including determining technical, connotative, and figurative meanings, and analyze how specific word choices shape meaning and tone.	**RI.6.4:** Determine the meaning of words and phrases as they are used in a text, including figurative, connotative, and technical meanings.	**RI.7.4:** Determine the meaning of words and phrases as they are used in a text, including figurative, connotative, and technical meanings; analyze the impact of a specific word choice on meaning and tone.	**RI.8.4:** Determine the meaning of words and phrases as they are used in a text, including figurative, connotative, and technical meanings; analyze the impact of specific word choices on meaning and tone, including analogies or allusions to other texts.
R.CCR.5: Analyze the structure of texts, including how specific sentences, paragraphs, and larger portions of the text (like a section, chapter, scene, or stanza) relate to each other and the style of a text.	**RI.6.5:** Analyze how a particular sentence, paragraph, chapter, or section fits into the overall structure of a text and contributes to the development of the ideas.	**RI.7.5:** Analyze the structure an author uses to organize a text, including how the major sections contribute to the whole and to the development of the ideas.	**RI.8.5:** Analyze in detail the structure of a specific paragraph in a text, including the role of particular sentences in developing and refining a key concept.
R.CCR.6: Assess how point of view or purpose shapes the content and style of a text.	**RI.6.6:** Determine an author's point of view or purpose in a text and explain how it is conveyed in the text.	**RI.7.6:** Determine an author's point of view or purpose in a text and analyze how the author distinguishes his or her position from that of others.	**RI.8.6:** Determine an author's point of view or purpose in a text and analyze how the author acknowledges and responds to conflicting evidence or viewpoints.

Source: Adapted from NGA & CCSSO, 2010a, pp. 35 and 39.

Seventh-grade English teacher Maureen Rogow discusses two pages of text with her students using a close-reading approach (Fisher, Frey, & Lapp, 2012; Richards, 1929). A guided close reading of a worthy passage consists of:

- An initial independent reading to gain familiarity with the text

- Annotations of the text to note patterns, confusions, and connections

- Teacher think-alouds to scaffold comprehension

- Text-dependent questions

- Discussion using evidence from the text
- Opportunities to re-read the passage, both in its entirety and using selective portions of the passage

Earlier in the week, the class read the Langston Hughes (1990) poem "Mother to Son." Knowing that biographical information about Hughes would further contextualize the poem, Ms. Rogow selects a chapter on the poet from *Black Stars of the Harlem Renaissance* (Haskins, Tate, Cox, & Wilkinson, 2002). After briefly introducing the reading, the students move into small groups to *read with a pencil* as Ms. Rogow calls it: underlining unfamiliar words and phrases and marking the text with arrows to signal connections. After students discuss their first reading with one another and then as a class, Ms. Rogow gains a sense of what she would need to model during think-alouds.

She projects a copy of the text on a document camera and reads aloud while students follow silently. In the first paragraph, she comes to this sentence: "Born in Joplin, Missouri, James Langston Hughes never seemed to be able to set down roots for himself" (Haskins et al., 2002, p. 95). After reading the next two paragraphs, she returns to this sentence and begins to think aloud.

"I'm drawn to that opening sentence because it's so jarring. As I read, I could see what the author was thinking when that was written. His dad left when he was young and moved to South America," she says, as she underlines the phrase. "Now there's more chaos. His mother moved around a lot and by the time he's six he's in Mexico City," she continues as she highlights more phrases. "But when I read the next sentence on page ninety-five, it stopped me in my tracks: 'He went to live with his maternal grandmother in Kansas City, while his mother continued her nomadic lifestyle on her own.'" She continues, "Wow! This poor child, shuffling around the continent, and then his mother leaves him at his grandmother's. I'm making a timeline in my head. I'd like you to re-read the next few paragraphs to continue his childhood timeline."

This time the instability of his childhood is more apparent to the students. Julio notes that shortly after the boy's grandmother dies, he has to live with friends. "What's the obvious question here?" Ms. Rogow asks. "Where was his mom?" several students ask. A few minutes later, Ms. Rogow asks several text-dependent questions to foster discussion and comments, "Let's look further, because she doesn't disappear completely." Corinne supplies a key detail: "His mother sent for him two years later." A paragraph later, comes the final event: "At age fourteen, he was on his own."

Ms. Rogow instructs the class, "Now let's pause on this and return to the poem for a few minutes. Read it again, and let's talk about whether you have a different perspective on this now." This time, the students are considering both the message of the poem and the poet's childhood. This time they see something different; a message beyond the written text. Ms. Rogow asks, "Knowing what you know about him now, do you believe this poem was borne out of personal experience?" Angelo is the first to answer: "I think he wished his mom would have been there to give him any advice," he offers. "He seems like a kid who's been on his own a lot, and there really wasn't anyone who would stick around long enough to give him advice."

Integration of Knowledge and Ideas in Informational Texts

This domain highlights the importance of being able to synthesize and integrate information from two or more sources (see table 2.11, page 53), especially to compare and contrast points of view and argument. Anchor standard seven (R.CCR.7) stresses the need to look at information shared across a variety of formats, including visual and digital media. Argumentation dominates anchor standard eight (R.CCR.8), requiring students to excise claims and evidence the author uses. Like standard seven, anchor standard nine (R.CCR.9) challenges students to critically analyze opposing information offered in two or more texts.

The eighth-grade students in Oscar Cruz's English class analyze the Carl Sandburg poem "Chicago" (1916/1994) in their Writers and Place unit. Their understanding of how the history of a place can fuel creativity included several readings concerning this Midwestern city. A short informational reading titled "Hustlers" from *Chicago: City on the Make* (Algren, 2011) grounds the city's rough-and-tumble atmosphere in the early encounters between explorers, traders, and the native Potawatomi who lived there. Mr. Cruz annotates the text for students in advance of the reading, including the words *Sauganash* (the name of a Mohawk-British fur trader) and *vermilion* (a red mineral pigment), but let them work out *portage* and *rigged* using context clues. After doing a close reading of the text, Mr. Cruz asks students to return to it to find evocative words and phrases that echoed the sentiments of the Sandburg (1916/1994) poem. They identify "Horse dealers and horse stealers" (p. 10) and compare this to the poem's line:

> Come and show me another city with lifted head singing so proud
>
> to be alive and coarse and strong and cunning.

One student, Jade, notices, "In both of them, they're proud that they're kinda nasty, like when you're proud that your neighborhood is tough."

Another student, D'Andre, reads a passage from the text: "'It's still the easiest joint in the country in which to jump bond, as well as for staying out of jail altogether. The price commonly being whatever you have in your wallet. If the wallet is empty, a fifty-cent cigar will usually do it'" (Algren, 2011, p. 13). Mr. Cruz asks, "That's really powerful. Can you link it to the poem?" The boy nods and reads:

> And they tell me you are crooked and I answer:
>
> Yes, it is true, I have seen the gunman kill and go free to kill again.

"Man, things don't change, right?" Mr. Cruz says. You've got Algren writing about things that happened two hundred years ago, and Sandburg writing about things that happened one hundred years ago, and they're both talking about the same idea: that this is a place where people don't always live by the rules. But Sandburg says that was also a good thing. Does Algren?"

Table 2.11: Informational Text Standards for Domain Integration of Knowledge and Ideas, Grades 6–8

Anchor Standards	Grade 6 Standards	Grade 7 Standards	Grade 8 Standards
R.CCR.7: Integrate and evaluate content presented in diverse media and formats, including visually and quantitatively, as well as in word.	**RI.6.7:** Integrate information presented in different media or formats (both visually and quantitatively), as well as in words to develop a coherent understanding of a topic or issue.	**RI.7.7:** Compare and contrast a text to an audio, video, or multimedia version of the text, analyzing each medium's portrayal of the subject (like how the delivery of a speech affects the impact of the words).	**RI.8.7:** Evaluate the advantages and disadvantages of using different mediums (like print or digital text, video, or multimedia) to present a particular topic or idea.
R.CCR.8: Delineate and evaluate the argument and specific claims in a text, including the validity of the reasoning as well as the relevance and sufficiency of the evidence.	**RI.6.8:** Trace and evaluate the argument and specific claims in a text, distinguishing claims that are supported by reasons and evidence from claims that are not.	**RI.7.8:** Trace and evaluate the argument and specific claims in a text, assessing whether the reasoning is sound and the evidence is relevant and sufficient to support the claims.	**RI.8.8:** Delineate and evaluate the argument and specific claims in a text, assessing whether the reasoning is sound and the evidence is relevant and sufficient; recognize when irrelevant evidence is introduced.
R.CCR.9: Analyze how two or more texts address similar themes or topics in order to build knowledge or to compare the approaches the authors take.	**RI.6.9:** Compare and contrast one author's presentation of events with that of another (such as a memoir and a biography on the same person).	**RI.7.9:** Analyze how two or more authors writing about the same topic shape their presentations of key information by emphasizing different evidence or advancing different interpretations of facts.	**RI.8.9:** Analyze a case in which two or more texts provide conflicting information on the same topic and identify where the texts disagree on matters of fact or interpretation.

Source: Adapted from NGA & CCSSO, 2010a, pp. 35 and 39.

The groups of students turn back to one another at their tables and to the text. Jasmine notices that the author refers to Jane Addams. "We learned about her in social studies, remember? She was the lady that helped the mothers and babies in . . . I forget the name of the place." Josh interjects, "Hull House!"

"Yeah, that's it—Hull House. Those are the do-gooders he's talking about," says Jasmine.

"And she didn't follow rules, either, because her folks just wanted her to get married and have grandkids for them," Josh says.

"But I don't think Algren's really saying a lot about the good side of breaking rules. Mostly it's just about breaking rules," comments D'Andre.

"Yeah, you're right," says Silvia. "There's that part about the crime-boss mayor they had. It says he 'greeted his fellow citizens correctly then with a cheery, "Fellow hoodlums!" on page fourteen.' Maybe it says it later in the book, but not here."

"That's what he means by a *rigged ball game* on the same page," says Jasmine. "Like sometimes cheating's just cheating, and maybe he doesn't see a good side to it, like Sandburg did."

Mr. Cruz is pleased with the discussion. He comments, "They're used to having information presented to them in a clear-cut way, like it's all black and white. I want them to see the gray. That's what English is about, right? Holding two conflicting ideas in your head at the same time and still being able to make sense of it. That's the world I want to show them this year."

Range of Reading and Level of Text Complexity in Informational Texts

With the exception of naming genres, the wording of anchor standard ten (R.CCR.10) is the same for informational texts as it is for literature (see table 2.12). As illustrated in previous examples, determining a text's complexity and then using it with other texts in such a way—using the staircase approach—so ideas build on one another is more complex. Not only are there quantitative measures to consider but also qualitative factors, individual factors about the reader, and the tasks that the reader is expected to complete.

Table 2.12: Informational Text Standards for Domain Range of Reading and Level of Text Complexity, Grades 6–8

Anchor Standard	Grade 6 Standard	Grade 7 Standard	Grade 8 Standard
R.CCR.10: Read and comprehend complex literary and informational texts independently and proficiently.	**RI.6.10:** By the end of the year, read and comprehend literary nonfiction in the grades 6–8 text complexity band proficiently, with scaffolding as needed at the high end of the range.	**RI.7.10:** By the end of the year, read and comprehend literary nonfiction in the grades 6–8 text complexity band proficiently, with scaffolding as needed at the high end of the range.	**RI.8.10:** By the end of the year, read and comprehend literary nonfiction at the high end of the grades 6–8 text complexity band independently and proficiently.

Source: Adapted from NGA & CCSSO, 2010a, pp. 35 and 39.

Your collaborative team can begin to establish a sequence of texts across grades 6–8 by beginning with the texts already in use. Figure 2.3 provides a protocol for teams to use as you make these determinations about text complexity.

Title of text: _____

Author: _____   **Publication date:** _____

Current Experiences

What is the current use of the text? (Include grade level, content area, and unit or topic.)

What have our experiences been with using this text?

What are its positive outcomes?

What are its drawbacks?

Quantitative Measures

What is the quantitative measure of this text? What measure did we use?

Qualitative Factors

1 = Comfortable (texts that are comfortable or build background, fluency, and skills)

2 = Grade level (texts that require grade-appropriate skills)

3 = Stretch (texts that stretch a reader's thinking or require instruction)

Levels of Meaning and Purpose	Rating
Density and complexity	
Figurative language	
Purpose	
Score	

Structure	Rating
Genre	
Organization	
Narration	
Text features and graphics	
Score	

Language and Conventionality	Rating
Standard English and variations	
Register	
Score	

Knowledge Demands	Rating
Background knowledge	
Prior knowledge	
Cultural knowledge	
Vocabulary knowledge	
Score	
Total qualitative score	

Figure 2.3: Collaborative team protocol for determining text complexity.

continued →

Questions for Considering the Reader and the Task

Will this text maintain our students' attention?

Will this text require specialized supports (such as language support or accommodations)?

Does the text's topic or genre interest our students?

Does the reader possess the needed metacognitive skills to comprehend the text?

Does the reader have sufficient background or prior knowledge to link to new information?

What direct experiences do our students have that may make this text more accessible?

Does this text require modeling of comprehension and word-solving strategies?

Does the task match the readers' collaborative learning and social skills?

Does the task provide sufficient challenge for our students, while avoiding protracted frustration?

Recommendations for Using This Text

For which grade is this text most appropriate, given the qualitative and quantitative analyses?

What are the specific teaching points necessary for student understanding?

Would this text be best for whole-class instruction, small-group learning, collaborative activities, or independent tasks?

Visit **go.solution-tree.com/commoncore** for a reproducible version of this figure.

A good starting place to begin the conversation about text complexity is to refer to the text exemplars in appendix B of the Common Core State Standards (NGA & CCSSO, 2010c). Ideally, some of the texts already in use will appear on this list, and can serve as placeholders for the texts team members have identified as needing further analysis. We suggest that the team discuss two or three texts at each meeting to alert team members to these considerations. As your team collectively becomes more adept at analyzing texts, pairs of teachers can collaborate to assess books for text complexity and suggest recommendations for using them in class. Over time, the collaborative planning team can use these assessments to create a sequence of texts to use at the beginning, middle, and end of each grade level to assure that texts are being used as a staircase from one year to the next.

Conclusion

The Common Core State Standards for reading build on content teachers already know. Students in grades 6–8 may still need instruction in the foundational skills of reading, such as decoding and fluency, as well as in how to read narrative and expository texts. But the Common Core for English language arts require that teachers raise their expectations and provide students with access to complex texts and scaffolded instruction so that they can justify their ideas and opinions. To ensure that students are prepared to meet these increased expectations, teachers have to plan new lessons that allow students to consolidate their understanding and apply what they have learned. This is a tall order for an individual teacher. However, when teachers work in collaborative teams within a professional learning community to plan instruction and review student performance, it is possible and even enjoyable to plan new lessons. As we have noted throughout this chapter, collaborative teams should focus their conversations around four questions.

1. What is familiar in the CCSS at each grade level?

2. What appears to be new based on prior standards?

3. What may be challenging for students?

4. What may be challenging for teachers?

In addition, collaborative teams should engage in lesson planning and a systematic review of student performance to determine which lessons are effective for which students, and what they need to do to ensure that all students reach the standard. We will focus on common formative assessment and responding to students who do not meet the expectations during initial instruction in the final chapter of this book. Before doing so, we will explore the Writing, Speaking and Listening, and Language standards.

CHAPTER 3

Implementing the Common Core State Standards for Writing

KEY QUESTIONS

- To what extent does your team understand the Writing standards: What is the essence of each standard? What teacher actions facilitate the standards in practice? What evidence will we accept that students are learning this standard?

- How do the three major text types influence the writing assignments students complete and the genres they must learn?

- How is technology used to allow students to produce and publish their writing such that they can interact and collaborate with others?

Seventh-grade English teacher Stephanie Tarpley asks, "Can social media affect social change? There has been lots of attention given to various charitable organizations and social causes that use social media like Facebook and Twitter, but does it have any long-lasting effects, or is it lots of hype for a short while?"

Using informational articles and persuasive essays, Ms. Tarpley and her students explore how social media may or may not be affecting charitable organizations and social causes. Inspired by materials from YCteen, a youth journalism organization, Ms. Tarpley assembles several short readings on the topic for her students to form a foundation of understanding. She uses Malcolm Gladwell's (2010) essay, "Small Change: Why the Revolution Will Not Be Tweeted" to build her own background knowledge, and identifies arguments he uses in the article to develop the unit. Following the author's lead, she located first-person accounts of sit-ins conducted across the American South during the civil rights movement and contrasted these with newspaper accounts of the same events. In addition, they viewed several Twitter feeds about the Arab Spring protests of 2011 and contrasted these with contemporary broadcast media reports. As part of this unit, students wrote daily. Sometimes they wrote short, informal exit slips that summarized the main points of a reading and discussion. But as students began to understand the complexities of the issue, they started to formulate their own arguments. Over the two-week unit, each student wrote a longer essay addressing the question Ms. Tarpley first posed to them. They cited evidence from the readings, Twitter feeds, and broadcasts to support their claims.

Ms. Tarpley notes, "I was really impressed with what they accomplished. Students at this age often think that whatever's new must automatically be better. This definitely is not a settled issue, and I want them to appreciate that the great writers wrestled with the issues of the day, just like they're doing. I like to think that they'll view this issue with a more critical eye."

A Collaborative Planning Team in Action

The genesis for Ms. Tarpley's social media unit came from collaborative conversations with her fellow team members in grades 6–8. After their analysis of the Common Core State Standards for writing, they identified several goals for improvement in their writing instruction. Writing for argumentation was at the top of their list.

"We looked at the kinds of writing we typically assigned, and we quickly realized our assignments were not up to snuff," Ms. Tarpley says. "Writing wasn't frequent enough, and it was mostly creative writing and personal response stuff. We knew we needed to create more formal writing opportunities that draw on students' critical-thinking skills."

In chapter 2, we introduced four planning questions for the collaborative team to use when analyzing and discussing the Common Core Reading standards: (1) What's new? (2) What's familiar? (3) What may be challenging for students? (4) What may be challenging for teachers? Collaborative teams may decide to continue using those questions as they investigate the writing standards. However, we propose a different tool for analysis of the writing standards, one that can facilitate discussion about the links between (1) standards, (2) instruction, and (3) formative assessment.

1. **Standards:** What is the essence or big idea of this standard?

2. **Instruction:** What teacher actions facilitate this standard in practice?

3. **Formative assessment:** What evidence will we accept that students are learning this standard?

Ms. Tarpley's collaborative team uses a similar method when first unpacking the writing standards. Figure 3.1 is a protocol for conducting this inquiry. Visit **go.solution-tree .com/commoncore** for a reproducible version of this figure that you can use in your collaborative team to analyze other writing standards.

Anchor Standards for Writing

The college and career readiness anchor standards for writing were designed to articulate the need for a strong foundation across disciplines, audiences, and purposes. Writing, like speaking, is also a form of communication; however, there are two important differences with writing: the audience is often unseen, and the product is often permanent. The fact is that we judge others by what they write and how they write. Too many misspellings and we wonder whether the person is careless; we assume disorganized discourse is the product of a jumbled mind. We often dismiss opinions altogether if writers do not back up their claims. Writers may be careful, organized, and articulate, but their

Writing anchor standard six (W.CCR.1): Write arguments to support claims in an analysis of substantive topics or texts, using valid reasoning and sufficient evidence.

CCSS grade band: Grades 6–8

CCSS grade strand: Writing

Anchor standard domain: Text Types and Purposes

Grade-Level Standard	Standard: What Is the Essence of This Standard?	Instruction: What Teacher Actions Facilitate This Standard in Practice?	Formative Assessment: What Evidence Will We Accept That Students Are Learning This Standard?
Grade 6 **W.6.1:** Write arguments to support claims with clear reasons and relevant evidence. a. Introduce claims and organize the reasons and evidence clearly. b. Support claims with clear reasons and relevant evidence, using credible sources and demonstrating an understanding of the topic or text. c. Use words, phrases, and clauses to clarify the relationships among claims and reasons. d. Establish and maintain a formal style. e. Provide a concluding statement or section that follows from the argument presented.			

continued →

Figure 3.1: Guiding questions for grade-by-grade analysis of the Writing standards.

Grade-Level Standard	Standard: What Is the Essence of This Standard?	Instruction: What Teacher Actions Facilitate This Standard in Practice?	Formative Assessment: What Evidence Will We Accept That Students Are Learning This Standard?
Grade 7 **W.7.1:** Write arguments to support claims with clear reasons and relevant evidence. a. Introduce claims, acknowledge alternate or opposing claims, and organize the reasons and evidence logically. b. Support claims with logical reasoning and relevant evidence, using accurate, credible sources and demonstrating an understanding of the topic or text. c. Use words, phrases, and clauses to create cohesion and clarify the relationships among claims, reasons, and evidence. d. Establish and maintain a formal style. e. Provide a concluding statement or section that follows from and supports the argument presented.			
Grade 8 **W.8.1:** Write arguments to support claims with clear reasons and relevant evidence. a. Introduce claims, acknowledge and distinguish the claims from alternate or opposing claims, and organize the reasons and evidence logically.			

b. Support claims with logical reasoning and relevant evidence, using accurate, credible sources and demonstrating an understanding of the topic or text.

c. Use words, phrases, and clauses to create cohesion and clarify the relationships among claims, counterclaims, reasons, and evidence.

d. Establish and maintain a formal style.

e. Provide a concluding statement or section that follows from and supports the argument presented.

Source: Adapted from NGA & CCSSO, 2010a, p. 42.

Visit go.solution-tree.com/commoncore for a reproducible version of this figure.

writing does not show this. The anchor standards are an effort to ensure that students are able to communicate effectively in written form in order to represent themselves in the classroom, workplace, and world. There are ten anchor standards for writing, extending from kindergarten through twelfth grade. These standards are organized into four domains: (1) Text Types and Purposes, (2) Production and Distribution of Writing, (3) Research to Build and Present Knowledge, and (4) Range of Writing (see NGA & CCSSO, 2010a, p. 41).

Text Types and Purposes

This domain has three anchor standards (W.CCR.1, 2, and 3) that define three major types of writing with specific purposes: (1) writing for argumentation, (2) writing to inform or explain, and (3) writing to convey real or imagined experiences. These basic text types are expressed through many writing genres, which are often a blend of two or more text types. For example, an opinion piece may include elements of argumentation, as well as narrative to describe the writer's perspective. Therefore, these text types should not be viewed too narrowly as a mandate to teach only three writing genres. Rather, it is an important reminder to us as educators that we need to clearly link purposes for writing, not just the format for a genre.

1. Write arguments to support claims in an analysis of substantive topics or texts, using valid reasoning and relevant and sufficient evidence. (W.CCR.1)

2. Write informative/explanatory texts to examine and convey complex ideas and information clearly and accurately through the effective selection, organization, and analysis of content. (W.CCR.2)

3. Write narratives to develop real or imagined experiences or events using effective technique, well-chosen details, and well-structured event sequences. (W.CCR.3) (NGA & CCSSO, 2010a, p. 41)

Production and Distribution of Writing

This domain focuses on the communicative nature of writing. Anchor standard four (W.CCR.4) encourages us to link the task, purpose, and audience to the selected genre or format. In anchor standard six (W.CCR.6), we can see how writing is lifted from a solitary and isolated act to one that involves peers, fellow writers, teachers, and experts across the classroom, community, and world. Anchor standard five (W.CCR.5) bridges the other two standards in this domain, articulating the processes a writer must necessarily engage with in order to communicate effectively.

4. Produce clear and coherent writing in which the development, organization, and style are appropriate to task, purpose, and audience. (WCCR.4)

5. Develop and strengthen writing as needed by planning, revising, editing, rewriting, or trying a new approach. (W.CCR.5)

6. Use technology, including the Internet, to produce and publish writing and to interact and collaborate with others. (W.CCR.6) (NGA & CCSSO, 2010a, p. 41)

Research to Build and Present Knowledge

The importance of academic writing is foregrounded in this domain, which has three anchor standards (W.CCR.7, 8, and 9). The standards encourage learners to gather information from a variety of sources in order to investigate worthwhile topics. These should be a natural extension of the learning students engage in across their academic career—not just as consumers of information, but also as users and producers of information. This requires that they critically analyze information sources, both literary and informational, and use it in their writing to conduct inquiry and research.

> 7. Conduct short as well as more sustained research projects based on focused questions, demonstrating understanding of the subject under investigation. (W.CCR.7)
>
> 8. Gather relevant information from multiple print and digital sources, assess the credibility and accuracy of each source, and integrate the information while avoiding plagiarism. (W.CCR.8)
>
> 9. Draw evidence from literary or informational texts to support analysis, reflection, and research. (W.CCR.9) (NGA & CCSSO, 2010a, p. 41)

Range of Writing

The key word in anchor standard ten (W.CCR.10) is *routinely*—writing is not something that is done only occasionally, but daily, and for extended periods of time so that writers increase their volume. As with reading, the intent is to build skill and stamina through frequent application and practice. This is a notable departure from the practices of many middle school teachers. Jennifer Gilbert and Steve Graham's (2010) national survey of teachers in grades 4–6 finds that only fifteen minutes a day are devoted to writing instruction, compared to forty minutes a day in primary grades. In addition, grades 4–6 students spent only twenty-five minutes a day producing writing of a paragraph or more in length. As the authors note, writing instruction truly is "the prisoner of time" (Gilbert & Graham, 2010, p. 511). The Common Core standards for grades 6–8 call for students to routinely engage in writing over extended periods of time, as well as during shorter periods (defined as a single sitting or a day or two).

Of course, writing is more than just assigning—purposeful instruction must occur. Steve Graham and Dolores Perin (2007) make eight recommendations for writing instruction in grades 4–12.

1. Teach students to plan, revise, and edit their writing. The authors found a large effect size (0.82) for struggling writers in grades 4–10, meaning that this was a *very* powerful approach that improved student performance.

2. Create opportunities for students to write summaries of their readings.

3. Make writing collaborative.

4. Set clear goals and establish purpose.

5. Allow students to write using word-processing tools.

6. Teach sentence combining as a method of composing more complex sentences.

7. Make writing part of the inquiry process.

8. Use writing models to discuss effective writing.

These recommendations do not comprise a writing curriculum, but rather aspects of writing instruction that should be included. Implementation of the Common Core State Standards in writing will require a concerted effort to address these eight recommendations.

The following is anchor standard ten for range of writing:

> 10. Write routinely over extended time frames (time for research, reflection, and revision) and shorter time frames (a single sitting or a day or two) for a range of tasks, purposes, and audiences. (W.CCR.10) (NGA & CCSSO, 2010a, p. 41)

The anchor standards frame a vision for writing across grades K–12. But before analyzing the standards for grades 6–8 in more detail, it is useful to gain a perspective on the development of writers from the primary grades to graduation. In understanding the behaviors of young adolescent writers, we can better interpret how these anchor standards link to grade-level expectations.

Characteristics of Writers

Classrooms are filled with students with different strengths and needs. In terms of writing, students do not all write equally well or share the same instructional needs. As we have noted, however, the Common Core State Standards provide teachers with information about appropriate grade-level expectations for writing acumen. These standards reflect an understanding about writing development and growth through four stages: (1) emergent, (2) early, (3) transitional, and (4) self-extending writers. Although there is a correlation between a student's age and his or her stage of writing development, it is important to recognize the writing behaviors at each stage of development, since classrooms are diverse places filled with students who have gaps in their experiences as well as extensive background knowledge. Table 3.1 describes characteristics for each writing stage.

Emergent Writers

These writers are just beginning to gain control of print and how it works. They are still learning that print carries a message and that they can create a new idea and then represent it on paper for others to appreciate. Emergent writers can generate text that retells a sequence of events in a story or in their personal lives, although the language they use is likely to be fairly simple, with few complex sentences containing more than one or two ideas. Their writing contains letters and words they know, and their name is likely to be prominently featured in their texts. Emergent writers:

- Learn how print works including spaces and punctuation

- Develop an understanding that their ideas can be written and re-read

- Integrate their ideas with known words

Table 3.1: Characteristics of Writers

Emergent Writers . . .	Early Writers . . .
• Are learning how print works • See the permanence of writing • Retell events in sequence • Use simple sentence construction • Use known words prominently	• Have rapid recall of letters and known words • Will use formulaic writing • Have writing constrained by limited known words • Use story grammar • Write longer texts, although ideas may not be consistent
Transitional Writers . . .	**Self-Extending Writers . . .**
• Apply text structures in their original writing • Recognize audience • Write longer texts with sustained ideas • Use more complex sentences • Use transition phrases and conjunctions	• Communicate a purposeful direction to audience • See writing as an extension of the writer • Write in multiple genres • Use words that are sophisticated and flexible • Engage in all aspects of editing

Visit **go.solution-tree.com/commoncore** for a reproducible version of this table.

Early Writers

Early writers are able to more rapidly recall letters, and they therefore can scribe their message more quickly. However, they are prone to formulaic writing that incorporates the limited number of words they can spell. (Any first-grade teacher can testify to the plethora of student-generated sentences that begin with "I like"). These early writers are engaging in editing, as evidenced by the increase in eraser marks and crossed-out words. They can generate their own ideas for writing topics and are applying some elements of story grammar, such as character, setting, plot, and problem and solution to their own writing. Later in this phase, students will begin writing multiparagraph texts, although the ideas introduced at the beginning of the piece may get lost along the way. Early writers:

- Increase their writing speed and accuracy

- Produce longer pieces of text, although they often lose the thread of their ideas

- Generate their own stories with increasingly complex plots and characters

Transitional Writers

Students in this phase of development are actively incorporating varied approaches for recognizing the audience in their original writing. For example, they create titles for their pieces, use *grabber* sentences to gain the reader's attention, and use descriptive vocabulary to evoke a response from the reader. Indeed, recognizing the role of the audience is a hallmark of writers in this phase of development. They are beginning to apply rudimentary structures to longer texts, such as listing directions for completing a task or writing a biography that contains the type of information expected in this literary form. Because their vocabulary has grown along with their language sophistication, they use more complex sentences containing multiple ideas. Students at this stage can use transition phrases and conjunctions to build these longer sentences. Their stamina has increased as well. Both mean sentence length and overall length of the text has increased. An important indicator of a transitional writer is his or her ability to sustain an idea or concept over the course of multiple paragraphs.

Students in the transitional phase of writing use a wide range of genres in their writing. They can write short informational reports using academic vocabulary, create multiparagraph essays on personal experiences, and construct original poems. They use conventional spelling and grammatical structures but often confuse irregular forms of words or grammar (for example, *gooses* instead of *geese*; *have went* instead of *have gone*). They use compound sentences.

Although this phase, like the others, is not strictly bound by grade level, many transitional writers emerge between grades 3–5. These transitional writers are more cognizant of the processes associated with writing. They are revising more of their work based on feedback from peers and the teacher, most likely at the sentence and paragraph level rather than at the document level. They are becoming more sophisticated in their use of multiple sources of information to support their own writing. Transitional writers:

- Write in multiple genres (for example, poetry, informational reports, narratives, and persuasive essays)

- Engage in author studies to examine the craft of writing (for example, studying Daniel Handler to learn to use irony in their writing or Christopher Paul Curtis to learn dialogue)

- Write rules and procedures for a variety of activities to practice technical writing (for example, directions for how to travel from school to the student's home)

- Create persuasive pieces to support a position (for example, "Why I should have a pet")

Self-Extending Writers

These sophisticated writers understand they are engaged in a complex process that is influenced by their application of specific strategies. This metacognitive awareness serves them well in being able to analyze their own writing and the writing of others.

Self-extending writers are expanding their repertoire of writing genres and can write narratives, persuasive essays, technical documents, responses to literature, and biographies and autobiographies. Importantly, they understand that each of these genres has specific rules; for example, the skills used to create a science lab report differ from writing a poem. Their control of the language, especially as it applies to vocabulary and multiple meanings, makes it easier for them to engage in a full editing process.

Students in this writing phase are notable for their ability to select the appropriate genre to match the task. They are learning to organize their ideas for longer pieces so that the plot moves well (for narrative) or the information is described in a logical manner (for expository). They increasingly use more complex sentences, and their word choice becomes more precise. Self-extending writers work toward two ideals: concise and precise. Their ability to edit is more sophisticated, and they are more likely to re-read their writing and retool sentences or sections. Self-extending writers:

- Operate flexibly between genres (that is, they can develop multiple forms of writing during the same day)

- Seek peer and teacher feedback and integrate it into their writing

- Recognize the value of using a wide variety of sources to develop their writing and seek original sources, not just those the teacher provides

- Use accurate and innovative punctuation, vocabulary, and grammatical structures

- Demonstrate individual voice and style

- Utilize writing as a means of clarifying their own thinking

Most students at the middle school level are in the late transitional and early self-extending phases of writing development, although individual students may be writing below or above expected levels. As we have noted, the Common Core State Standards articulate expectations for students across grade levels based on a common set of anchor standards. We'll explore the specific writing standards for grades 6–8 in the following section.

Samples of Student Writing

Observing how students are developing as writers is an important aspect of teaching writing well. The Common Core ELA contain a collection of student writing examples that will enable you and your collaborative team to gain added insights into what student writing looks like at various stages. As a future task for your team, use the annotated student writing examples for grades 6–8 featured in appendix C (NGA & CCSSO, 2010d). Collectively, these samples reflect a range of writing ability and were constructed under several conditions, including on-demand writing, as well as more polished pieces that were developed through several rounds of editing and revision. These include narrative and informative and explanatory pieces at all three grade levels, as well as argumentative pieces from writers in grades 6 through 8. We encourage your team to examine these samples together across the grade-level band in order to gain a better sense of the progression to look for as writers develop their craft and skill. These samples can serve as anchor papers for developing a consensus scoring procedure to be used at each grade level. These consensus scoring events serve as a tuning process for educators and provide valuable formative assessment data for making instructional decisions.

As we have noted previously, the Common Core State Standards articulate expectations for students across grade levels based on a common set of anchor standards. We'll explore the specific writing standards for grades 6–8 in the following section.

Writing Standards for Grades 6–8

The grade-level standards for writing are organized in the following domains: Text Types and Purposes, Production and Distribution of Writing, Research to Build and Present Knowledge, and Range of Writing (NGA & CCSSO, 2010a). We hope that teachers meet in their collaborative team to discuss these standards using the protocol introduced at the beginning of this chapter.

1. **Standards:** What is the essence of this standard?

2. **Instruction:** What teacher actions facilitate this standard in practice?

3. **Formative assessment:** What evidence will we accept that students are learning this standard?

Text Types and Purposes

The first three standards in this domain define three basic text types used in and out of school—(1) opinion and persuasive, (2) informative and explanatory, and (3) narrative (see table 3.2). Although the first anchor standard uses the term *argument*, the NGA and CCSSO (2010b) acknowledge that young writers are not yet developmentally situated to write for formal arguments:

> They develop a variety of methods to extend and elaborate their work by providing examples, offering reasons for their assertions, and explaining cause and effect. These kinds of expository structures are steps on the road to argument. (p. 23)

This has implications, especially for sixth-grade teachers, because their incoming students will not have had experience with argumentation as a formal process. Therefore, teachers must introduce it to their students. In addition, content teachers should consistently use the argumentation framework teachers design for your school, as well as across English classrooms, so that students are grounded in a solid foundation of rhetorical writing processes.

The three standards parallel one another, with each devoted to a specific text type. Anchor standard one (W.CCR.1) focuses on writing for argumentation, and in grade 7 also includes counterclaims. By grade 8, students should be able to formally organize claims, counterclaims, reason, and evidence. Anchor standard two (W.CCR.2) similarly focuses on writing for informative and explanatory purposes.

Table 3.2: Writing Standards for Domain Text Types and Purposes, Grades 6–8

Anchor Standards	Grade 6 Standards	Grade 7 Standards	Grade 8 Standards
W.CCR.1: Write arguments to support claims in an analysis of substantive topics or texts, using valid reasoning and relevant and sufficient evidence.	**W.6.1:** Write arguments to support claims with clear reasons and relevant evidence. a. Introduce claims and organize the reasons and evidence clearly. b. Support claims with clear reasons and relevant evidence, using credible sources and demonstrating an understanding of the topic or text. c. Use words, phrases, and clauses to clarify the relationships among claims and reasons. d. Establish and maintain a formal style. e. Provide a concluding statement or section that follows from the argument presented.	**W.7.1:** Write arguments to support claims with clear reasons and relevant evidence. a. Introduce claims, acknowledge alternate or opposing claims, and organize the reasons and evidence logically. b. Support claims with logical reasoning and relevant evidence, using accurate, credible sources and demonstrating an understanding of the topic or text. c. Use words, phrases, and clauses to create cohesion and clarify the relationships among claims, reasons, and evidence. d. Establish and maintain a formal style. e. Provide a concluding statement or section that follows from and supports the argument presented.	**W.8.1:** Write arguments to support claims with clear reasons and relevant evidence. a. Introduce claims, acknowledge and distinguish the claims from alternate or opposing claims, and organize the reasons and evidence logically. b. Support claims with logical reasoning and relevant evidence, using accurate, credible sources and demonstrating an understanding of the topic or text. c. Use words, phrases, and clauses to create cohesion and clarify the relationships among claims, counterclaims, reasons, and evidence. d. Establish and maintain a formal style. e. Provide a concluding statement or section that follows from and supports the argument presented.

continued →

Anchor Standards	Grade 6 Standards	Grade 7 Standards	Grade 8 Standards
W.CCR.2: Write informative or explanatory texts to examine and convey complex ideas and information clearly and accurately through the effective selection, organization, and analysis of content.	**W.6.2:** Write informative or explanatory texts to examine a topic and convey ideas, concepts, and information through the selection, organization, and analysis of relevant content. a. Introduce a topic; organize ideas, concepts, and information, using strategies such as definition, classification, comparison and contrast, and cause and effect; include formatting (like headings), graphics (like charts or tables), and multimedia when useful to aiding comprehension. b. Develop the topic with relevant facts, definitions, concrete details, quotations, or other information and examples. c. Use appropriate transitions to clarify the relationships among ideas and concepts. d. Use precise language and domain-specific vocabulary to inform about or explain the topic.	**W.7.2:** Write informative or explanatory texts to examine a topic and convey ideas, concepts, and information through the selection, organization, and analysis of relevant content. a. Introduce a topic clearly, previewing what is to follow; organize ideas, concepts, and information, using strategies such as definition, classification, comparison and contrast, and cause and effect; include formatting (like headings), graphics (like charts or tables), and multimedia when useful to aiding comprehension. b. Develop the topic with relevant facts, definitions, concrete details, quotations, or other information and examples. c. Use appropriate transitions to create cohesion and clarify the relationships among ideas and concepts. d. Use precise language and domain-specific vocabulary to inform about or explain the topic.	**W.8.2:** Write informative or explanatory texts to examine a topic and convey ideas, concepts, and information through the selection, organization, and analysis of relevant content. a. Introduce a topic clearly, previewing what is to follow; organize ideas, concepts, and information into broader categories; include formatting (like headings), graphics (like charts or tables), and multimedia when useful to aiding comprehension. b. Develop the topic with relevant, well-chosen facts, definitions, concrete details, quotations, or other information and examples. c. Use appropriate and varied transitions to create cohesion and clarify the relationships among ideas and concepts. d. Use precise language and domain-specific vocabulary to inform about or explain the topic.

W.CCR.3	W.6.3	W.7.3	W.8.3
W.CCR.3: Write narratives to develop real or imagined experiences or events using effective technique, well-chosen details and well-constructed event sequences.	**W.6.3:** Write narratives to develop real or imagined experiences or events using effective technique, relevant descriptive details, and well-structured event sequences.	**W.7.3:** Write narratives to develop real or imagined experiences or events using effective technique, relevant descriptive details, and well-structured event sequences.	**W.8.3:** Write narratives to develop real or imagined experiences or events using effective technique, relevant descriptive details, and well-structured event sequences.
	a. Engage and orient the reader by establishing a context and introducing a narrator or characters; organize an event sequence that unfolds naturally and logically.	a. Engage and orient the reader by establishing a context and point of view and introducing a narrator or characters; organize an event sequence that unfolds naturally and logically.	a. Engage and orient the reader by establishing a context and point of view and introducing a narrator or characters; organize an event sequence that unfolds naturally and logically.
	b. Use narrative techniques, such as dialogue, pacing, and description, to develop experiences, events, or characters.	b. Use narrative techniques, such as dialogue, pacing, and description, to develop experiences, events, or characters.	b. Use narrative techniques, such as dialogue, pacing, description, and reflection, to develop experiences, events, or characters.
	c. Use a variety of transition words, phrases, and clauses to convey sequence and signal shifts from one time frame or setting to another.	c. Use a variety of transition words, phrases, and clauses to convey sequence and signal shifts from one time frame or setting to another.	c. Use a variety of transition words, phrases, and clauses to convey sequence, signal shifts from one time frame or setting to another, and show the relationships among experiences and events.
	e. Establish and maintain a formal style.	e. Establish and maintain a formal style.	e. Establish and maintain a formal style.
	f. Provide a concluding statement or section that follows from the information or explanation presented.	f. Provide a concluding statement or section that follows from and supports the information or explanation presented.	f. Provide a concluding statement or section that follows from and supports the information or explanation presented.

continued →

Anchor Standards	Grade 6 Standards	Grade 7 Standards	Grade 8 Standards
W.CCR.3: Write narratives to develop real or imagined experiences or events using effective technique, well-chosen details and well-constructed event sequences.	**W.6.3:** Write narratives to develop real or imagined experiences or events using effective technique, relevant descriptive details, and well-structured event sequences. d. Use precise words and phrases, relevant descriptive details, and sensory language to convey experiences and events. e. Provide a conclusion that follows from the narrated experiences or events.	**W.7.3:** Write narratives to develop real or imagined experiences or events using effective technique, relevant descriptive details, and well-structured event sequences. d. Use precise words and phrases, relevant descriptive details, and sensory language to capture the action and convey experiences and events. e. Provide a conclusion that follows from and reflects on the narrated experiences or events.	**W.8.3:** Write narratives to develop real or imagined experiences or events using effective technique, relevant descriptive details, and well-structured event sequences. d. Use precise words and phrases, relevant descriptive details, and sensory language to capture the action and convey experiences and events. e. Provide a conclusion that follows from and reflects on the narrated experiences or events.

Source: Adapted from NGA & CCSSO, 2010a, pp. 41 and 43.

Middle school students will have more experience writing these forms, but they are not yet adept at using text features, sophisticated vocabulary, and transitions in their work. Instruction on the use of introductions and conclusions should emphasize how they are tied to the body of the piece and to one another. Anchor standard three (W.CCR.3) addresses narrative writing and requires students to use techniques, transitions, and vocabulary to create a cohesive storyline.

As stated earlier in this chapter, text *type* should not be confused with writing *genre*. Students will encounter a multitude of genres in their lives. Specifically what constitutes a genre has been debated, but most people agree that there should be similarities in form, style, or subject matter for something to be called a genre (Coker, 2007; Kress, 1999; Miller, 1984; Short, Schroeder, Kauffman, & Kaser, 2004; Turbill & Bean, 2006). In other words, a genre has defining characteristics that are unique to a group of works. The genres students read may not be the genres that they learn to write, at least at grades 6–8. For example, students may read westerns, science fiction, horror, fantasy, realistic fiction, biographies, poetry, and a host of other genres.

As previously noted, Common Core State Standards identify three major text types: (1) opinion and persuasive, (2) informative and explanatory, and (3) narrative (NGA & CCSSO, 2010b). For each text type, there are specific genres that students should know and be able to use. Students are taught the characteristics of these genres so they can use these characteristics in their own writing. Skillful use of these elements allows the writer to convey ideas in a way that the intended audience understands. Table 3.3 (page 76) contains a summary of common features of each text type and its genres, features, and writing characteristics.

Opinion and Persuasive Writing

Everyone has an opinion, but not everyone can support his or her opinion with reasons and information. Likewise, not everyone can share an opinion in a way that encourages discussion about different viewpoints or use information to convince others. In kindergarten through grade 5, students develop persuasive abilities as they learn to share their opinions with others. In the opinion pieces and persuasive writing of elementary school, students learn to support their point of view and convince others to agree with the facts as they present them, share their values, accept specific arguments and conclusions, or adopt a way of thinking. In middle school, the focus shifts to more formal argumentation. George Hillocks (2011) cautions not to confuse the two, noting that persuasive techniques of opinion writing are also present in advertising and propaganda: He notes the following about formal argumentation:

> Argument . . . is mainly about logical appeals and involves claims, evidence, warrants, backing, and rebuttals. . . . Argument is at the heart of critical thinking and academic discourse; it is the kind of writing students need to know for success in college and in life. (p. xvii)

This type of writing is often regarded as the most difficult for students to master. Students must commit to a line of reasoning and not introduce new topics.

Table 3.3: CCSS Text Types and Genres

Text Type	Genres	Features	Writing Characteristics
Opinion and Persuasive	Essay, speech, editorial, and letters to the editor	States an opinion or point of view and provide reasons and information Seeks to convince a reader about the validity of a position or action	Defines a position Offers supporting evidence using primary and secondary sources Addresses concerns of the reader
Informative and Explanatory	Report of information, summary, and technical analysis and literary analysis	Conveys factual reports containing information or observations Briefly restates a text's main ideas Presents instructions and procedures	Uses multiple sources and document sources Refrains from expressing opinions Identifies sequence accurately Uses correct format for document
Narrative	Autobiography biography, creative fiction, and memoir	Uses time as a deep structure Has a narrator Establishes a situation and sequence	Informs, instructs, persuades, or entertains Uses monologue or dialogue, visual details, and actions

Source: Adapted from NGA & CCSSO, 2010a, pp. 23–24.

In addition, they need to demonstrate clear thinking through convincing arguments and support their statements with ample, credible evidence. At the end of the piece, they must summarize their logic and thinking in a conclusion.

Informative and Explanatory Writing

A *factual report*—often referred to as an *essay*—conveys information or observations. The purpose of this type of writing is to inform, not to persuade or react. Students must learn not to interject themselves or their opinions into this type of writing and instead use credible sources to support the facts they present. Typically, a factual report has a common structure that includes an opening paragraph that explains to readers what they will find in the paper, a body that leads readers through the pertinent information, and a conclusion that summarizes the report's information. In other words, an informative or explanatory piece provides a forum for writers to report the information they have analyzed, summarize conclusions they have drawn from the information, consider alternatives to the information presented, and make a series of recommendations based on the information.

Narrative Writing

Students are also expected to write accounts of their lives and the lives of others, real or imagined. In our experience, students particularly like this text type. They enjoy reading about others and take pleasure in writing about themselves and people they find interesting. The key to writing good narratives is to collect enough information to tell a good story about a person, event, or experience. Students should learn to use descriptive language to capture the readers' interest and employ a variety of narrative techniques such as story grammar, dialogue, and literary devices. As students get older and become more skilled writers, they will be asked to produce papers in which they analyze a piece of literature or a poem. Typically, a series of questions guides their writing, such as:

- What happened in the story?

- What point do you think the author is making in the story?

- Do you think the story mirrors real life?

To respond to these types of questions, students need experience writing these responses, talking about literature, and receiving feedback.

Using George Hillocks's (2011) suggestions for introducing argumentation in writing through mystery, sixth-grade English teacher Brenda Schultz uses *Silent to the Bone* (Konigsberg, 2000) to engage students in thinking critically about the elements of argument. She begins by introducing the two-minute video *Test Your Awareness: Whodunnit?*, which contains twenty-one unexpected changes to a fictional crime scene (Rudolph, 2010). Although the original purpose for the video was a public service announcement about the importance of being a vigilant driver, Ms. Schultz finds it to be useful for linking close observation to argument development. Afterward, she connects the topic of the book with the argumentation paper students will write later: "You'll swear out a warrant for the arrest of the person who has committed a crime, using claims, evidence, and backing to do so," she explains.

Ms. Schultz begins by telling students, "This book, *Silent to the Bone*, is about a crime and a boy who may or may not be wrongfully accused of committing it. Fortunately, there's another character, his best friend, who is going to help us solve it."

During the next two weeks, she and her students list the evidence they glean from the book and propose various solutions. Because the author reveals information strategically, and not in chronological order, students' hypotheses vary. With Ms. Schultz's help, they begin to organize the information in the same way a detective would. In this case, the best friend of the accused is the one doing the sleuthing, and his conversations with his older sister make his use of logic transparent to the readers.

Whenever possible, Ms. Schultz links the elements of argumentation to students' critical thinking as they process the information. At the end of the novel, the true criminal is revealed to the reader. But by that time, her students are ready to swear out a warrant for the arrest of the reprehensible character who hurt an infant and was willing to let a young boy take the fall.

The process of working through a mystery novel also reveals the basic elements of argumentation that students will apply many more times in their schooling and beyond.

Production and Distribution of Writing

This domain describes the procedural and technical aspects of writing (NGA & CCSSO, 2010a). Anchor standard four (W.CCR.4) stresses the importance of organization and its effect on coherence in writing, and it relates much of this back to standards one to three in the domain Text Types and Purposes discussed in the previous section. Keep in mind that as writing becomes more nuanced, a student paper may contain two or three text types. For instance, it may open with a short narrative about a heroic person, go on to inform about the person's accomplishments, and then use elements of argumentation derived from the first two sections to support the writer's argument that this person should be honored.

Anchor standard five (W.CCR.5) foregrounds writing as a public and collaborative process that requires oral and written communication skills and refers further to the Language standards as they relate to grammar and the Conventions of Standard English (these will be more fully explored in the next chapter). Finally, anchor standard six (W.CCR.6) extends the groundwork laid in the previous standard by defining the public space beyond the classroom and into digital environments. Table 3.4 presents the anchor standards and grade-level standards. These standards represent a shift in how writing is taught. The technical skills of keyboarding and word processing need to be viewed as basic skills, in the same way that we view holding a pencil correctly. Sure, it's important for a time, but it's not our endpoint. No one would confuse a good pencil grip with good written communication; likewise, we should not confound operating a word-processing program well with good writing.

These first two domains of the anchor standards for writing—(1) Text Types and Purposes (2) and Production and Distribution of Writing—reset our vision of what writing should be. It's not the *tools* of writing that matter as much as it is the *functions*: we find, use, produce, and share information (Frey, Fisher, & Gonzalez, 2010). Young adolescent writers will encounter tools we can't even imagine at this point in the history of the information era, but if sufficiently equipped with a deep understanding of the functions of writing, they can adopt these new tools more quickly and more fully. For example, the students in eighth-grade English teacher Alexa Oxford's class read several short stories, including "An Occurrence at Owl Creek Bridge" (Bierce, 1891, 2011). Students then rewrite the short story as a play, producing it using a variety of online tools, such as a digital storyboard at VoiceThread (www.voicethread.com), digital animation at Animoto (www.animoto.com), or a digital avatar at Voki (www.voki.com). According to Ms. Oxford, "Bierce's short story contains several motifs that should be represented visually, like the distortion of time and the color gray. By writing and producing visual representations of the story, students were able to demonstrate their understanding of these deep structures in multiple ways."

Table 3.4: Writing Standards for Domain Production and Distribution of Writing, Grades 6–8

Anchor Standards	Grade 6 Standards	Grade 7 Standards	Grade 8 Standards
W.CCR.4: Produce clear and coherent writing in which the development, organization, and style are appropriate to task, purpose, and audience.	**W.6.4:** Produce clear and coherent writing in which the development, organization, and style are appropriate to task, purpose, and audience. (Grade-specific expectations for writing types are defined in standards one to three.)	**W.7.4:** Produce clear and coherent writing in which the development, organization, and style are appropriate to task, purpose, and audience. (Grade-specific expectations for writing types are defined in standards one to three.)	**W.8.4:** Produce clear and coherent writing in which the development, organization, and style are appropriate to task, purpose, and audience. (Grade-specific expectations for writing types are defined in standards one to three.)
W.CCR.5: Develop and strengthen writing as needed by planning, revising, editing, rewriting, or trying a new approach.	**W.6.5:** With some guidance and support from peers and adults, develop and strengthen writing as needed by planning, revising, editing, rewriting, or trying a new approach. (Editing for conventions should demonstrate command of Language standards one to three up to and including grade 6.)	**W.7.5:** With some guidance and support from peers and adults, develop and strengthen writing as needed by planning, revising, editing, rewriting, or trying a new approach, focusing on how well purpose and audience have been addressed. (Editing for conventions should demonstrate command of Language standards one to three up to and including grade 7).	**W.8.5:** With some guidance and support from peers and adults, develop and strengthen writing as needed by planning, revising, editing, rewriting, or trying a new approach, focusing on how well purpose and audience have been addressed. (Editing for conventions should demonstrate command of Language standards one to three up to and including grade 8).
W.CCR.6: Use technology, including the Internet, to produce and publish writing and to interact and collaborate with others.	**W.6.6:** Use technology, including the Internet, to produce and publish writing as well as to interact and collaborate with others; demonstrate sufficient command of keyboarding skills to type a minimum of three pages in a single sitting.	**W.7.6:** Use technology, including the Internet, to produce and publish writing and link to and cite sources as well as to interact and collaborate with others, including linking to and citing sources.	**W.8.6:** Use technology, including the Internet, to produce and publish writing and present the relationships between information and ideas efficiently as well as to interact and collaborate with others.

Source: Adapted from NGA & CCSSO, 2010a, pp. 41 and 43.

The public and collaborative nature of writing requires that students see themselves as both readers and writers. They are readers of published works, of course, but they are also readers of each other's writing. In addition, writers need to understand the importance of audience in shaping their writing. As students write longer pieces, they need to find out what a reader understands. This is consistent with the practices of professional writers, who seek the feedback of an editor to refine their work. Peer response allows students to come together as fellow writers to read each other's work and discuss it. Peer response is not peer editing or peer teaching. Peer response is discussion between a writer and a reader about the ideas in a piece and how they are understood. The teacher, and only the teacher, is responsible for editing and providing the feedback that goes with it. Novice writers lack the ability to edit sufficiently well for it to be helpful to writers, and they lack the communication skills to negotiate feedback conversations. In addition, there are essential conditions regarding when and how to use peer response.

- The writer determines when he or she needs peer feedback.

- The teacher and students recognize that not all writing needs peer feedback.

- Students, not teachers, should offer feedback focused on a reader's needs and a writer's strategies.

- Teachers, not students, should offer editing feedback about the details of a piece as it relates to mechanics, conventions, and flow.

This means that the writer decides when he or she is ready for peer response. Few things are more dispiriting than receiving criticism about a piece a writer knows is not ready for review. This can serve to discourage the writer and prevent him or her from seeking peer responses in the future.

Some peer responses are less helpful than others. In particular, global praise does little to provide the writer with any feedback that might be useful. Additionally, feedback that only focuses on word- and sentence-level editing mirrors what the teacher often does and may not be welcome by fellow students. Rather, the purpose of seeking peer responses is not to have the work evaluated but to hear what a reader understood and where the reader became confused (Simmons, 2003).

How Fellow Writers Talk

1. Tell your fellow writer what you liked best.

2. Retell the story or main ideas in your own words.

3. Ask questions about the parts you don't understand.

4. Give your fellow writer your good ideas about making it even better.

5. Thank the writer for sharing his or her writing with you.

How Fellow Writers Listen

1. Listen to the ideas your fellow writer offers.

2. Ask questions about ideas you don't understand.

3. Thank your fellow writer for reading your writing.

4. Use the ideas you like in your writing.

Visit **go.solution-tree.com/commoncore** for a reproducible version of these feature boxes.

Once teachers instruct students on the types of appropriate responses, students can use a simple peer response form to give back to the writer. It is helpful for writers to receive comments in writing so they have an idea of what to do next. The teacher should also review these peer comments in order to monitor whether students are offering helpful feedback. Figure 3.2 is a sample peer response feedback form.

Peer Response for Writing

Reader: _____ Writer: _____

Title: _____ Date: _____

What are the best things about this writing?

Retell the main ideas of the story using your own words.

What questions do you have for the writer so you can understand the story better?

What specific suggestions do you have for the writer to make the piece stronger?

Figure 3.2: Peer response feedback form.

Visit **go.solution-tree.com/commoncore** for a reproducible version of this figure.

Research to Build and Present Knowledge

Anchor standards seven, eight, and nine in this domain set students on a writing path they will use throughout the remainder of their school and work lives: the ability to report experiences and information (see table 3.5, page 82). Anchor standard seven (W.CCR.7) sets the stage for research projects, and seventh and eighth grade requires students to include insights about future questions or lines of investigation. This can be a challenge for students who are accustomed to reaching the end of a line of inquiry but not necessarily considering the new questions that have been exposed. Anchor standard eight (W.CCR.8) addresses the issue of formal citation, paraphrasing, and academic writing requirements that prevent plagiarism. This is another challenge for middle school writers, who are unfamiliar with the formal demands of writing styles like the Modern Language Association (MLA) style or the *Chicago Manual of Style* (2010). Adept use of these styles takes many years of consistent exposure and practice. Teachers should use these styles in classroom materials and draw students' attention to them to witness how the styles work in a variety of formats.

Building on the ideas from grades 3–5, students in grades 6–8 are expected to understand how to take notes and use the information they gather in their writing. A student's ability to take and organize notes is a significant predictor of success.

A Focus on Annotation and Note Taking

Over time, students not only use their notes for externally storing information but also for encoding their ideas. This builds comprehension and understanding of the content (Ganske, 1981). Note taking is also a critical skill for college success (Pauk, 1974), so it's an important skill to master.

Table 3.5: Writing Standards for Domain Research to Build and Present Knowledge, Grades 6–8

Anchor Standards	Grade 6 Standard	Grade 7 Standard	Grade 8 Standard
W.CCR.7: Conduct short as well as more sustained research projects based on focused questions, demonstrating understanding of the subject under investigation.	**W.6.7:** Conduct short research projects to answer a question, drawing on several sources and refocusing the inquiry when appropriate.	**W.7.7:** Conduct short research projects to answer a question, drawing on several sources and generating additional related, focused questions for further research and investigation.	**W.8.7:** Conduct short research projects to answer a question (including a self-generated question), drawing on several sources and generating additional related, focused questions that allow for multiple avenues of exploration.
W.CCR.8: Gather relevant information from multiple print and digital sources, assess the credibility and accuracy of each source, and integrate the information while avoiding plagiarism.	**W.6.8:** Gather relevant information from multiple print and digital sources; assess the credibility and accuracy of each source; and quote or paraphrase the data and conclusions of others while avoiding plagiarism and providing basic bibliographic information for sources.	**W.7.8:** Gather relevant information from multiple print and digital sources, using search terms effectively; assess the credibility and accuracy of each source; and quote or paraphrase the data and conclusions of others while avoiding plagiarism and following a standard format for citation.	**W.8.8:** Gather relevant information from multiple print and digital sources, using search terms effectively; assess the credibility and accuracy of each source; and quote or paraphrase the data and conclusions of others while avoiding plagiarism and following a standard format for citation.
W.CCR.9: Draw evidence from literary or informational texts to support analysis, reflection, and research.	**W.6.9:** Draw evidence from literary or informational texts to support analysis, reflection, and research. a. Apply grade 6 Reading standards to literature (such as "Compare and contrast texts in different forms or genres [like stories and poems; historical novels and fantasy stories] in terms of their approaches to similar themes and topics").	**W.7.9:** Draw evidence from literary or informational texts to support analysis, reflection, and research. a. Apply grade 7 Reading standards to literature (such as "Compare and contrast a fictional portrayal of a time, place, or character and a historical account of the same period as a means of understanding how authors of fiction use or alter history").	**W.8.9:** Draw evidence from literary or informational texts to support analysis, reflection, and research. a. Apply grade 8 Reading standards to literature (such as "Analyze how a modern work of fiction draws on themes, patterns of events, or character types from myths, traditional stories, or religious works such as the bible, including describing how the material is rendered new").

| W.CCR.9: Draw evidence from literary or informational texts to support analysis, reflection, and research. | b. Apply grade 6 Reading standards to literary nonfiction (such as "Trace and evaluate the argument and specific claims in a text, distinguishing claims that are supported by reasons and evidence from claims that are not"). | b. Apply grade 7 Reading standards to literary nonfiction (such as "Trace and evaluate the argument and specific claims in a text, assessing whether the reasoning is sound and the evidence is relevant and sufficient to support the claims"). | b. Apply grade 8 Reading standards to literary nonfiction (such as "Delineate and evaluate the argument and specific claims in a text, assessing whether the reasoning is sound and the evidence is relevant and sufficient; recognize when irrelevant evidence is introduced"). |

Source: Adapted from NGA & CCSSO, 2010a, pp. 41 and 44.

Edgar Allan Poe (1844/1988), an unapologetic note maker in the margins of texts, writes, "In the marginalia, too, we talk only to ourselves; we therefore talk freshly— boldly—originally—with abandonment—without conceit" (p. 7). In their seminal text *How to Read a Book*, Mortimer Adler and Charles Van Doren (1972) lay out a case for engaging in repeated readings with accompanying annotation:

> Why is marking a book indispensable to reading it? First, it keeps you awake—not merely conscious, but wide awake. Second, reading, if active, is thinking, and thinking tends to express itself in words, spoken or written. The person who says he knows what he thinks but cannot express it usu- ally does not know what he thinks. Third, writing your reactions down helps you remember the thoughts of the author. (p. 49)

They go on to describe the most common annotation marks (Adler & Van Doren, 1940/1972).

- **Underlines** for major points

- **Vertical lines** in the margin for statements that are too long to be underlined

- **Star, asterisk, or other symbol** in the margin to emphasize the ten or twelve most important statements (folding the corner or bookmarking the page is a helpful way to quickly turn back to these)

- **Numbers** in the margin to indicate a sequence of points the author makes to develop an argument

- **Page numbers** in the margin to indicate where else the author makes the same points

- **Circles** for key words or phrases

- **Questions (and perhaps answers)** in the margin or at the top or bottom of the page that come to mind while reading

Additionally, Susan Vanneman (2011) suggests that note taking is as easy as ABC LOU, a mnemonic device that stands for *abbreviations, bullets, caveman language, lists, one word for several,* and *use your own words.* Using annotations and mnemonics are just a couple ways students can take quick but efficient notes.

However, the question remains, what kind of note-taking system works? As Jean Faber, John Morris, and Mary Lieberman (2000) find, the Cornell note-taking system increases comprehension (and test scores). Using this system, students divide a piece of paper into three sections: (1) the right side to take notes and complete tasks, (2) the left side as a guide for questions and key points (cues), and (3) the bottom for a sum- mary. Key points help students quickly find information, locate references, conduct research projects, "gather relevant information from multiple print and digital sources" (W.CCR.8), and "draw evidence from literary or informational texts to support analysis, reflection, and research" (W.CCR.9; NGA & CCSSO, 2010a, p. 41). See figure 3.3 (page 85) for an example of the Cornell note-taking system.

Cues	Notes
• Note key points.	• Record notes here during class or while reading.
• Phrase notes as questions.	• Use meaningful abbreviations and symbols.
• Write questions within twenty-four hours after class.	• Leave space to add additional information.
Summary	
• Record main ideas and major points.	
• Write during review sessions.	

Figure 3.3: Cornell note-taking system template.

Visit **go.solution-tree.com/commoncore** for a reproducible version of this figure.

Other Note-Taking Methods

Of course, there are other ways for students to take notes. For example, students can learn to take notes digitally using laptops or tablets (Horney et al., 2009). Daniel Callison and Leslie Preddy (2006) identify four note-taking strategies for web pages: (1) highlight key terms and statements, (2) write a summary, (3) recite information learned, and (4) cite the source. The website NoteStar (http://notestar.4teachers.org) allows students to collect and organize their notes using some given fields that teachers create or assign.

Regardless of the format, students should learn the five Rs of note taking: (1) record meaningful facts and ideas; (2) reduce the text to main ideas and summaries; (3) recite the most important terms, concepts, ideas, and conclusions; (4) reflect on personal opinion and perspective; and (5) review. The key for teachers is to instruct students to extract meaningful information and record the sources.

Additionally, anchor standard nine (W.CCR.9) requires middle school writers to extract evidence, including direct quotes, from the literary and informational texts they read in order to write about them. Importantly, students are asked to draw information from *multiple* pieces of text—not just a single reading. Again, this last standard may challenge teachers and their students, who may have grown accustomed to responding to, but not analyzing, the literature and informational texts they read. Even more so, many middle school educators have not routinely required students to draw information from multiple texts, aside from formal research papers. Stating that one likes (or does not like) a book doesn't especially challenge the writer to read deeply. Keep in mind that the reading standards call on students to read critically as they compare and contrast, describe problems and solutions, and so forth. However, much of this critical analysis occurs when the writer has to put these ideas down on paper. Understanding follows action; it rarely precedes it. We come to understandings when we try things out, even when our initial attempts are unsuccessful. In order for readers to deeply understand a text, they must write about it at a comparably complex level.

Writers invariably compose orally before they put their ideas into written form; they carry critical-analysis skills from conversation into their writing. Discussion has great value across several dimensions. Discussions are an important source of information for learners, who can benefit from structures that give students an opportunity to formulate opinions, consider alternative views, and reach conclusions. An excellent technique for accomplishing all of these goals is the *discussion web* (Alvermann, 1991). A discussion web converges on a central question and is conducted in three distinct stages similar to the think-pair-share approach.

First, students write responses in favor of and opposed to a proposal. The group members then discuss their responses with one another. Next, they read several pieces of text, looking for evidence defending both positions. Once again, the group discusses both sides of the issue, now utilizing evidence from the text to support the positions. After the discussion, the group members return to the discussion web to note any points they may have overlooked. Students now have an excellent tool to use to when writing an opinion piece for either position. This tool is especially useful because effective persuasion requires that the writer acknowledge the other side of the issue. See figure 3.4 for a sample discussion web form.

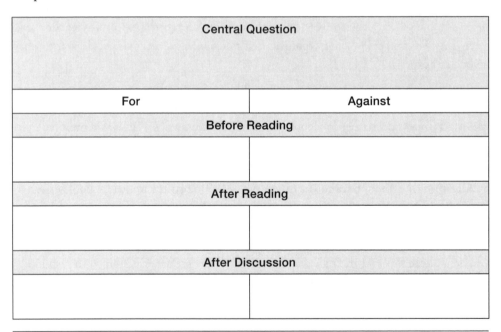

Figure 3.4: Sample discussion web.

Visit **go.solution-tree.com/commoncore** for a reproducible version of this figure.

Graphic organizers, such as discussion webs, concept maps, semantic webs, cause-and-effect charts, and the like, help students organize information presented in print and digital sources (Kirylo & Millet, 2000). The idea is to visually organize key points (Vasilyev, 2003). In addition, graphic organizers are a good way to summarize information so students can easily remember and recall content (Wilson, 2002). Graphic organizers have been used successfully with English learners (Carlson, 2000), struggling readers or students with special needs (Dexter & Hughes, 2011), and students who are gifted and talented (Cassidy, 1989; Howard, 1994). In other words, the use of graphic organizers is well-documented and is a powerful way to ensure students learn to recall relevant information and categorize that information.

Range of Writing

Like independent reading, this domain with its single anchor standard (W.CCR.10) provides students with a chance to write and then discuss their writing with others (see table 3.6). Importantly, this standard profiles students' growing ability to write for extended periods of time, both in a single sitting, as well as with writing that develops over the course of time. But it doesn't mean that a student is simply stuck in a corner for forty-five minutes and told to write something while the teacher paces anxiously the whole time.

Table 3.6: Writing Standards for Domain Range of Writing, Grades 6–8

Anchor Standard	Grade 6 Standard	Grade 7 Standard	Grade 8 Standard
W.CCR.10: Write routinely and for extended time frames (time for research, reflection, and revision) and shorter time frames (a single sitting or a day or two) for a range of tasks, purposes, and audiences.	**W.6.10:** Write routinely over extended time frames (time for research, reflection, and revision) and shorter time frames (a single sitting or a day or two) for a range of discipline-specific tasks, purposes, and audiences.	**W.7.10:** Write routinely over extended time frames (time for research, reflection, and revision) and shorter time frames (a single sitting or a day or two) for a range of discipline-specific tasks, purposes, and audiences.	**W.8.10:** Write routinely over extended time frames (time for research, reflection, and revision) and shorter time frames (a single sitting or a day or two) for a range of discipline-specific tasks, purposes, and audiences.

Source: Adapted from NGA & CCSSO, 2010a, pp. 41 and 44.

Students need instructional conditions that build toward independence. This includes finding out how other authors compose, especially in their close analysis of reading materials. Students require practice under the guidance of their teacher. In addition, students need a classroom climate that communicates a belief that writing is an expressive channel that is as equally important as speaking. In order for students to meet the writing standard routinely over extended time frames, they must write frequently and fluently to build their stamina for independent writing.

The Writing Process

As with other strands in the Common Core State Standards, Writing doesn't isolate one standard while ignoring others within or across strands. Young adolescent writers require ongoing multidimensional instruction that fulfills the expectations of the

CCSS. Students need to learn effective writing habits, the kinds of writing and the resulting genres, conventions and language use, and the processes writers use to produce writing. Interactive and personal writing experiences enable students to grow in their understanding of what they need to do to write well. Writing behavior is modeled in shared and guided writing activities during which students take turns contributing ideas, dictating words or sentences, or transcribing the message. As students observe writing and participate in the development of a piece, they become aware of appropriate writing behaviors and can begin to apply what they have observed to their personal and independent writing.

- Good writers know effective habits of writing will increase the efficiency and quality of their writing. Young writers need to learn how to organize materials, how to utilize reference materials to support content, and what skills they need to get their ideas down on paper.

- Good writers know how to move from ideas to words to sentences and paragraphs. The less adept writer will be frustrated with his or her inability to transmit ideas to the reader. Writing craft includes word choice and perspective and recognizing that different genres require different approaches.

- Good writers use punctuation, spelling, and grammatical structures to ensure that readers understand their message. Selecting the correct genre of writing to fit the purpose goes hand in hand with the conventions associated with clear writing.

Aspects of the Writing Process

Good writers understand that there is a process to writing and that their awareness of the process can facilitate writing. Writing teacher and researcher Donald Graves (personal communication as cited in Nagin, 2003) writes:

> The writing process is anything a writer does from the time the idea came until the piece is completed or abandoned. There is no particular order. So it's not effective to teach writing process in a lock-step, rigid manner. What a good writing teacher does is help students see where writing comes from; in a chance remark or an article that really burns you up. I still hold by my original statement: if kids don't write more than three days a week they're dead, and it's very hard to become a writer. If you provide frequent occasions for writing then the students start to think about writing when they're not doing it. I call it a constant state of composition. (p. 23)

While we do not advocate for a strictly sequential approach to writing that moves students through a lockstep system, we do believe that students will benefit from learning common writing techniques. Five common writing dimensions are the following.

1. **Prewriting:** Formulating (or brainstorming) ideas that may or may not be utilized later in a writing piece

2. **Drafting:** Committing brainstormed ideas to paper to produce a first draft

3. **Revising:** Revisiting the draft to add, delete, or change what has been drafted

4. **Editing:** Approaching the piece's final form and asking teachers or peers for corrections and feedback on content

5. **Publishing:** Finalizing the piece and sharing it with others

These dimensions build on one another to contribute to the writer's growing stamina and fluency in order to *get in the zone.* If you like sports, you know what it means to be *in the zone.* Athletes in the zone report feeling that time is suspended and that their movements are fluid. Similarly, some people report *getting lost* in a book or good movie. Mihaly Csikszentmihalyi (1997) calls this phenomenon *flow.* He believes that flow is an optimal experience for humans. Fluent writers also gain a sense of flow as they write.

The Characteristics of Flow

In simple terms, Csikszentmihalyi's research suggests that people are generally unhappy doing nothing, happy doing things, and uncertain about what makes them happy. However, people fully engaged in a task *get lost* in the activity or *get in the zone* or what he likes to call *flow.* According to Csikszentmihalyi (1997), there are a number of characteristics of flow, which include the following.

- **Complete involvement, focus, and concentration:** Being innately curious or as the result of having training

- **A sense of ecstasy:** Being outside everyday reality

- **A great inner clarity:** Knowing what needs to be done and how well it is going

- **Knowledge that the activity is doable:** Knowing that one's skills are adequate and that the task does not create anxiety or boredom

- **A sense of serenity:** Not worrying about self; feeling of growing beyond the boundaries of ego—afterward feeling of transcending ego in ways not thought possible

- **Timeliness:** Thoroughly focusing on the present; not noticing time passing

- **Intrinsic motivation:** Using whatever produces flow as a reward

---

Source: Adapted from Csikszentmihalyi, 1997.

As you can imagine, a goal of teachers is to keep students in flow for as much of the school day as possible. Csikszentmihalyi (1997, 2000) notes humans cannot be in flow all of the time—it is an optimal state, not necessarily a common state of being. When the challenge is relatively high and skills are relatively low, students become anxious. Importantly, when the challenge is relatively low and skills are relatively high, students become bored. When both are low, a profound sense of apathy is apparent.

We believe that flow is influenced in part by fluency in reading and writing. Not being able to read smoothly and accurately is frustrating, causes anxiety, and results in poor comprehension. The message as the brain processes becomes halting, choppy, and disjointed. A similar phenomenon occurs with disfluent writing. When ideas are coming faster than one can write, students become frustrated. If they do not have good command of spelling and vocabulary, they oversimplify their sentences with low-level words and ideas or give up altogether on their writing. Alternatively, smooth and accurate reading allows the reader to concentrate on the meaning of the message, an important contributor to motivation and interest. Likewise, the ability to compose a message without having to stop after every word to recall spelling or syntax allows the writer to concentrate on more sophisticated writing behaviors, such as planning, composing, and revising to create the best message. Without a doubt, fluency in reading and writing are important because they contribute to the learner's ability to fully engage with the literacy activity.

Aspects of Writing Fluency

Writing fluency has received significantly less research attention compared with reading fluency. However, it stands to reason that not writing quickly enough would be frustrating for students. Imagine having all kinds of ideas in your head, but having them leave you before you can record them! Similarly, poor writing volume results in few words to edit. After all, if a student only generates a few dozen words after fifteen minutes of writing, he or she will not have much to edit and revise. Most importantly, a focus on writing fluency requires that students move on with the task and not procrastinate. We've all watched a student staring off into space after being asked to respond in writing to a question or comment. When asked, this student will respond, "I'm thinking" or "I'm not sure what to write." A focus on writing fluency provides students with the skills to record their thoughts, supplies them with ideas to edit and revise, and addresses the frequent delays associated with writing performance. (See pages 92–94 for sample activities to focus on writing fluency.)

While there are a number of theories about writing and how to write, writers generally use three interactive and recursive components: "*planning* what to say, *translating* those plans into written text, and *reviewing* those written texts or plans" (McCutchen, Covill, Hoyne, & Mildes, 1994, p. 256). We maintain that a focus on writing fluency requires attention to each of these three components.

Planning the Message

During planning students must develop the skills to rapidly organize their thinking and develop a scheme for their ideas. Naturally there are a number of strategies that focus on this component, including brainstorming ideas, talking to a partner, thinking and searching through texts, and developing concept maps. A study of fourth- and fifth-grade students reveals those who receive intentional instruction in planning activities produce higher-quality writing than those who receive only process writing instruction in which students revise papers based on teacher feedback (Troia & Graham, 2002).

Translating the Message

As students translate their plans into text, they must have developed the motor skills for extended writing tasks, have the stamina to write for extended periods, and be able to make connections between what they've written and what they're thinking. Predictably, there are specific instructional strategies to help students develop this component, including quick writes, freewrites, timed writings, and power writing (Fearn & Farnan, 2001). (See pages 92–94 for more information on these instructional strategies.)

Reviewing the Message

In terms of reviewing, students need to be able to read what they've written and revise accordingly. Again, it's important to note that writing is recursive and interactive—writers revise as they write and think as they revise and so on. Once again, intentional instruction in revision has been shown to produce longer and more sophisticated essays. Gary Robert Muschla (1993) suggests that all students be taught a simple five-step plan for revision.

1. Read the piece silently and then aloud. Reading it aloud can highlight the flow and rhythm of the words.

2. Consider the whole piece first. What are its strengths? What parts do you like best? What are its weaknesses? How can the weaknesses be improved? What can be added? What can be eliminated?

3. Focus on the paragraphs. Are they well organized? Does each have a main idea supported by details? Do the paragraphs follow each other logically? Are the transitions between them smooth?

4. Consider the sentences. Do they follow logically? Are they clear?

5. Focus on the words and phrases. Which should be changed? What are examples of clutter? (pp. 62–63)

There is no expected writing fluency rate that can provide teachers guidance with determining how many words per minute students should be able to write. However, a large study of elementary and middle school students found that middle school writers averaged forty-three words in three-minute timed writing samples collected in the fall. By the spring of grade 8, they averaged seventy-three words in the same time period (Malecki & Jewell, 2003). At some point, fluency is sufficient, and further attempts to increase written production will compromise writing quality. The point is that students need practice getting their ideas on paper such that they have content to edit and revise.

Fluency and Writing Maturity

As with reading, writing fluency is not only about writing more words. As students become more fluent writers, they also become more sophisticated writers. V. Andee Bayliss and Nancy Walker (1990) and Bayliss (1994) identify signs of maturing writing fluency, including:

- Providing details

- Elaborating on the subject

- Varying sentence patterns

- Deepening and unfolding the presentation

- Sustaining focus

As writers become more fluent, they are able to use these devices to produce more sophisticated pieces of writing. When a writer adds detail, the reader can visualize the setting and characters. Elaboration on a subject helps the reader more fully understand what the writer is discussing (the sentences in this paragraph are examples of elaboration). Additionally, a mature writer can deepen and unfold a presentation by building on concepts in a logical manner. Finally, a good writer does not wander from topic to topic. Taken together, these characteristics form the definition of good writing and an effective writer. Think back to our description of the characteristics of a self-extending writer (page 69). Educators in grades 6–8 play an important role in establishing the foundations students will need to become mature writers.

Writing fluency is important in the middle school classroom because it contributes to more sophisticated expression of ideas. Reading fluency contributes to more sophisticated understanding of ideas. Neither reading nor writing fluency exist in isolation, but rather are influenced by a learner's control of phonics, syntax, comprehension, and vocabulary. However, fluency serves as an important bridge between these processes. Instruction in reading and writing fluency contributes to improving literacy skills of students.

Power Writing

Power writing is a daily instructional routine to build writing fluency. It involves brief, timed writing events. Leif Fearn and Nancy Farnan (2001) describe it as "a structured free-write where the objective is quantity alone" (p. 501). Typically, this exercise is performed daily in three rounds of timed writes, each one minute in length. Students are given a word or phrase to use somewhere in their writing and are reminded to "write as much as you can, as well as you can" (Fearn & Farnan, 2001, p. 196). At the end of one minute, they count the number of words they have written and note the total in the margin. This cycle is repeated two more times using different words or phrases. After the last cycle, they re-read what they have written and circle words they believe they may have misspelled. This allows the teacher to evaluate students' self-monitoring of their spelling. They keep a graph where they list the highest number of words for the day.

The purpose of tracking progress is not to establish a competitive atmosphere; these graphs are kept in the writer's notebook and are viewed only by the teacher and student. These simple charts can be constructed on graph paper. See figure 3.5 for a sample graph. The words per minute are recorded on the vertical axis and should begin with a number that is just below the writer's current range of words. The teacher establishes this value based on the student's power writing average and his or her goal for each student. For instance, if a writer currently averages thirty-two words per minute, the vertical axis might begin with twenty.

Students completing three sessions of power writing are likely to observe another unexpected benefit. Typically, performance increases between the first and third rotation. Like physical exercise, the repetitions result in increased fluidity of writing. By assessing their own progress, students internalize their own motivation as they seek to improve on their last effort. This is especially important for struggling writers, who commonly say, "I don't know what to write about." If they are stuck, they should be instructed to write the prompt word repeatedly until an idea forms. As they do so, they begin to think of related words and often start to generate ideas, even if it is only a list of words at the start.

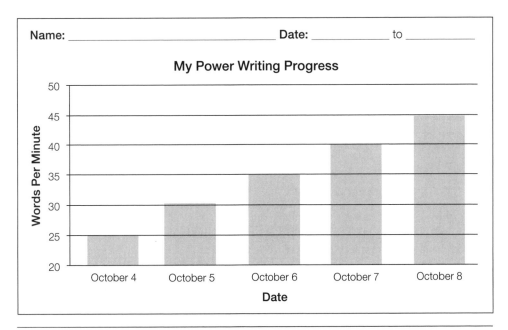

Figure 3.5: Sample power writing graph.

Visit **go.solution-tree.com/commoncore** for a reproducible version of this figure.

Journal Writing

An effective instructional program provides many opportunities for children to write across subjects and throughout the school day and week. As Graves notes, "If you provide frequent occasions for writing then the students start to think about writing when they're not doing it" (personal communication as cited in Nagin, 2003, p. 23). To help children observe and appreciate their growth as writers, we believe that every student should have a place to keep his or her writing. This is often accomplished through the use of a writing journal. Although organization of the writer's notebook varies by teacher, grade level, and purpose, most are arranged chronologically. Therefore, the various writing exercises during shared, guided, and collaborative writing are likely to be in there. We recommend devoting a section of the notebook to fluency exercises like power writing. During independent writing, we sometimes invite students to review past power writing work in the journal and select one to expand into a more finished piece. Students frequently discover a good idea that they had previously overlooked.

Freewriting

Students also need time to write for their own purposes and should be encouraged to write for their own motivation. We return to the concept we discussed earlier—*flow.* Peter Elbow (1981) describes a process called *freewriting* as a method for opening creative pathways. For ten minutes a day, students write independently on a topic of their own choice. During this time, no editing takes place. The sole purpose is to get words down on paper. This differs somewhat from power writing in that it is not viewed as a competition against the clock but rather a way of accessing ideas. When stuck, writers are instructed to write anything—even squiggles—until the words come again. Sometimes the squiggles give the brain a little time to focus and produce. If a student struggles with language, the teacher may need to meet individually with the student to develop some ideas in collaboration that can be used in future writing sessions. Freewriting can be valuable for students to tap into their understanding of the world and themselves.

Conclusion

Learning to write is not a matter of simply brainstorming, drafting, editing, revising, and publishing. It's much messier than that and occasionally (if we are lucky) reaches a state of flow. Our efforts to foster young writers are focused on enabling them to move closer to that *constant state of composition*. In order for students to become writers who are adept at using different text types, and with different purposes and audiences in mind, they must write throughout the day. If they are to produce and distribute their writing across the classroom and the world, they must write frequently. If students are to engage in research in order to build their knowledge and present it to others, they must write across disciplines. Only fifteen minutes of daily instruction (Gilbert & Graham, 2010) is woefully inadequate if students are to attain these expectations. Simply stated, writing needs to be part of the air that is breathed in every classroom.

Writing is a time when students are provided an opportunity to apply the skills they have been learning to create original texts. Students write for a variety of purposes and have a voice in the choice of topics and in making editing decisions. The type of writing a student engages in is influenced by the developmental level of the student and the purpose for writing. Transitional writers in grades 6–8 use multiple sources of information to influence their writing and utilize techniques for writing to improve the message. The CCSS for writing highlight the importance of writing as a communicative channel across disciplines. Like other aspects of these standards, writing should not be confined to the literacy block, but should be incorporated across the learning day.

As with the Reading standards, the Common Core State Standards for writing build on content teachers already know. Writing is a major facet of students' schooling, but the question we have to ask ourselves is, are they getting any better at writing? Research evidence from large-scale writing assessments, such as the National Assessment of Educational Progress, suggests that there is still a lot of work to be done in this area (Salahu-Din, Persky, & Miller, 2008). Overall, the writing that students do in school is not sufficient for them to be successful in college and careers. Rather than assign writing, teachers have to focus on writing *instruction*. This is where the collaborative planning team can help. As we have noted throughout this chapter, collaborative teams can focus their planning conversations around three questions about the writing standards.

1. **Standards:** What is the essence of this standard?

2. **Instruction:** What teacher actions facilitate this standard in practice?

3. **Formative assessment:** What evidence will we accept that students are learning this standard?

By focusing on these questions, teams will develop a scope and sequence of writing curriculum that is connected with the reading students are doing. Teams will also ensure that writing is integrated into the speaking and listening activities students engage in and that language development is occurring so students can write increasingly sophisticated pieces. As we have noted, the Common Core State Standards are interconnected. The Writing standards must be taught in the context of all of the other standards so student competence and confidence are routinely raised.

CHAPTER 4

Implementing the Common Core State Standards for Speaking and Listening and for Language

KEY QUESTIONS

- To what extent does your collaborative team understand the Speaking and Listening standards and the Language standards: What is our current level of knowledge about this standard? How can we increase our expertise? How will we measure our growth?

- How much classroom speaking do students do that is academic in nature? Do they use argumentation and provide evidence for their claims when they share their thinking?

- How sophisticated is the language students use in speaking and writing? Are there language structures that students need to learn to be successful?

Sixth graders Merrill, Joseph, Angela, and Rukiya—students in Mya Harrison's English class—have been learning about courage. As part of a unit on courageous acts, these students have learned about baseball legend Lou Gehrig. Stricken with amyotrophic lateral sclerosis (ALS), a fatal motor neuron disease, Gehrig saw his brilliant career abruptly end at the age of thirty-six. His farewell speech to the crowd at Yankee Stadium on July 4, 1939, demonstrated a remarkable outlook for a man who would die two years later. The students had previously heard the audio broadcast of Gehrig's speech and watched Gary Cooper's recreation in the 1942 film *The Pride of the Yankees* (Wood, 1942). Now, students have a handout with the text of Gehrig's speech in front of them, formatted so that the left margin allows for them to make notes directly on the page. Their task is to identify evidence of courage in the face of adversity.

After the students read the short text to themselves several times, Rukiya comments, "Well, first off, there's that sentence about being 'the luckiest man on the face of the earth.' That's something right there. I mean, he knew he was going to die, and it would be a horrible death, too." All the students highlight this sentence on their copies of the speech.

"And so did everyone else. He starts by saying that they've been 'reading about a bad break.' It's there in the first sentence," says Merrill. "So let's add that to our list. What

Rukiya said about him being the luckiest man, and saying that knowing that everyone in the stadium knew how bad the disease was."

As Joseph prepares the list for the group, he says, "Here's another thing, too. It's gotta be a terrible day, and he takes the time to thank the people he's worked with on the team. Like, I don't know who all these dudes are: Jacob Ruppert, Joe McCarthy, but he does, and he thanks them." In the margin of the speech, the students note that he is taking the time to show his gratitude to his colleagues.

"He says, 'Which of you won't consider it the highlight of his career just to associate with them for even one day?'" says Angela. "Joseph, add that to the evidence part of the list." The other three highlight this sentence, and some make a note in the margin about this.

The group continues to identify acts of courage found in Gehrig's unprepared remarks. Rukiya points out that he thanks a rival team, and Angela adds that he praises his mother-in-law. "Yep, he's thanking people that other people might fight with," says Merrill.

After listing evidence drawn from the speech, the group looks over the list for patterns. Using discussion questions Ms. Harrison prepared, the students focus on motivation. "So why would he say all this?" asks Joseph. "Man, I would just be crying my eyes out and feeling sorry for myself."

"I think he felt bad about everyone else feeling bad," says Rukiya. Angela follows with, "I agree, and I think he didn't want people to feel sorry for him, even though they all knew he was gonna die." Merrill nods and adds, "Yeah, he tells them, 'I've got an awful lot to live for.' He wants to give them . . .'"

"Hope," says Joseph. "He wants to give them hope."

A Collaborative Planning Team in Action

It should come as no surprise that the unit of instruction on courage Ms. Harrison developed began with her collaborative team's conversations about the Common Core State Standards for English language arts.

"We were struck by the presence of speeches in the list of text exemplars. Frankly, we just never used speeches as texts with our students. When we did, which was rarely, we just had students watch or listen to them," Ms. Harrison says. The team's discussion about this genre led it to identify other examples members could use in their units of instruction, including Gehrig's farewell to baseball speech that Ms. Harrison's students used.

The team approached its study of the Speaking and Listening standards, as well as the Language standards, somewhat differently. "We feel more solid about developing collaborative skills. In fact, we've been doing this for several years, but we need to bump up the task complexity in order to get kids really discussing content, and not just how to get the task itself done. So we've been collectively making sure that text discussion processes like literature circles and reciprocal teaching are in place." However, the Language standards are more problematic. Ms. Harrison comments, "When we first started looking at the standards, we couldn't even agree on what language is: is it linguistics, or vocabulary, or semantics? We use three guiding questions to keep our work on track."

1. What is our current level of knowledge about this standard?

2. How can we increase our expertise?

3. How will we measure our growth?

Ms. Harrison continues, "We need to be able to build our own knowledge before we could ever hope to build our students' knowledge."

Figure 4.1 (page 100) and figure 4.2 (page 102) offer sample protocols you can use in your collaborative team to analyze the Language standards and Speaking and Listening standards, using the three guiding questions from Ms. Harrison and her collaborative team. (Visit **go.solution-tree.com/commoncore** for online-only reproducibles of these figures.)

In this chapter, we will examine two domains: (1) Speaking and Listening and (2) Language. We have chosen to do so because they are tied so closely together. While language is not confined only to the oral and verbal domains, it serves as the underpinning to them. Like Ms. Harrison's collaborative planning team, we hope this lens is useful in reducing the temptation to isolate the Common Core State Standards to the extent that they lose their usefulness. In other words, when planning lessons, collaborative teams should not focus only on one strand, be that Reading, Writing, Speaking and Listening, or Language. Instead, they should identify opportunities to address appropriate standards from each area.

Anchor Standards for Speaking and Listening

The anchor standards for speaking and listening spotlight the quality of transactions students have across the table, classroom, and world. NGA and CCSSO (2010a) note, "Students must have ample opportunities to take part in a variety of rich, structured conversations—as part of a whole class, in small groups, and with a partner" (p. 22). In the 21st century, in which digital communications have become a feature of everyday life, these communication skills extend to virtual environments. These anchor standards are divided into two domains: (1) Comprehension and Collaboration and (2) Presentation of Knowledge and Ideas. Together, they outline the expectations for the informal and formal talk of an effective classroom. As you and your collaborative team examine these standards, notice how they clearly link to those discussed in Reading and Writing strands in chapters 2 and 3.

Language anchor standard five (L.CCR.5): Demonstrate understanding of figurative language, word relationships, and nuances in word meanings.

CCSS grade band: Grades 6–8

CCSS strand: Language

Anchor standard domain: Vocabulary Acquisition and Use

Grade-Level Standard	What Is Our Current Level of Knowledge About This Standard?	How Can We Increase Our Expertise?	How Will We Measure Our Growth?
Grade 6			
L.6.5: Demonstrate understanding of figurative language, word relationships, and nuances in word meanings. a. Interpret figures of speech (like personification) in context. b. Use the relationship between particular words (like cause and effect, part and whole, or item and category) to better understand each of the words. c. Distinguish among the connotations (associations) of words with similar denotations (definitions) (like *stingy, scrimping, economical, unwasteful,* and *thrifty*).			
Grade 7			
L.7.5: Demonstrate understanding of figurative language, word relationships, and nuances in word meanings. a. Interpret figures of speech (in literary, biblical, and mythological allusions) in context.			

b. Use the relationship between particular words (like synonym and antonym or analogy and metaphor) to better understand each of the words. c. Distinguish among the connotations (associations) of words with similar denotations (definitions) (like *refined, respectful, polite, diplomatic,* and *condescending*).	
Grade 8 **L.8.5:** Demonstrate understanding of figurative language, word relationships, and nuances in word meanings. a. Interpret figures of speech (such as verbal irony and puns) in context. b. Use the relationship between particular words to better understand each of the words. c. Distinguish among the connotations (associations) of words with similar denotations (definitions) (like *bullheaded, willful, firm, persistent,* and *resolute*).	

Source: Adapted from NGA & CCSSO, 2010a, p. 29.

Figure 4.1: Guiding questions for grade-by-grade analysis of the Language standards.

Visit **go.solution-tree.com/commoncore** for a reproducible version of this figure.

Language anchor standard five (L.CCR.5): Demonstrate understanding of figurative language, word relationships, and nuances in word meanings.

CCSS grade band: Grades 6–8

CCSS strand: Speaking and Listening

Anchor standard domain: Comprehension and Collaboration

Grade-Level Standard	What Is Our Current Level of Knowledge About This Standard?	How Can We Increase Our Expertise?	How Will We Measure Our Growth?
Grade 6 **SL.6.3:** Delineate a speaker's argument and specific claims, distinguishing claims that are supported by reasons and evidence from claims that are not.			
Grade 7 **SL.7.3:** Delineate a speaker's argument and specific claims, evaluating the soundness of the reasoning and the relevance and sufficiency of the evidence.			
Grade 8 **SL.8.3:** Delineate a speaker's argument and specific claims, evaluating the soundness of the reasoning and relevance and sufficiency of the evidence and identifying when irrelevant evidence is introduced.			

Source: Adapted NGA & CCSSO, 2010a, p. 49.

Figure 4.2: Guiding questions for grade-by-grade analysis of the Speaking and Listening standards.

Visit go.solution-tree.com/commoncore for a reproducible version of this figure.

Comprehension and Collaboration

The three anchor standards in this domain focus on the students' growing ability to collaborate with others in a meaningful way, using the content as the platform for their work. Anchor standard one (SL.CCR.1) describes the dispositions of the prepared student who can fully participate in academic discussions. Anchor standard three (SL.CCR.3) is reminiscent of the work on accountable talk, which describes the habits of speakers and listeners as they engage in academic discourse, such as incorporating the statements of others into the discussion, asking questions, using evidence and examples, and even disagreeing with one another (Michaels, O'Connor, & Resnick, 2008). Anchor standard two (SL.CCR.2) bridges the other two standards, as it reminds us of the role that content knowledge plays in these conversations.

1. Prepare for and participate effectively in a range of conversations and collaborations with diverse partners, building on others' ideas and expressing their own clearly and persuasively. (SL.CCR.1)

2. Integrate and evaluate information presented in diverse media and formats, including visually, quantitatively, and orally. (SL.CCR.2)

3. Evaluate a speaker's point of view, reasoning, and use of evidence and rhetoric. (SL.CCR.3) (NGA & CCSSO, 2010a, p. 48)

Presentation of Knowledge and Ideas

The second domain of anchor standards for the Speaking and Listening strand profiles the essential nature of presenting information to one another in more formal ways. Anchor standard four (SL.CCR.4) discusses the ways a speaker organizes and presents information, always keeping the audience and the purpose for the presentation in mind. Anchor standard six (SL.CCR.6) is a reminder that presenters are also listeners and consumers of information. As such, they need to use critical-thinking skills in order to make judgments about the information being shared. Anchor standard five (SL.CCR.5) serves to bridge these two ideas, and it focuses on the presenter's skills in using digital media and visual displays of information, as well as the listener's ability to understand it.

4. Present information, findings, and supporting evidence such that listeners can follow the line of reasoning and the organization, development, and style are appropriate to task, purpose, and audience. (SL.CCR.4)

5. Make strategic use of digital media and visual displays of data to express information and enhance understanding of presentations. (SL.CCR.5)

6. Adapt speech to a variety of contexts and communicative tasks, demonstrating command of formal English when indicated or appropriate. (SL.CCR.6) (NGA & CCSSO, 2010a, p. 48)

Taken together, the anchor standards for speaking and listening highlight the integral role of peers in the learning process. Long gone is the notion that all knowledge emanates from the teacher, and that the student's chief role is to listen quietly and take it all in (Frey et al., 2009). Peer learning has become a dominant feature in 21st century classrooms, which carries implications for tomorrow's citizens. These standards are not about being able to pass on pleasantries to one another in conversation; they are the engine of learning. Before we examine the specific Speaking and Listening standards for grades 6–8, consider what is known about peer learning.

The Power of Peer Learning

Perhaps the most influential theorist on the role of peer-assisted learning is Lev Vygotsky (1978), who states that all learning is the product of sociocultural phenomena mediated by interactions with others. These social interactions shape the learner's view of the world. Therefore, collaboration with peers becomes a necessary part of a child's learning process. Indeed, Vygotsky identifies both the teacher and peers as important agents in the learning process (Crain, 2000).

One of Vygotsky's most enduring contributions to education is the concept of a *zone of proximal development*, which describes tasks a learner can successfully complete with minimal assistance. Students who assist one another in completing a task that might otherwise be too difficult to complete alone are considered to be working within their zone of proximal development. Many of us have found ourselves working in a group in which the problem is solved through discussion. This is why collaborative planning teams are so powerful; we all enjoy learning and producing in the presence of our peers. So it is with peer learning.

In addition to solving the task at hand, another goal of this type of learning is to foster mastery of skills and strategies that can be used independently in the future. This learning occurs when these "external and social activities are gradually internalized by the child . . . creat[ing] internal dialogues that form the processes of mental regulation" (Wood, 1998, p. 98). Stated differently, the language two students use to figure out a task together eventually becomes part of the internal problem-solving processes each child uses independently.

The power of peer-to-peer learning has been well documented in the research base on effective instruction, and it lies at the heart of all academic discussions (Mueller & Fleming, 2001; Stevens & Slavin, 1995). When students work collaboratively on a task, they are able to clarify one another's understandings, explore possible solutions, analyze concepts, and create new products (Frey et al., 2009). Additionally, they provide an ideal arena for the teacher to observe learning as it takes place, especially through listening to the problem-solving strategies that students use as they wrestle with concepts, skills, and ideas. The anchor standards articulate a path for students to regularly engage in these kinds of collaborative learning processes so that students can construct—not just assimilate—knowledge, and share it with others. In the next section, we will examine how peer learning forms the basis for the Speaking and Listening standards for grades 6–8.

Speaking and Listening Standards for Grades 6–8

The six grade-level standards for the Speaking and Listening strand are organized in two domains: (1) Comprehension and Collaboration and (2) Presentation of Knowledge and Ideas. Using the protocol in figures 4.1 and 4.2, consider the following questions in your collaborative team.

- What is our current level of knowledge about this standard?

- How can we increase our expertise?

- How will we measure our growth?

Alternatively, you and your team may prefer to use the analysis questions from chapters 2 and 3 (pages 27 and 60). Whichever set of questions you select to guide your discussions, you will be working within a framework that enables you to better understand and implement the CCSS.

Comprehension and Collaboration

The three standards in this domain describe the dispositions and purposes of informal talk in the classroom (see table 4.1, page 106). Throughout grades 6–8, students are expected to be prepared to participate with peers, especially as it applies to the norms of discussion. For example, if any of the students in Ms. Harrison's sixth-grade English class had failed to engage in collegial conversation, the quality of the group's talk would have suffered. Instead, it was elevated because students were able to cite examples from the text of Lou Gehrig's speech as evidence for their comments and questions.

Another notable feature of this domain is that its standards are intertwined with other domains of the Common Core ELA standards. For example, collaborative reading experiences provide students with opportunities to make meaning of a text with their peers. When students read and discuss texts together, they apply comprehension strategies and support the understanding of others. We use *collaborative reading* as an umbrella term to describe a number of peer-reading activities, including partner reading, literature circles, and reciprocal teaching. While each of these peer-reading arrangements possesses unique features, there are common elements.

First, students work in pairs or groups of no more than five. Second, the work they do is outside the immediate supervision of the teacher. Instead, they guide their own discussions and make decisions about how they will complete a task. A third element common to these collaborative reading practices is that students work with text to deepen their understanding of the content and the processes they use to comprehend. The Comprehension and Collaboration standards should be viewed through the lens of the content being taught, not held in isolation of other literacy and discipline-specific expectations.

Both anchor standard one (SL.CCR.1) and anchor standard two (SL.CCR.2) in this domain acknowledge the vital role of gaining information from other sources. In the previous domain, the attention is on how students gain information in conversations and discussions with others. In the second domain, the focus is on acquiring information from informational displays and other forms of multimedia technology. Anchor standard two (SL.CCR.2) reflects the increasing importance of visual and media literacies and

Table 4.1: Speaking and Listening Standards for Domain Comprehension and Collaboration, Grades 6–8

Anchor Standards	Grade 6 Standards	Grade 7 Standards	Grade 8 Standards
SL.CCR.1: Prepare for and participate effectively in a range of conversations and collaborations with diverse partners, building on others' ideas and expressing their own clearly and persuasively.	**SL.6.1:** Engage effectively in a range of collaborative discussions (one-on-one, in groups, and teacher-led) with diverse partners on grade 6 topics, texts, and issues, building on others' ideas and expressing their own clearly. a. Come to discussions prepared, having read or studied required material; explicitly draw on that preparation by referring to evidence on the topic, text, or issue to probe and reflect on ideas under discussion. b. Follow rules for collegial discussions, set specific goals and deadlines, and define individual roles as needed. c. Pose and respond to specific questions with elaboration and detail by making comments that contribute to the topic, text, or issue under discussion.	**SL.7.1:** Engage effectively in a range of collaborative discussions (one-on-one, in groups, and teacher-led) with diverse partners on grade 7 topics, texts, and issues, building on others' ideas and expressing their own clearly. a. Come to discussions prepared, having read or researched material under study; explicitly draw on that preparation by referring to evidence on the topic, text, or issue to probe and reflect on ideas under discussion. b. Follow rules for collegial discussions, track progress toward specific goals and deadlines, and define individual roles as needed. c. Pose questions that elicit elaboration and respond to others' questions and comments with relevant observations and ideas that bring the discussion back on topic as needed.	**SL.8.1:** Engage effectively in a range of collaborative discussions (one-on-one, in groups, and teacher-led) with diverse partners on grade 8 topics, texts, and issues, building on others' ideas and expressing their own clearly. a. Come to discussions prepared, having read or researched material under study; explicitly draw on that preparation by referring to evidence on the topic, text, or issue to probe and reflect on ideas under discussion. b. Follow rules for collegial discussions and decision making, track progress toward specific goals and deadlines, and define individual roles as needed. c. Pose questions that connect the ideas of several speakers and respond to others' questions and comments with relevant evidence, observations, and ideas.

SL.CCR.1: Prepare for and participate effectively in a range of conversations and collaborations with diverse partners, building on others; ideas and expressing their own clearly and persuasively.	d. Review the key ideas expressed and demonstrate understanding of multiple perspectives through reflection and paraphrasing.	d. Acknowledge new information expressed by others and, when warranted, modify their own views.	d. Acknowledge new information expressed by others and, when warranted, qualify or justify their own views in light of the evidence presented.
SL.CCR.2: Integrate and evaluate information presented in diverse media and formats, including visually, quantitatively, and orally.	**SL.6.2:** Interpret information presented in diverse media and formats (such as visually, quantitatively, or orally) and explain how it contributes to a topic, text, or issue under study.	**SL.7.2:** Analyze the main ideas and supporting details presented in diverse media and formats (such as visually, quantitatively, or orally) and explain how the ideas clarify a topic, text, or issue under study.	**SL.8.2:** Analyze the purpose of information presented in diverse media and formats (such as visually, quantitatively, or orally) and evaluate the motives (such as social, commercial, or political) behind its presentation.
SL.CCR.3: Evaluate a speaker's point of view, reasoning, and use of evidence and rhetoric.	**SL.6.3:** Delineate a speaker's argument and specific claims, distinguishing claims that are supported by reasons and evidence from claims that are not.	**SL.7.3:** Delineate a speaker's argument and specific claims, evaluating the soundness of the reasoning and the relevance and sufficiency of the evidence.	**SL.8.3:** Delineate a speaker's argument and specific claims, evaluating the soundness of the reasoning and relevance and sufficiency of the evidence and identifying when irrelevant evidence is introduced.

Source: Adapted from NGA & CCSSO, 2010a, pp. 48 and 49.

informational graphics for displaying and comprehending information (Frey & Fisher, 2008). The 21st century textbooks are filled with more photographs, charts, and diagrams than ever before. Even the ancillary materials rely on multimedia presentations. Short video clips are designed to build background knowledge at the beginning of a unit. Interviews with experts on the topic being studied supplement print resources. More than ever before, these print resources are being converted to digital texts.

However, these digital formats can tax the listening-comprehension skills of students. The eighth-grade version of standard two is especially challenging, as it asks students to consider the social, commercial, and political motives of the person or organization that has created the presentation.

Manuel Hinojosa, an eighth-grade English teacher, introduces media literacy early in the school year so that students can draw on this critical lens through all their learning. He begins by creating an online learning experience for students using My Pop Studio (www.mypopstudio.com), a free interactive game for middle school students. Mr. Hinojosa pairs students and assigns each group one of the site's four learning environments: music studio, magazine studio, television studio, or digital studio.

According to Mr. Hinojosa, "In each of these online environments, students learn about how editing changes the message, whether it is by touching up a photograph, autotuning a song, or using product placement in a TV show. They also gain some knowledge about the role of public relations and marketing in a celebrity culture."

After they have explored their assigned environment, individual students join groups with other learning environments to explore each studio. Each time, students reconvene in their original group, and the focus questions change.

"By the time students have explored each studio, they are getting to those critical-thinking questions about media. How is the message shaped and altered through editing and digital manipulation? What are the useful and harmful effects? And most importantly, how can we become sophisticated media consumers?" Mr. Hinojosa adds.

Activities like the one Mr. Hinojosa uses have the additional benefit of addressing standard three's focus on critically analyzing a speaker's arguments and claims. "One of the activities we do together is to analyze advertisements that are thinly disguised as journalism," he says. "Some of the weekly celebrity and sports magazines are notorious for doing this. I love it when my students start to bring in examples. They say, 'Mr. Hinojosa, look at this magazine story! It's nothing but an ad!'" He chuckles, "Those are the days when I really know I'm having a positive effect on their thinking."

Presentation of Knowledge and Ideas

Standards four through six of this domain focus on the student's ability to present information more formally. In addition, they describe the necessary skills the speaker should exhibit (see table 4.2). Efficient presentation skills, whether face-to-face or in a digital environment, require the speaker to follow these constructs:

- Organize information into a logical sequence so that listeners and viewers can comprehend it

- Have deep and accurate subject knowledge of the topic

- Ensure graphically displayed information is coherent, accurate, well designed, grammatically correct, and free of misspellings

- Deliver information smoothly and give attention to the audience's needs (for example, eye contact, elocution, and so on)

Table 4.2: Speaking and Listening Standards for Domain Presentation of Knowledge and Ideas, Grades 6–8

Anchor Standards	Grade 6 Standards	Grade 7 Standards	Grade 8 Standards
SL.CCR.4: Present information, findings, and supporting evidence such that listeners can follow the line of reasoning and the organization, development, and style are appropriate to task, purpose, and audience.	**SL.6.4:** Present claims and findings, sequencing ideas logically and using pertinent descriptions, facts, and details to accentuate main ideas or themes; use appropriate eye contact, adequate volume, and clear pronunciation.	**SL.7.4:** Present claims and findings, emphasizing salient points in a focused, coherent manner with pertinent descriptions, facts, details, and examples; use appropriate eye contact, adequate volume, and clear pronunciation.	**SL.8.4:** Present claims and findings, emphasizing salient points in a focused, coherent manner with relevant evidence, sound valid reasoning, and well-chosen details; use appropriate eye contact, adequate volume, and clear pronunciation.
SL.CCR.5: Make strategic use of digital media and visual displays of data to express information and enhance understanding of the presentations.	**SL.6.5:** Include multimedia components (like graphics, images, music, and sound) and visual displays in presentations to clarify information.	**SL.7.5:** Include multimedia components and visual displays in presentations to clarify claims and findings and emphasize salient points.	**SL.8.5:** Integrate multimedia and visual displays into presentations to clarify information, strengthen claims and evidence, and add interest.
SL.CCR.6: Adapt speech to a variety of contexts and communicative tasks, demonstrating command of formal English when indicated or appropriate.	**SL.6.6:** Adapt speech to a variety of contexts and tasks, demonstrating command of formal English when indicated or appropriate. (See grade 6 Language standards one and three for specific expectations.)	**SL.7.6:** Adapt speech to a variety of contexts and tasks, demonstrating command of formal English when indicated or appropriate. (See grade 7 Language standards one and three for specific expectations.)	**SL.8.6:** Adapt speech to a variety of contexts and tasks, demonstrating command of formal English when indicated or appropriate. (See grade 8 Language standards one and three for specific expectations.)

Source: Adapted from NGA & CCSSO, 2010a, pp. 48 and 49.

It's helpful for collaborative teams to tie formal presentations to writing standards, as students must write presentations before delivering them. Given that there is a parallel emphasis on organization in the writing standards, students should be encouraged to convert written products into formal presentations. The *paragraph frame* is a useful instructional scaffold for doing both. It is a series of sentence stems intended to scaffold original writing while furnishing an organizational structure. Paragraph frames are not intended as a fill-in-the-blank exercise. Instead, they should be introduced after rich oral development of ideas and concepts. This preliminary stage of oral composition assists writers in organizing their own thoughts about a topic as they engage in informal talk (see standards one to three in table 4.1, page 106). The paragraph frame is introduced, and students are instructed to add original sentences within or after it. This procedure is more sophisticated than traditional story starters, which begin with a sentence stem, like "It was a dark and stormy night," because it provides more structure for the writer. A paragraph frame might look like this:

"Many people call _____ a hero, but few know that _____. I was surprised to learn that _____, but I can see how this incident made _____ the person [he or she] became. Nevertheless, most biographical accounts of _____ don't include this incident. That is unfortunate, because _____. I believe that if more people knew about _____, they would understand this heroic story more deeply."

Notice that the frame establishes a direction for the writer without being prescriptive. Furthermore, the writer does not need to use these sentences in sequence but can add his or her own original writing within the frame. Once written, these paragraph frames organize formal presentations as well, especially in sequencing facts, events, or concepts in a logical order. Other sample paragraph frames appear in figure 4.3.

Narrative
Carla's heart began to pound as she heard the _____. She trembled, thinking that _____ would be inevitable. Carla silently recounted the things she was most thankful for: _____, _____, and _____. She also listed her regrets: _____ and _____. Why is it that only when we are confronted with an awful event that we suddenly become reflective about our life?
Biographical and Autobiographical
_____ has been the most life-changing event in my life. Before _____ occurred, I believed that _____. But after this happened, I would never look at the world in the same way again. Now I understood that _____.
Informative and Explanatory
Without question, the development of the _____ has changed the world profoundly. Before _____ was invented, people had to rely on _____ to _____. However, the development of _____ has also had some unintended consequences. First and foremost, _____.

Figure 4.3: Sample paragraph frames for writing and formal presentations.

Anchor standard six (SL.CCR.6) for Speaking and Listening specifically references Language standards one and three on using the conventions of English in speech and in writing. In terms of the speaking portion of the standard, this means using the correct grammar and syntax of conventional English. This can be challenging for students who are learning English, or for some students with language disabilities that make learning English difficult. These students might require more support.

Seventh-grade teacher Robert Crenshaw uses a simple technique for supporting his students who require additional language support. "We do lots of group presentations in our class, because the collaboration is so valuable," he says. "But it can be difficult for some students. We do what I like to call *human captioning* to draw on a little more support." As groups organize their presentations into key ideas, they create sentence strips to match. These strips are written in complete sentences, and as a speaker discusses his or her portion of the speech, he or she holds the sentence strip under him. "Like when you watch a news program, and there's that text on the bottom of the screen that gives the viewer the main idea of the topic," Mr. Crenshaw explains. This has an added benefit for the speaker, as the back of the sentence strip is the place where he or she can write notes. "It keeps the speaker organized to state his ideas correctly, and it helps organize the listeners, too." Mr. Crenshaw also uses presentation tools available on the computer for added support. "Students use these as a digital storytelling tool, but they also allow students to record their presentations. They speak into the built-in microphone and then play back the recording. If it doesn't sound right to them, they can record it again," says Mr. Crenshaw. "I encourage students to do this, because it's so valuable to hear yourself. They get immediate feedback about whether their pronunciation, vocal quality, and syntax are sufficient."

Anchor Standards for Language

A final set of Common Core ELA standards is dedicated to language. Speech and language are closely related, but they do have distinct features that make them unique. Speech concerns verbal expression; language describes what words mean (vocabulary), how they are strung together to make sense using the rules of the language (grammar and syntax), how new words are made (conjugation), and what word combinations work best for a situation (pragmatics and register) (American Speech-Language-Hearing Association, 2012). Language is foundational to what we do, and we are so enmeshed in it that it can be difficult to distance ourselves in order to observe it. As the saying goes, "The last thing a fish notices is the water it swims in." Language is to humans as water is to fish. (By the way, your ability to understand that last idiom and its analogy speaks to your command of language.) The NGA and CCSSO (2010a) put it a different way:

> The inclusion of Language standards in their own strand should not be taken as an indication that skills related to conventions, effective language use, and vocabulary are unimportant to reading, writing, speaking, and listening; indeed, they are inseparable from such contexts. (p. 25)

The overall intent of the Language standards speaks to the need to raise students' awareness of language, something they are not likely to be able to do without the intentional instruction of a teacher who already possesses this awareness. As a reminder, you may want to analyze the standards for the grades 6–8 band with these questions in mind: (1) What is our current level of knowledge about this standard? (2) How can we increase our expertise? (3) How will we measure our growth? In the next section, we will examine the anchor standards for language, which are foundational to the grade-level standards. They are organized into three domains: (1) Conventions of Standard English, (2) Knowledge of Language, and (3) Vocabulary Acquisition and Use.

Conventions of Standard English

This first domain of standards concerns itself with the grammatical rules of spoken and written language, especially as they pertain to parts of speech, written conventions, and spelling. The following standards are essential to communication, and involve issues related to the development of complex sentences, as well as voice and mood:

1. Demonstrate command of the conventions of standard English grammar and usage when writing or speaking. (L.CCR.1)

2. Demonstrate command of the conventions of standard English capitalization, punctuation, and spelling when writing. (L.CCR.2) (NGA & CCSSO, 2010a, p. 25)

A unique feature of the CCSS is a table that provides a graphic representation of the language progression for Language standards one to three (see table 4.3). The CCSS expect attention to language demands to continue throughout the grades as they are applied to increasingly sophisticated writing and speaking situations. The table highlights particular skills that are likely to need many years of attention to refine and expand. For example, while recognizing and correcting inappropriate shifts in pronoun number and person is initially introduced in sixth grade, it is continued through twelfth grade.

Knowledge of Language

This single anchor standard covers quite a bit of territory. Beginning in grade 2 (there isn't a grade-level standard for this domain in kindergarten or first grade), students begin to attend to the registers of language, especially in comparing formal and informal modes of communication. By high school, students are applying their knowledge of language through the use of style guides, like MLA. This anchor standard is strongly linked to those in Writing and in Speaking and Listening:

3. Apply knowledge of language to understand how language functions in different contexts, to make effective choices for meaning or style, and to comprehend more fully when reading or listening. (L.CCR.3) (NGA & CCSSO, 2010a, p. 25)

Table 4.3: Language Progressive Skills by Grade

Standards	Grades							
	3	4	5	6	7	8	9–10	11–12
L.3.1f: Ensure subject-verb and pronoun-antecedent agreement.								
L.3.3a: Choose words and phrases for effect.								
L.4.1f: Produce complete sentences, recognizing and correcting inappropriate fragments and run-ons.								
L.4.1g: Correctly use frequently confused words (such as to/too/two and there/their).								
L.4.3a: Choose words and phrases to convey ideas precisely.[1]								
L.4.3b: Choose punctuation for effect.								
L.5.1d: Recognize and correct inappropriate shifts in verb tense.								
L.5.2a: Use punctuation to separate items in a series.[2]								
L.6.1c: Recognize and correct inappropriate shifts in pronoun number and person.								
L.6.1d: Recognize and correct vague pronouns (such as ones with unclear or ambiguous antecedents).								
L.6.1e: Recognize variations from standard English in their own and others' writing and speaking, and identify and use strategies to improve expression in conventional language.								
L.6.2a: Use punctuation (like commas, parentheses, and dashes) to set off nonrestrictive and parenthetical elements.								
L.6.3a: Vary sentence patterns for meaning, reader and listener interest, and style.[3]								

continued →

Standards	Grades							
	3	4	5	6	7	8	9–10	11–12
L.6.3b: Maintain consistency in style and tone.								
L.7.1c: Place phrases and clauses within a sentence, recognizing and correcting misplaced and dangling modifiers.								
L.7.3a: Choose language that expresses ideas precisely and concisely, recognizing and eliminating wordiness and redundancy.								
L.8.1d: Recognize and correct inappropriate shifts in verb voice and mood.								
L.9–10.1a: Use parallel structure.								

[1] Subsumed by L.7.3a
[2] Subsumed by L.9–10.1a
[3] Subsumed by L.11–12.3a
* The Language standards one to three, are particularly likely to require continued attention in higher grades as they are applied to increasingly sophisticated writing and speaking.

Source: Adapted from NGA & CCSSO, 2010a, p. 30. © Copyright 2010. National Governors Association Center for Best Practices and Council of Chief State School Officers. All rights reserved.

Vocabulary Acquisition and Use

This domain has received considerable attention in the education community because of the emphasis in anchor standard four (L.CCR.4) on word solving. While this approach to vocabulary development has been widely researched (for example, Baumann, Font, Edwards, & Boland, 2005; Blachowicz & Fisher, 2002), in practice there has been a more prominent focus on vocabulary lists. As anchor standard six (L.CCR.6) illustrates, grade-level vocabulary lists are valuable. Every teacher should have a strong sense of the grade-level vocabulary expectations. Additionally, this should be coupled with purposeful instruction on how to solve for unknown words.

A second area of attention has been on nuanced use of language in standard six. Note that it defines vocabulary as *words and phrases*, not single words alone. In addition, it describes these words and phrases as *general academic* and *domain specific*. These terms align with the work of Beck et al. (2002) and their description of tier two words (in the language of CCSS, they are general academic words and phrases like *motionless* and *endearing qualities*) that mature language users use in several contents. In addition, tier three words are those domain-specific words and phrases that are tied to a discipline, like using *nebula* and *recessive genes* in science. Anchor standard five (L.CCR.5) draws attention to the need to appreciate the artistry of words that convey just the right meaning, tone, and mood. The standards in the Vocabulary Acquisition and Use domain are as follows:

4. Determine or clarify the meaning of unknown and multiple-meaning words and phrases by using context clues, analyzing meaningful word parts, and consulting general and specialized reference materials, as appropriate. (L.CCR.4)

5. Demonstrate understanding of figurative language, word relationships, and nuances in word meanings. (L.CCR.5)

6. Acquire and use accurately a range of general academic and domain-specific words and phrases sufficient for reading, writing, speaking, and listening at the college and career readiness level; demonstrate independence in gathering vocabulary knowledge when encountering an unknown term important to comprehension or expression. (L.CCR.6) (NGA & CCSSO, 2010a, p. 25)

Language Standards for Grades 6–8

The anchor standards frame a pathway for language development from kindergarten through twelfth grade, with an eye toward systematically preparing students for the language demands of career and college. In the next section, we will analyze the specific standards for grades 6–8 in more detail.

The six grade-level standards for language are organized in the same manner as the domains they are derived from: Conventions of Standard English, Knowledge of

Language, and Vocabulary Acquisition and Use. As noted previously, refer to figures 4.1 and 4.2, consider the following questions in your collaborative team.

- What is our current level of knowledge about this standard?
- How can we increase our expertise?
- How will we measure our growth?

Alternatively, you and your team may prefer to use the analysis questions from chapters 2 and 3 (pages 27 and 60). Whichever set of questions you select to guide your discussions, you will be working within a framework that enables you to better understand and implement the CCSS.

Conventions of Standard English

The grade-level standards for this domain speak to the growing command students gain in middle school as they apply formal rules of grammar and conventions to their spoken and written communication (see table 4.4). A challenge with teaching grammar is that the number of rules can quickly overwhelm most learners. Grammar instruction calls for teaching within the context of authentic reading, writing, and speaking demands (Weaver, 1996). Of course, students should be able to identify parts of speech, punctuation, and writing conventions. However, learning fewer but powerful rules deeply is more effective than trying to memorize a bewildering list of rules that is soon forgotten. A challenge in grades 6–8 is that some grammar instruction needs to be direct, and not all English teachers are confident in their ability to provide direct instruction for more complex grammatical structures, such as the use of gerunds, participles, and infinitives in grade 8. From an instructional standpoint, identify the most important labels and rules for your students to know, and place a stronger emphasis on teaching grammar and conventions in context, rather than confining it to workbook pages of lessons. Use these formal grammar lessons as a basis for helping students understand their own writing, especially in using authentic examples for revision.

Generative Writing

One way to teach these essential language skills in context is through generative writing instruction. This teacher-directed instruction offers a valuable opportunity to provide carefully designed lessons that lead students through an organized process for writing with clarity and originality. However, this does not mean that writing should be reduced to isolated skills at the expense of purpose, voice, content, and conventions. We know that problems can occur when a student is full of ideas but does not possess the means to put the message on paper. Likewise, the student who has mastered the conventions but has difficulty with generating ideas is equally at risk. Through generative writing instruction, teachers provide students with strategies for creating cohesive writing while engaged in authentic tasks. Linda Dorn and Carla Soffos (2001) describe a continuum of difficulty when completing generative writing:

Table 4.4: Language Standards for Domain Conventions of Standard English, Grades 6–8

Anchor Standards	Grade 6 Standards	Grade 7 Standards	Grade 8 Standards
L.CCR.1: Demonstrate command of conventions of standard English grammar and usage when speaking and writing.	**L.6.1:** Demonstrate command of the conventions of standard English grammar and usage when writing or speaking. a. Ensure that pronouns are in the proper case (subjective, objective, or possessive). b. Use intensive pronouns (like *myself* or *ourselves*). c. Recognize and correct inappropriate shifts in pronoun number and person.* d. Recognize and correct vague pronouns (like ones with unclear or ambiguous antecedents).* e. Recognize variations from standard English in their own and others' writing and speaking, and identify and use strategies to improve expression in conventional language.*	**L.7.1:** Demonstrate command of the conventions of standard English grammar and usage when writing or speaking. a. Explain the function of phrases and clauses in general and their function in specific sentences. b. Choose among simple, compound, complex, and compound-complex sentences to signal differing relationships among ideas. c. Place phrases and clauses within a sentence, recognizing and correcting misplaced and dangling modifiers.*	**L.8.1:** Demonstrate command of the conventions of standard English grammar and usage when writing or speaking. a. Explain the function of verbals (like gerunds, participles, and infinitives) in general and their function in particular sentences. b. Form and use verbs in the active and passive voice. c. Form and use verbs in the indicative, imperative, interrogative, conditional, and subjunctive mood. d. Recognize and correct inappropriate shifts in verb voice and mood.*

continued →

Anchor Standards	Grade 6 Standards	Grade 7 Standards	Grade 8 Standards
L.CCR.2: Demonstrate command of conventions of standard English capitalization, punctuation, and spelling when writing.	**L.6.2:** Demonstrate command of the conventions of standard English capitalization, punctuation, and spelling when writing. a. Use punctuation (like commas, parentheses, and dashes) to set off nonrestrictive and parenthetical elements.* b. Spell correctly.	**L.7.2:** Use knowledge of language and its conventions when writing, speaking, reading, or listening. a. Choose language that expresses ideas precisely and concisely, recognizing and eliminating wordiness and redundancy.* b. Spell correctly.	**L.8.2:** Use knowledge of language and its conventions when writing, speaking, reading, or listening. a. Use verbs in the active and passive voice and in the conditional and subjunctive mood to achieve particular effects (like emphasizing the actor or the action; expressing uncertainty or describing a state contrary to fact). b. Spell correctly.

* The Language standards one to three are particularly likely to require continued attention in higher grades as they are applied to increasingly sophisticated writing and speaking.

Source: Adapted from NGA & CCSSO, 2010a, pp. 51 and 52.

- Adding words to a text is easier to do
- Deleting words from a text is harder to do; deleting lines or phrases is even more difficult
- Substituting words for other words is still more difficult because it requires writers to know multiple meanings for words
- Rearranging sentences and paragraphs is the most difficult skill (pp. 6–7)

Generative sentences draw the writer's attention to the ways grammar, conventions, and vocabulary work together to convey a message. They are initially brief pieces of text that are systematically expanded under the guidance of the teacher. The strategy is based on Fearn and Farnan's (2001) work with *given word sentences* and can be extended through additional scaffolding. A series of prompts are offered to move students from one idea formulated first at the word level to a more fully developed piece of connected text. These prompts are usually paced with a timer to keep the lesson moving and to increase fluency at both the written and creative levels.

A generative sentence session for middle school writers begins at the word level. For example, ask students to compare and contrast the use of gerunds and infinitives by asking them to use *learning* and *to learn* in sentences. Begin by asking them to construct a sentence with the word *learning* in the fourth position in the sentence, and they'll develop sentences like:

- Students are always *learning* new ideas in English class.
- I like the *learning* that happens to me when I watch the news.

Now ask students to write a similar sentence using the infinitive version, *to learn*, in the fourth and fifth positions, such as:

- For a student *to learn* new ideas, she must go to English class.
- Watching the news *to learn* makes me happy.

In this case, the most likely way to use the infinitive in the fourth position is to use the passive voice, and now the discussion can focus on the merits of each. Generative sentences can be made more challenging by introducing more conditions, such as the:

- Position of the word within the sentence
- Length of the sentence (more than, less than, or the exact number of words)
- Sentence pattern (parts of speech, punctuation, or elements of style)

For example, students might be asked to use an adverb in the second position in a sentence (parts of speech), to embed a parenthetical expression (punctuation), or to write an imperative using a particular word (elements of style). This method can also be used for learning content because the teacher chooses the focus word. For example, students can be given the words *metaphor* and *simile* to construct a syntactically and semantically accurate sentence. These can then serve as a topic sentence for two more detailed paragraphs that compare and contrast the two, thereby providing the teacher with information about students' content knowledge as well as writing skills.

Spelling

Anchor standard two (L.CCR.2) describes writing conventions such as punctuation and capitalization and spelling. The process of encoding in writing parallels decoding development as students gain control of their reading. As with all expressive language domains (speaking and writing), development will always lag behind our receptive skill levels (listening and reading). You probably notice this with your own literacy as you struggle to spell a word you rarely write, but fully know the meaning and can read it with no difficulty at all.

Researchers have examined the spelling patterns children use and have named each stage of spelling development in grades K–12: emergent, letter name, within word pattern, syllable juncture, and derivational constancy (Templeton, Johnston, Bear, & Invernizzi, 2008).

- **Emergent stage:** Students at this stage recognize that print conveys a message, but they are not yet reading. Most kindergarteners begin at this stage.

- **Letter name stage:** Students entering this stage have started to master the sound-symbol relationships and the concept of a word.

- **Within word pattern stage:** At this stage, students are consolidating their growing knowledge of how combinations of letters can be used to figure out the spelling of unknown ones.

- **Syllable juncture stage:** Students at this stage are becoming more skillful readers and writers. They spell most common words correctly and have a growing oral vocabulary. Advanced grade 2 and most grades 3–5 students fall into this stage. However, English learners and students who struggle with reading and writing in grades 6–8 may still be in this stage.

- **Derivational constancy stage:** Students at this stage rarely spell the majority of words incorrectly, and they are beginning to learn that words with similar meanings share common spelling patterns (such as *demonstrate*, *demonstration*, and *demonstrable*). Students at this stage learn about this history of the language as well as the etymology (word origins). Most middle school and high school students fall into this stage.

However, the Common Core standards in grades 6–12 state simply that students should "spell correctly," but don't call for specific spelling instruction. This has been an area of criticism regarding the standards, as a notable number of middle school students still require spelling instruction. By the time they reach sixth grade, most students are in the derivational constancy phase of spelling (Templeton et al., 2008)—the final stage of spelling development that typically begins in middle school and continues through adulthood. The basis for this stage is formed in the intermediate grades.

The instructional implications for students at this stage allow the teacher to teach students to scrutinize words for their histories. Importantly, the teacher will often learn a lot about words as his or her students engage in this level of word study. Students should be encouraged to keep word journals and to capture the related etymology for the words in these journals. Often students like to record the first known use of the word, related words, and a typical sentence in which the word is used. Templeton, Johnston, Bear, and Invernizzi (2009) suggest that the teacher can initiate the word study with a simple question, "Did you find any interesting words in your reading?" (p. 20). Although spelling is not addressed directly in the Common Core standards, the needs of the students should dictate the extent to which spelling instruction occurs in the English classroom.

Knowledge of Language

The key word in this domain is *precision* in use of written and oral language, especially in being able to create a mood (see table 4.5). Students learn written language by building words into sentences that represent ideas. They also learn to write through taking away what is not necessary. This taking away process is critical for good editing. A hallmark of effective writing is the way sentences *hang together* to support the reader's understanding of the message the writer is attempting to convey. An effective technique for teaching about the nuances involved in transforming adequate sentences into those that resonate is sentence combining.

Table 4.5: Language Standards for Domain Knowledge of Language, Grades 6–8

Anchor Standard	Grade 6 Standards	Grade 7 Standards	Grade 8 Standards
L.CCR.3: Apply knowledge of language to understand how language functions in different contexts, to make effective use of choices for meaning or style, and to comprehend more fully when reading or listening.	**L.6.3:** Use knowledge of language and its conventions when writing, speaking, reading, or listening. a. Vary sentence patterns for meaning, reader and listener interest, and style.* b. Maintain consistency in style and tone.*	**L.7.3:** Use knowledge of language and its conventions when writing, speaking, reading, or listening. a. Choose language that expresses ideas precisely and concisely, recognizing and eliminating wordiness and redundancy.*	**L.8.3:** Use knowledge of language and its conventions when writing, speaking, reading, or listening. a. Use verbs in the active and passive voice and in the conditional and subjunctive mood to achieve particular effects (such as emphasizing the actor or the action; expressing uncertainty or describing a state contrary to fact.)

* The skills in Language standards one to three are particularly likely to require continued attention in higher grades as they are applied to increasingly sophisticated writing and speaking.

Source: Adapted from NGA & CCSSO, 2010a, pp. 51 and 52.

Sentence combining provides students with an opportunity to utilize syntactic knowledge to create more sophisticated sentences. In a typical activity, students work with a passage of syntactically correct but choppy sentences and rework them to create sentences that preserve the original meaning while increasing the flow of the language. It is important to keep in mind what sentence combining can and cannot do. The effectiveness of sentence combining is diminished in the absence of other components of writing instruction. However, like spoken language, a complex weaving of skills must take place in order to result in a meaningful written message. Syntax is an important part of the fabric of language, and these syntactic lessons should be used as one part of a balanced writing program.

Vocabulary Acquisition and Use

The three remaining Language standards are under the domain Vocabulary Acquisition and Use (see table 4.6). The vocabulary demands on students skyrocket during the school years, ballooning to an estimated 88,500 word families by the time a student is in high school (Nagy & Anderson, 1984). Word families are groups of words related by a common root or pattern, such as *sign*, *significant*, and *signify*. Given the number of word families, it is estimated that students are exposed to over 500,000 words while they are in grades 3 to 9. While these academic language demands are high, it is estimated that everyday speech consists of only 5,000–7,000 words (Nagy & Anderson, 1984). Thus, there is a huge difference between the number of words a student uses commonly as he or she speaks and the number of words needed to be successful in school. This difference in word knowledge is problematic because of its impact on content learning and reading comprehension. In fact, knowledge of vocabulary is a strong predictor of how well a reader will comprehend a text.

The fact is that no one could teach 88,500 word families—that's 154 words a day from kindergarten to eighth grade!—nor would it be effective. Fortunately, students acquire many words and phrases through wide reading and experiences. In addition, they need to know how to resolve unknown words outside the company of an adult. Anchor standard four (L.CCR.4) emphasizes teaching students a problem-solving approach using structural and contextual analysis, as well as resources. We refer to this as looking inside a word (structure) and outside a word (context and resources) (Frey & Fisher, 2009).

Looking Inside a Word: Structure

Students use analysis of structural components such as prefixes, suffixes, and the root and base words to figure out unfamiliar words that contain familiar morphology. When elementary students understand common prefixes like *re-*, *dis-*, and *un-*, as well as suffixes such as *-s/-es*, *-ing*, and *-er/-or*, they can use this knowledge when they encounter a new word. In middle school, students are learning how more complex affixes such as *fore- intra-*, *-eous*, and *-ative* are used to build derivatives. Roots of words are also helpful in understanding the meaning of a new word. For instance, when a student is able

Table 4.6: Language Standards for Domain Vocabulary Acquisition and Use, Grades 6–8

Anchor Standards	Grade 6 Standards	Grade 7 Standards	Grade 8 Standards
L.CCR.4: Determine or clarify the meaning of unknown and multiple-meaning words and phrases by using context clues, analyzing meaningful word parts, and consulting general and specialized reference materials, as appropriate.	**L.6.4:** Determine or clarify the meaning of unknown and multiple-meaning words and phrases based on grade 6 reading and content, choosing flexibly from a range of strategies. a. Use context (such as the overall meaning of a sentence or paragraph; a word's position or function in a sentence) as a clue to the meaning of a word or phrase. b. Use common, grade-appropriate Greek or Latin affixes and roots as clues to the meaning of a word (such as *audience, auditory,* and *audible*). c. Consult reference materials (like dictionaries, glossaries, and thesauruses), both print and digital, to find the pronunciation of a word or determine or clarify its precise meaning or its part of speech.	**L.7.4:** Determine or clarify the meaning of unknown and multiple-meaning words and phrases based on grade 7 reading and content, choosing flexibly from a range of strategies. a. Use context (such as the overall meaning of a sentence or paragraph; a word's position or function in a sentence) as a clue to the meaning of a word or phrase. b. Use common, grade-appropriate Greek or Latin affixes and roots as clues to the meaning of a word (such as *belligerent, bellicose,* and *rebel*). c. Consult general and specialized reference materials (like dictionaries, glossaries, and thesauruses), both print and digital, to find the pronunciation of a word or determine or clarify its precise meaning or its part of speech.	**L.8.4:** Determine or clarify the meaning of unknown and multiple-meaning words or phrases based on grade 8 reading and content, choosing flexibly from a range of strategies. a. Use context (such as the overall meaning of a sentence or paragraph; a word's position or function in a sentence) as a clue to the meaning of a word or phrase. b. Use common, grade-appropriate Greek or Latin affixes and roots as clues to the meaning of a word (such as *precede, recede,* and *secede*). c. Consult general and specialized reference materials (like dictionaries, glossaries, and thesauruses), both print and digital, to find the pronunciation of a word or determine or clarify its precise meaning or its part of speech.

continued →

Anchor Standards	Grade 6 Standards	Grade 7 Standards	Grade 8 Standards
L.CCR.4: Determine or clarify the meaning of unknown and multiple-meaning words and phrases by using context clues, analyzing meaningful word parts, and consulting general and specialized reference materials, as appropriate.	d. Verify the preliminary determination of the meaning of a word or phrase (such as by checking the inferred meaning in context or in a dictionary).	d. Verify the preliminary determination of the meaning of a word or phrase (such as by checking the inferred meaning in context or in a dictionary).	d. Verify the preliminary determination of the meaning of a word or phrase (such as by checking the inferred meaning in context or in a dictionary).

Source: Adapted from NGA & CCSSO, 2010a, pp. 51 and 53.

to recognize the root in the word *patronize*, he or she can make a good prediction about related words such as *expatriate* and *compatriot*.

Looking Outside a Word: Context

Context clues are the signals authors use to explain a word meaning. There are several types of contextual clues readers use to understand a word, including definitions, synonyms, antonyms, and examples. In the following list, the vocabulary word is underlined and the contextual clue is italicized.

- **Definition:** Many American <u>expatriates</u> assembled in Paris after World War I. *An expatriate is a person who is temporarily living in a country other than the one in which he or she was raised.*

- **Synonym:** These expatriates formed a *group* of artists, writers, and intellectuals who experimented with new forms of literature and thought. This <u>cohort</u> included writers like Ernest Hemingway and poets like Langston Hughes. We will read their works this year in English.

- **Antonym:** Many of these expatriates were drawn to Paris's <u>tolerant</u> climate, which *differed from the <u>strict</u> rules* of American culture, especially in its attitudes about gender, race, and politics.

- **Example:** For instance, the women's <u>suffrage</u> movement in the United States took more than seventy years. Women were not *granted the right to vote* in the United States until 1920. But in France, women had been voting since 1871, and did not have to engage in a prolonged suffrage movement to protest for equal voting rights for both genders. Female expatriate artists and writers enjoyed living in a country where this issue had been resolved generations earlier.

Looking Outside a Word: Resources

Another way that students figure out unfamiliar words is by using a resource. We don't encourage students to turn to the dictionary first, because we want them to practice their word-solving strategies. We do encourage students to use structural and contextual analysis first, because even if they can't figure out the word's meaning using those two strategies, they at least know something about the word by the time they turn to the resource. Glossaries are especially good because, unlike dictionaries, they limit the given meaning to the one used in the related text. In addition, we keep developmental dictionaries in the classroom for students to consult, and bookmark online dictionaries. Finally, asking another peer is also a legitimate resource, which we use frequently ourselves.

Anchor standard five (L.CCR.5) in the domain Vocabulary Acquisition and Use for grades 6–8 details the importance of word relationships in verbal and written language. Relationships between words can be particularly challenging when interpreting figures of speech, as well as nuanced associations between words. The differences between *tolerant*, *liberal*, and *charitable* are fine but distinct ones. This ability to discern between gradient of meaning is a skill assessed on many achievement tests. The difference between the right word and the almost right word can impact the student's ability to use precise language. These *shades of meaning* require students to know both the denotation (definition) of a word or phrase, as well as its connotation (association) to other concepts or ideas.

Mr. Hinojosa extends his students' understanding of connotation through his media literacy unit. His students find example advertisements and develop lists of key words within the advertisements that have a strong impact. Using Visual Thesaurus (www .visualthesaurus.com), an online interactive dictionary and thesaurus, students create word maps of their identified words, and then sort them into those that have positive and negative connotations. After analyzing a print ad from a pharmaceutical company about a prescription cosmetic treatment, they determine that the words and phrases *clinically significant*, *proven*, and *safety* have strongly positive connotations. In the fine print, they also found *toxin*, *serious side effects*, and *temporary results* to have negative connotations. Mr. Hinojosa comments, "This is a great way for students to pay close attention to the use of words in advertising. Our use of the online dictionary helped to push our discussion further by letting them see other words associated with the target words."

The text itself can also be an outside resource, when used as a reference to compare to predicted content. This can be accomplished using the *list-group-label* method, which emphasizes the link between words and their relationship to content (Taba, 1967). This instructional technique encourages students to first make predictions about the vocabulary they expect to encounter during a reading then categorize those predictions into an organized frame. By doing this, students will create more detailed predictions. After the reading, they revisit the chart to add information and make corrections. Barbara Moss and Virginia Loh (2010) advise using the following steps to conduct a successful list-group-label lesson.

1. Select an informational text.

2. Before reading the text, invite students to list vocabulary words they know about the topic of the informational text. Record their ideas on the board.

3. Once the list has been created, discuss how the words and phrases can be grouped.

4. Develop labels for each of the groups they have created. Arrange in a grid and write the words and phrases again under the appropriate categories.

5. Read the text.

6. After the reading, add new words and phrases to the existing categories. New categories can be created as well.

Before reading the Simple English Wikipedia entry about Ernest Hemingway, which uses fewer words and easier grammar than standard Wikipedia entries (http://simple .wikipedia.org/wiki/Ernest_Hemingway), Mr. Hinojosa asks his students to list what they knew about the author. "We were getting ready to read *The Old Man and the Sea*

(Hemingway, 1952, 1996), and students needed to understand how the personality of the author melds with the main character," he says. "But what they knew about Hemingway was pretty minimal, so I used an instructional routine to let them build their knowledge." Mr. Hinojosa uses the Simple English version of the Wikipedia entry as an introductory text. As the unit progresses, he asks them to read the more extensive entry. He explains, "I often use vocabulary and a gradient of texts to scaffold student knowledge and build their ability to read more complex texts." His students make predictions, which are then organized as categories into a chart (see figure 4.4). After the students read and discuss the Simple English entry, they add other facts to the same chart. The information they add after the reading is in the shaded boxes.

Who Was He?	When Did He Live?	Why Was He Famous?	How Did He Contribute to His Profession?
Writer	A long time ago	He wrote stories that are still read today.	He is considered to be a great American writer.
Member of the Lost Generation	In the United States	There's a poem about him.	He used discussion between characters to tell a story.
Journalist	He was born in 1899 and committed suicide in 1961.	Many of his stories were about his own fears.	He won a Nobel Prize in Literature in 1954.
Married and divorced many times	In many locations, including Key West, Chicago, and Paris	"The author himself was his best creation."	His last important book is *The Old Man and the Sea*.

Figure 4.4: Sample list-group-label for Ernest Hemingway.

Anchor standard six (L.CCR.6) is the final one in this domain and references grade-appropriate general academic and domain-specific words, and is worded exactly the same across the three grade levels. As you have already realized, providing direct instruction for each vocabulary word a student might encounter would be an impossible task. In addition, the source words identified within a grade level will vary according to materials used, student need, and the local context. It is, however, essential to have a method for selecting the words that *will* be taught. It is not uncommon for teachers to use a more haphazard approach such as choosing all the "big words" or those that are unusual. However, this is particularly inefficient for ensuring that students are focusing on critical vocabulary. Therefore, we offer the following considerations for choosing vocabulary words to teach.

- **Conceptual value:** Does the word represent an important concept that is needed in order to understand the reading? For example, Hattie's reference to *the Kaiser* was important for the sixth-grade students in the opening pages of *Hattie Big Sky* (Larson, 2006) to more fully appreciate the anti-German sentiment during the World War I time period of the novel. However, it's likely that they will come to understand this concept as the story unfolds. Therefore, it is sufficient to briefly explain what Hattie is referring to. An important consideration in choosing vocabulary relates to the usefulness of the word. Some words are concepts, while others are labels. Given that students need to acquire a tremendous volume of vocabulary words each year, it seems careless to squander valuable instructional time on words that function only as labels in a particular reading.

- **Repeatability:** Is the word going to be used throughout the school year? Some words are worth teaching because they will be used often. For instance, it is worth taking the time to instruct students on the meaning of *argumentation* because it will be used throughout the year as students write, read, and discuss.

- **Transportability:** Some words should be selected because they will appear in many subjects or content areas. Teaching students the term *homestead claim* as it appears in *Hattie Big Sky* (Larson, 2006) is useful because students will also be using this word in social studies.

- **Contextual analysis:** If students can use context clues to determine the word meaning then direct instruction is not necessary. In *Hattie Big Sky* (Larson, 2006), readers can use context clues to determine the meaning of *cultivate* in the following sentences: "Your uncle tell you that you need to cultivate one-eighth of this claim? That's forty acres" (p. 25).

- **Structural analysis:** Words that contain affixes and Latin or Greek root words students are familiar with can be analyzed through structural analysis. For example, the word *resolution* may not need to be included in the list of vocabulary words if students understand the meaning of *resolve* and recognize that the suffix *-tion* is used to change verbs into nouns.

- **Cognitive load:** While there is debate about the number of vocabulary words that teachers should introduce to students at a given time, most agree that the number should reflect the developmental level of the students and the length of the reading (Baumann, 2009; Graves & Watts-Taffe, 2002; Nagy & Scott, 2000; Padak, Bromley, Rasinski, & Newton, 2012). In a brief reading, two to three words is often sufficient for emergent and early readers, while transitional readers can utilize five or more.

Teachers must create a balance between students learning words in context and learning words through systematic, explicit instruction. Our experience suggests that students will learn a great number of words from well-chosen texts *and* from a thoughtful selection of words for intentional instruction.

Conclusion

The Common Core State Standards for ELA contain several resources that are of value for your collaborative teams to draw on in future activities. The research supports for the standards are located in appendix A of the CCSS (NGA & CCSSO, 2010b). For example, one possible path for your collaborative planning team to follow concerns language, grammar, and conventions, as well as vocabulary. Appendix A of the CCSS provides a discussion of the relationship between these domains in the Reading, Writing, Speaking and Listening, and Language strands and further articulates how these threads weave through them. There is a solid discussion of grammar in this document, which may be helpful for teams whose members do not feel as well grounded in current methods of grammar instruction. Further, the document offers extensive information on vocabulary and the identification of tier one (everyday speech), tier two (general academic), and tier three (domain specific) words and phrases. The team may decide to identify vocabulary in tiers two and three that will be taught across the grade band using a schoolwide approach to vocabulary development (Frey & Fisher, 2009).

The Speaking and Listening and Language strands are integral to English language arts, both within the Reading and Writing strands, and across the disciplines. Never again should we tell students that "spelling doesn't count" when in mathematics instruction, or that communication skills don't need instruction because now it's time for social studies. These are foundational to how people learn; all learning is language based. Speaking and listening skills are used most prominently in the classroom, and the quality of discourse in the classroom is directly related to increased achievement. James Britton (1983) says, "Writing floats on a sea of talk" (p. 1), and we fully agree. In fact, we would go one step further: *learning* floats on a sea of talk.

CHAPTER 5

Implementing Formative Assessments to Guide Instruction and Intervention

KEY QUESTIONS

- In your preparations for teaching the lesson, chapter, or unit, to what extent does your collaborative team use the standards and aligned assignments to guide your planning?

- What assessment instruments have you developed collaboratively? Do these instruments accurately reflect the expectations for student achievement that the standards define?

- How do you use your assessment practices to enable students to better understand their learning strengths as well as their needs? In what ways do your assessment activities build students' confidence and motivation?

- To what extent do your schedules provide for timely assessment feedback to students? If changes are needed, how can you go about making them?

- How can you use your assessment data more effectively to modify instruction and help students achieve success?

I t is the end of the first week of school, and papers surround seventh-grade teacher Frank diCarlo. These papers are the screening assessments that have been administered to all students as part of their first week of school. Mr. diCarlo is comparing student performance on the screening assessments, students' end-of-year grades from the previous year, and their state assessment scores as he enters the information into the school data-management system. For example, every student has responded to the writing prompt, and their papers were evaluated using an analytic writing inventory.

In discussing the results with his colleagues, Mr. diCarlo comments, "I'm really looking forward to this year. The average length of sentences written by my students this year is 8.4, which is up from last year. And their correct word choice is off the charts. These students really know their vocabulary and how to create complex sentences. I did notice a few students with significant grammar errors, but we can take care of that. I also think that I'll focus more on the opening paragraph of their papers because so many of them were dry and almost formulaic. We've got a little work to do there. Did any of you see this in your assessment data?"

A Collaborative Planning Team in Action

Mr. diCarlo's collaborative planning team makes a commitment to fold ongoing assessment into its instructional practices, beginning the first day of school. Initially, team members collect information about each student as an individual in order to establish a baseline for where to begin. These early assessments allow them to group students and get them started with using complex texts, writing for extended periods, and engaging in informal and formal talk. Their instructional units are peppered with formative assessments that make it possible for them to gauge student progress toward goals before the unit has ended. Mr. diCarlo's team uses the key questions at the opening of the chapter (page 131) to shape its assessment plan. Likewise, we encourage you to use these same questions as you identify, design, and analyze the formative and summative assessments you will use in your classrooms.

In the first part of this chapter, we will discuss how a formative assessment plan guides instruction. In the latter half of the chapter, we will discuss the use of data to guide an RTI plan for students who struggle.

The Role of Assessment and the Common Core State Standards

Why do teachers assess students? Think about this for a minute. Is it because they want to find out what students do not know? Or is it because assessments and testing are part of the official behaviors of teachers? Or maybe it's because teachers don't know where to begin instruction without good assessment information. Diane Lapp, Douglas Fisher, James Flood, and Arturo Cabello (2001) suggest that teachers assess students for at least four reasons, including to:

1. Diagnose individual student needs (for example, assessing developmental status, monitoring and communicating student progress, certifying competency, and determining needs)

2. Inform instruction (for example, evaluating instruction, modifying instructional strategies, and identifying instructional needs)

3. Evaluate programs

4. Provide accountability information

As educators, we make numerous decisions about instruction that matter in very significant ways. We believe that these decisions must be based on the assessment information that we gather throughout the learning cycle. This means the teacher doesn't merely march lockstep through the content of a standards-based curriculum, but rather balances the content with the learner needs. These needs are identified through ongoing assessment that is linked to subsequent instruction. In this model, assessment and instruction are considered to be recursive because they repeat as students learn new content. In learner-centered classrooms, teachers first assess to establish what students know and do not know, then they plan instruction based on this information. Next, they deliver the instruction they have designed and observe how learners respond. Based on these observations, educators reflect on the results and assess again to determine what needs to be taught next. Figure 5.1 represents this concept.

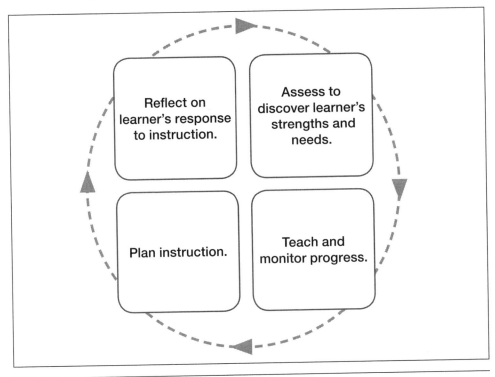

Figure 5.1: Relationship between assessment and instruction.

This model may sound as if it would take a lot of time to complete; in fact, effective teachers perform many of these complex tasks fluidly within the course of their instruction. In well-organized classrooms, assessment happens throughout the day as teachers use questions, discussions, and assignments to measure progress. In addition, teachers administer assessments to monitor progress and formulate future instruction. Assessment equips them with specific information about students who struggle and further informs them about the conditions and content of intervention needed. Teachers are also informed of those students who would benefit from instruction that deepens and enriches their learning. This lies at the very heart of what collaborative planning teams do—they monitor the progress of their students, analyze the results of their teaching, and design intervention supports.

In this chapter, we will concentrate on illustrating assessment events that occur and inform future teaching, so that students can thrive within a Common Core-framed educational system.

Preparing for and responding to large-scale assessments can consume much of the focus and effort of grades 6–8 teachers, school principals, and school district administrators. Implementing the CCSS is unlikely to alter the scrutiny and pressure teachers and administrators face from large-scale assessments.

In 2010, the U.S. Department of Education awarded $330 million in Race to the Top funds to two consortia, representing the majority of states, to develop assessments aligned with the CCSS. (See page 12.) SBAC, representing more than thirty states, received $160 million, and PARCC, representing more than twenty-five states, received $176 million. As of this publication, eleven states are members of both consortia (Porter, McMaken, Hwang, & Yang, 2011). Both consortia intend to implement their new state-level common assessments for grades 3–8 and high school during the 2014–2015 school year.

Both assessment consortia aim to design *common* state assessments that are consistent with the vision of the CCSS to include items that assess higher-order thinking, complex texts, writing with evidence, and comparisons across texts. If the assessments take the form their designers intend, then these new state assessments will promote desired instructional changes in favor of an emphasis on deep understanding and reasoning.

Both PARCC and SBAC intend to provide adaptive online tests that will include a mix of constructed-response items, performance-based tasks, and computer-enhanced items that require the application of knowledge and skills. Both assessment consortia are intending to provide summative- and interim-assessment options within the assessment system. You should check your state website for the latest information about progress of the assessment consortia, or visit www.parcconline.org/about-parcc or www.smarterbalanced.org for more information.

For the interim assessments to function as a potential learning tool, teachers will need to ensure they are used for formative purposes—that they are used to provide students and teachers with accurate, timely, fair, and specific information that can move learning forward. This will require that collaborative planning team members are provided time to plan instructional adjustments and that students are supported in relearning content not yet mastered.

However, overreliance on the PARCC and SBAC interim assessments to provide a school district's formative assessment system is not recommended since the effectiveness of this structure to improve student learning is questionable (Popham, 2008). What will make the most difference in terms of student learning is the formative assessment system described later in this chapter. As Wiliam (2007) writes, "If students have left the classroom before teachers have made adjustments to their teaching on the basis of what they have learned about students' achievement, then they are already playing catch-up" (p. 191).

It will be important for team members to become engaged in their state and school's transition to the SBAC or PARCC assessment initiative as part of the full implementation of the Common Core State Standards. The team will need to discuss the following questions.

- How and when will interim assessments be used?
- How will collaborative teams inform families and other members of the school community?
- How will collaborative teams prepare all children in each grade level or school?

Such questions are appropriate as your district- and school-level collaborative teams begin to link state-supported CCSS-related assessments to your implementation of the Common Core State Standards for English language arts. All of this starts with the development and implementation of a formative assessment system. More than formative assessment tools, a system allows teachers and teams to systematically evaluate student performance data and make instructional adjustments accordingly. It also allows teams to identify students in significant need and allocate additional support, often through RTI. A formative assessment system that comes from synthesis of research about the use of student work to inform instruction requires teachers to feed up, feed back, and feed forward.

Feed Up, Back, and Forward

Assessment doesn't begin when the test is passed out; it starts the moment instruction begins. Yet too often assessment is an afterthought, administered mostly to assign a grade. John Hattie and Helen Timperley (2007) have an elegant way of describing a model of ongoing assessment: feed up, feed back, and feed forward. We have taken this model a step further to articulate a concrete plan for doing so, one in which we add checking for understanding to the mix (Frey & Fisher, 2011) as a way to *feed up* by using methods to analyze and assess student understanding. Additionally, we offer a protocol for developing common pacing guides and curricula.

Feed Up by Establishing Purpose

When learners know what is expected of them, what they should be learning, and how they will demonstrate their mastery, their knowledge acquisition is accelerated. This requires clear statements of purpose in order to orient students and make learning intentional. As teachers, we are long accustomed to the practice of defining learning objectives for a lesson. For example, "Students will be able to compare and contrast a fictional character with a historical account of the same period." But how often are these objectives shared with the people who are supposed to demonstrate them? Establishing purpose means that these intentions are shared with the students and are used as a guideline for the formative assessment that follows.

We advise further identifying your purpose across three dimensions: (1) content, (2) language, and (3) social purpose. Content is usually the easiest and the one we often think of first when relating it to objectives. It is the discipline-specific knowledge students should acquire *today*. Comparing and contrasting fictional characters with historical accounts from the same period is an example of a content purpose. But how will students demonstrate this knowledge? Will they use a graphic organizer? Will they describe the similarities and differences in their collaborative groups using evidence from the text? Will they summarize the similarities and differences in written form? All of these are related to the language purpose. As we discussed in chapter 4, language is pervasive and includes written and verbal forms, as well as levels of cognition. Finally, a social purpose is useful for grades 6–8 students, who are still developing their ability to learn collaboratively. A social purpose in this lesson might be to provide evidence and examples to help others understand, or to demonstrate listening comprehension by building on the comments of others during a class discussion.

Sixth-grade teacher Rachel Young uses a feed-up process with every lesson she teaches. She comments, "This has been a focus of our collaborative team for a while. We developed purpose statements to accompany each of our lessons. Most of us write them on the board so that the students can see them. This helps to ensure students know what we'll be doing and why."

She goes on to say that initially it was a daunting task: "We made the mistake of leaving establishing purpose up to individual teachers to do, but we quickly realized there was a lot of duplication of effort."

She comments on the team's guiding questions, featured at the beginning of this chapter: "That first question about understanding the student learning targets *in advance of the lesson* was crucial for us. Developing purpose statements together led to lots of good discussion about what we were teaching, and for what purposes. And now our students come in and look to see what they'll be learning. It's just part of the culture of the school."

Checking for Understanding

This is an ongoing process of assessment to determine to what extent students understood the lesson, and to find out what gaps remain. As such, checking for understanding lies at the heart of formative assessment and is probably the first thing that comes to mind when teachers think about assessment. There are a variety of methods to check for understanding, including using oral language activities, questions, writing, projects and performances, and tests (Fisher & Frey, 2007a).

Oral Language Activities

When students are doing the talking, the teacher has a chance to assess understanding. There are a number of classroom structures that provide students an opportunity to talk, including think-pair-share, reciprocal teaching, literacy circles, discussion prompts, and Socratic seminars. For example, as Ms. Young listens to her students discussing a book they are reading as part of their book club, she notices that they are not justifying their responses with evidence from the text. They are skilled at summarizing, but the lack of evidence in their discussions indicates a need to devote additional instructional time to this practice.

Questions

Questioning, which can be done orally or in writing, is the most common way teachers check for understanding. Unfortunately, not all questions are worthy of instructional time. To be useful, the initial questions teachers ask should be planned in advance. Of course, additional questions that probe student understanding will come to mind during the interactions teachers have with students, but these initial questions form the expectations for student understanding. Less helpful questions are those we like to call *guess what's in the teacher's head*. More formally known as *initiate-respond-evaluate* or *IRE* (Cazden, 2001), this cycle privileges students who are willing to play the game. For example, when sixth-grade teacher Scott Bradford asks students to name one literary device, three or four students raise their hands, and Mario is selected to respond. Mario says, "Personification," to which the teacher responds, "Good." IRE is typically used with recall information and provides only a few students an opportunity to respond.

Instead, quality checking for understanding suggests that teachers need to ask questions that require more complex and critical thinking and that lots of students need to respond. A number of instructional routines provide students with practice in questioning habits, such as *reciprocal questioning* or *ReQuest* (Manzo, 1969), in which students read with a partner, taking turns asking and answering questions. As they practice, their teacher analyzes the types of questions they are asking and the appropriateness of the answers. Over time (and with instruction and practice) students tire of the literal and recall questions and move toward more interesting questions that require synthesis and evaluation.

Another way to question is to invite students to create their own questions. Student-generated questions are a powerful way to engage students in reading and discussion about texts. For example, while reading the short story "Salvador Late or Early" (Cisneros, 1991), the students in Ms. Dunlap's eighth-grade class create their own questions, including:

- Why does the author say the homes are "the color of bad weather" (p. 10) rather than gray?

- What does "the business of the baby" (p. 10) mean connotatively?

- What's a normal day like for Salvador?

Similar to reciprocal questioning, these student-generated questions allow the teacher to check student understanding through both the questions students create as well as through their responses to the questions that their peers ask.

Writing

When students are writing, they are thinking. In fact, it's nearly impossible to write and *not* think. Writing to learn "involves getting students to think about and to find the words to explain what they are learning, how they understand that learning, and what their own processes of learning involve" (Mitchell, 1996, p. 93). As Edward Jenkinson (1988) explains, "Writing should be a process in which writers discover what they know and do not know about their topics, their language, themselves, and their ability to communicate with specific audiences" (p. 714).

For example, following a shared reading of a newspaper article on hepatitis A, Mr. Green asked his eighth-grade students to respond to the following writing-to-learn prompt: "Explain to your younger brother or sister why hand washing is important." Responding to this prompt requires that students consider their prior knowledge about germs, the cognitive development of their younger siblings, what they have read or listened to about the topic, and how to best convey this information in writing.

A writing-to-learn prompt can be open ended (for example, "What did you think was confusing about this topic?") or fairly specific (for example, "Discuss the role of photosynthesis in plant life"). The range of writing-to-learn opportunities can include the following (Fisher & Frey, 2012).

- **Admit slips:** Upon entering the classroom, students write on an assigned topic, such as "In our reading today, will Anne Frank be discovered?"

- **Crystal ball:** Students describe what they think class will be about, what will happen next in the novel they are reading, and so on.

- **Found poems:** Students re-read an assigned text and find key phrases that speak to them, then arrange these into a poem structure without adding any of their own words.

- **Awards:** Students recommend someone or something for an award that the teacher has created, such as "The best writer of the century, living or dead."

- **Cinquains:** Students write a five-line poem in which the first line is the topic (a noun), the second line is a description of the topic in two words, the third line is three gerunds, the fourth line is a description of the topic in four words, and the final line is a synonym of the topic word from line one.

- **Yesterday's news:** Students summarize the information presented the day before, either from a video, discussion, or reading.

- **"What if?" scenarios:** Students respond to prompts in which information is changed from what they know to predicting outcomes. For example, students may be asked to respond to the prompt, "What would be different if Anne Frank had escaped detection and survived the war?"

- **Take a stand:** Students debate about a controversial topic such as school uniforms.

- **Letters:** Students write letters to others, including elected officials, family members, friends, people who made a difference, and so on. For example, students may respond to the prompt, "Write a letter to Dr. Martin Luther King Jr. informing him of the progress we have made on racism since his death."

- **Exit slips:** Students write on an assigned prompt as a closure activity at the end of the period, such as "The three best things I learned today are . . .").

A specific type of writing-to-learn prompt is a RAFT (Santa & Havens, 1995), which requires students to consider the role, audience, format, and topic in their writing; this is an excellent way to check for understanding. There are, of course, many other writing prompts that can be used, but RAFT is flexible and teaches perspective. For example, after discussing sportsmanship, Mr. Davenport asks his students to respond to the following RAFT:

    R Bronze medal winner

    A Gold medal winner

    F Greeting card

    T Victory

Projects and Performances

On a larger scale, teachers can use projects and performances to check for understanding. Importantly, this should not be done at the end when the project is completed, but rather as students work on these types of activities. A wide range of appropriate projects and performances allow students an opportunity to engage in meaningful work aligned with content standards. As we have noted in chapter 4, the Speaking and Listening standards require that students present, and this category is important for checking for understanding as students learn to demonstrate mastery of these standards. Useful projects and performances range from presentations to group tasks like creating PowerPoint slides.

Tests

Although tests are typically considered a summative assessment tool used for grading and evaluating student performance, they can also be used to check for understanding. Incorrect answers on a test provide teachers with information about what students still need to learn. Tests can be developed in a number of different formats, ranging from multiple-choice to dichotomous choice (like true/false, yes/no, and agree/disagree) to essays.

Developing Common Pacing Guides and Curricula

Assessments that are used to check for understanding are designed and implemented by the collaborative planning team in order to gather and analyze data. The Common Core State Standards for English language arts will present a new set of challenges for teachers and administrators. Common assessments, consensus scoring, and item analysis will figure prominently in developing new pacing guides and curricula. You can use the protocol in figure 1.2 (page 11) to do so. The five steps include (Fisher & Frey, 2007a) the following.

1. Construct an initial pacing guide for instruction. Designed to frame the team's work, this guide should be aligned to the expectations in the CCSS.

2. Identify instructional materials such as texts, websites, and media for each unit of study in the pacing guide.

3. Develop common assessments and a schedule for administering them. These should include formative and summative measures and will provide the collaborative team with data to analyze.

4. Engage in consensus scoring and item analysis. These actions serve to determine how students did and to explore the relationship between teaching and learning. It is useful to disaggregate the data to identify trends within and across significant subpopulations. The intent of this process is not to drill down to the individual teacher level, but rather to look across the grade level and grade band to locate patterns. For example, if students with disabilities are making good progress, then what accommodations can this be attributed to? Remember that these data-analysis events are also intended for identifying areas of instructional strength, not just locating areas of need.

5. Make revisions to instruction and curriculum and the formation of intervention groups. The outcomes of these team meetings should have dual purposes. The first is to refine instruction for all students in order to improve acquisition of knowledge. In addition, the team needs to examine the circumstances that might be preventing identified students from making sufficient progress. For some students, this may be a matter of reteaching. For those who are displaying a pattern of difficulties that may warrant more formal intervention. Later in this chapter, we will discuss RTI as a model for meeting the needs of students who struggle.

Feed Back to Build Student Agency

It would be a mistake to isolate checking for understanding from the feedback loop. Think about the third planning question for a moment: How do we use our assessment practices to enable students to better understand their learning strengths as well as their needs? In what ways do our assessment activities build students' confidence and motivation? Students need feedback to guide their learning throughout the process. But not all feedback is useful. The evidence on scoring as feedback suggests that when done in isolation from other types of feedback, such as feedback about processing of the task, it undermines future achievement (Wiliam, 2011). To make feedback more robust, use it judiciously (Hattie & Timperley, 2007). Consider the following forms of feedback.

- **Feedback about the task** (corrective feedback) is effective for alerting a learner to errors. But it is not effective when the student lacks the skills or the knowledge needed to complete the task.

- **Feedback about the processing used in the task** is highly effective because it reminds the learner about his or her cognitive and metacognitive thinking. For example, "I see you're underlining the parts of the story that are important for telling us about the character. That's keeping your ideas organized."

- **Feedback about self-regulation** is also very effective because it assists the learner in self-assessing. For instance, "You were frustrated earlier when your group wasn't listening to your ideas, but you stayed cool and tried again. Did you notice how your peers listened when you gave them another chance?"

- **Feedback about the person** is considered ineffective because it doesn't provide the learner with any information about what to do next. For example, "Way to go!"

The fourth planning question is also related to feedback: To what extent do our schedules provide for timely assessment feedback to students? If changes are needed, how can we go about making them? Even the best feedback will lose its effectiveness if it is not *timely*. In addition, the feedback must be *actionable*; that is, the learner must have a clear sense of direction about what he or she should do next. Additionally, feedback should be *specific* so that the learner is equipped with a necessary level of detail about his or her next actions. Of course, it should be *understandable* in the sense that it should be developmentally and cognitively appropriate for the learner. Taken together, feedback that is well thought out and delivered in a timely fashion will build the agency of the learner and encourages him or her to assume more responsibility for his or her own learning—because he or she *can*. After all, "Feedback should cause thinking" (Wiliam, 2011, p. 127).

Feed Forward to Inform Instruction

The process of formative assessment is incomplete unless it feeds forward into future instruction. The classroom is the unit of analysis, and the purpose is to locate students who need further instruction *during* (not after) the unit of study. This requires some recordkeeping in order to analyze errors students are making. In our efforts to get to know students as individual learners, we can lose track of patterns that are otherwise right in front of us. Call it the phenomenon of not seeing the forest through the trees, if you will. Error analysis allows us to gain a bit of perspective on who is having difficulty and further prevents us from expending so much effort attending to individual learning problems that we run out of time to instruct everyone.

Error analysis can be accomplished in a number of ways, from a commercially prepared checklist to one the teacher makes. This links back to being clear about the purpose, and these purpose statements can be used as a platform for clarifying what exactly students should be able to do. By creating a list of specific skills, teachers can not only gather data at the individual level but can also look across these checklists to identify groups of students who need further instruction. This may include building background knowledge or simply reteaching. In addition, these teacher-directed small-group arrangements provide the added benefit of having students apply their speaking, listening, and language skills in the service of content.

Formative and Summative Assessments

The usefulness of every assessment is dependent on a proper fit between purpose and type of assessment used. It is important to remember that every assessment is useful and not useful *at the same time*. Any given assessment is useful in the hands of a conscientious educator who understands the limitations of the tool being used. Any given assessment is useless if it is interpreted to show something it was not intended to show. You would be very suspicious of a doctor who ordered a chest x-ray when you were seeking help for a sprained ankle. There is nothing inherently wrong with a chest x-ray; it is simply the wrong test for the task. In the same regard, the type of reading or writing assessment selected must match its intended use. Andrea Guillaume (2004) offers these considerations for selecting an assessment. Each assessment needs to be:

- Tied to your stance on learning

- Driven by learning goals

- Systematic

- Tied to instruction

- Connected to the learner

- Integrated into a manageable system

Tied to Your Stance on Learning

Every teacher brings a philosophy of education and a view of literacy to his or her practice. It is important to recognize how assessment choices fit into that perspective. For example, an educator who possesses a viewpoint of learning as a developmental phenomenon will be interested in assessment instruments that reflect benchmarks of developmental phases of learning. Teachers with a skills-based orientation will find skills measures to be useful.

Driven by Learning Goals

Classroom assessments should be consistent with the expectations of the grade-level Common Core State Standards. The standards are outcome-based and articulate the *what* of learning. As educators, we make the decisions about *how* we get there.

Systematic

Teachers select assessments that can be administered and analyzed in a systematic way at both the individual and class levels. Good assessments should possess data recording and analysis protocols that make it easy for the teacher to interpret the information at a later date. In addition, the teacher must determine how often they will be administered. Finally, each assessment should measure what it purports to measure (it should be valid) and yield results that are consistent across administrations and assessors (it should be reliable).

Tied to Instruction

Although this seems apparent, it is worth stating again: assessment should be linked directly to instruction, either to determine what should be taught next (pretesting) or to check for understanding of skills or strategies that have just been taught (post-testing). Assessments that are not connected to instruction are likely to be frustrating for students because they appear purposeless and inadequate for teachers because they do not provide relevant information.

Connected to the Learner

Assessments are intended to be completed in conjunction with the learners' needs. They should be designed to capture the work of students in the act of learning. Whether through listening to a student reading text (as is the case with running records and informal reading inventories) or using a rubric to discuss a student's writing (analytic writing assessment), these tools are intended to involve the learner in their own measures of progress.

Integrated Into a Manageable System

No teacher can devote all of his or her time to collecting and analyzing assessment data. The demands of assessment on the time available can become overwhelming and even crowd out equally valuable instructional time. Therefore, it is in the teacher's interest to understand what each assessment does, then select the one that best fits the needs of the students, teacher, and curriculum. The collaborative planning team is the ideal forum for selecting and designing formative assessments that inform instruction.

One of the challenges teachers and teams often encounter with feed-forward systems is creating a manageable system. When teachers evaluate students' work, they often provide individual students with feedback. As we have discussed, this is helpful for the student, and perhaps his or her parents, in understanding areas of strength and need. But it is less helpful for teachers in terms of determining what to teach next. Frankly, it's hard for any of us to remember the range of errors and misconceptions that students have and then to organize instruction around those instructional needs. To effectively implement a formative assessment system, teachers and their collaborative teams need to regularly examine student work and identify patterns in the strengths and needs identified in the data.

For example, seventh-grade teacher Jane Clark and her collaborative team developed an error-analysis tool based on their efforts to teach compare and contrast essays to use in the beginning of the year to determine students' skills and needs (see figure 5.2, page 144). The input they received from their colleagues in grades 6 and 8 was instrumental in designing the tool in anticipation of likely errors. They use this tool to analyze student's writing to determine areas of strength and need. The challenge is then to figure out what to do with the information once it has been collected.

	Period One	Period Two	Period Three	Period Four	Period Five
Student includes an introductory paragraph.					
Student includes at least one comparison paragraph (topic sentence and three details).					
Student includes at least one contrast paragraph (topic sentence and three details).					
Student includes transitions between paragraphs.					
Student includes contrast words.					
Student includes compare words.					
Student includes appropriate punctuation.					

Figure 5.2: Error analysis for seventh-grade compare-and-contrast essay.

Visit **go.solution-tree.com/commoncore** for a reproducible version of this figure.

Without some analysis of the patterns that emerge in each classroom, teachers will have a hard time teaching students based on need and are at risk of teaching the whole class content that some students have already mastered.

We recommend that collaborative teams develop an error-analysis system that includes all student information on a single sheet of paper. In this case, teachers list student initials for those students who have not yet met the standard on any indicator (see figure 5.3).

In one classroom, there were three students who made excessive errors in punctuation. These students need additional instruction, probably small-group instruction, but the rest of the class does not. The majority of the students in this class made mistakes with transitions between paragraphs. As such, the whole class could benefit from additional instruction, specifically on how writers use transitions to guide their readers.

If there are specific students who fail to respond to quality core instruction, including the re-teaching that comes from careful analysis of student work, the teacher should

	Period One	Period Two	Period Three	Period Four	Period Five
Student does not include an introductory paragraph.					
Student does not include at least one comparison paragraph (topic sentence and three details).					
Student does not include at least one contrast paragraph (topic sentence and three details).					
Student does not include transitions between paragraphs.					
Student does not include contrast words.					
Student does not include compare words.					
Student does not include appropriate punctuation.					

Figure 5.3: Revised error analysis for seventh-grade compare-and-contrast essay for students not meeting learning target.

Visit **go.solution-tree.com/commoncore** for a reproducible version of this figure.

present this situation and the data that has been collected to the team for consideration. The team may recommend that an RTI committee evaluate each student, as will be discussed in the next section. Or the team may decide that the student needs to receive some additional instruction from the classroom teacher or from another team member. The key here is to realize that no teacher is alone in this process. Students fail to respond to quality instruction for a whole host of reasons and when teams of teachers get together to problem solve these situations, students benefit. Unfortunately, in some schools, asking other teachers for assistance or advice is seen as a weakness. If we are to implement the Common Core State Standards well, we are going to have to talk and collaborate with our colleagues much more often—including specifically about students who struggle, despite our best efforts to ensure their success.

What to Do When Students Struggle

Sometimes the assessment information that teachers collect will indicate that a student, or group of students, has failed to make progress. Sometimes this happens because the student did not receive adequate quality core instruction, perhaps due to absences or a specific teaching situation. In that case, the student needs to be retaught the content using evidence-based practices that ensure success. Sometimes students fail to make progress despite solid core instruction. In this case, the student likely needs some sort of supplemental or intensive intervention. RTI is a system to respond when students fail to progress. As with other efforts to implement the Common Core State Standards, RTI requires the mobilization of collaborative teams and entire school systems (Buffum et al., 2009).

Although RTI has become more broadly known through its inclusion in the Individuals With Disabilities Education Improvement Act of 2004, RTI is a well-known theory and practice. As described in federal legislation, the intent is twofold: (1) to provide early intervention for students who are struggling and (2) to allow for an alternate means of identifying the presence of a learning disability. Unfortunately, in some schools the latter purpose has overshadowed the former. In an effort to establish a balance between the two, a growing number of states are investing in a response to instruction and intervention (RTI^2) model. Before focusing on the major components of an RTI model, we will explore five mistakes that are commonly made when school systems attempt to establish and implement an RTI^2 program.

Mistake One: Thinking Intervention, Not Instruction

An effective RTI effort begins with a quality core program—this is the first tier of the widely known three-tier model of RTI (for more information, visit the RTI Action Network at www.rtinetwork.org). A quality core program includes the kind of scaffolded learning experiences expressed through a gradual release of responsibility instructional framework (Frey & Fisher, 2010). This framework includes establishing the purpose of the lesson for students, modeling one's cognitive processes by thinking aloud, and providing guided instruction through the use of questions, prompts, and cues. In addition, students spend much of their time learning collaboratively with their peers in productive group work before attempting independent learning. Without these practices firmly in place in all classrooms, the supplemental and intensive intervention efforts of any school will be quickly overwhelmed by students who are failing simply because they are not receiving quality core instruction.

Consider the practices of seventh-grade teacher Mr. Davenport who skillfully weaves these instructional practices throughout his lesson on supporting claims with evidence. He starts with a clear purpose, namely that students will introduce a claim and then provide evidence that links to the claim. As part of the lesson, he models his thinking while writing aloud. Mr. Davenport explains, "One of the problems I have to watch out for is that sometimes I just list the evidence, and I forget that I have to interpret it for the reader. I can't just let the evidence stand for itself. I have to tell the reader why this piece of evidence supports my claim."

As groups of students get to work, Mr. Davenport meets with students who have experienced difficulty, as shown in the error-analysis data, thus far in the unit for additional guided instruction. They leave their group when he calls them to have a discussion with him. At one point, he meets with Hector, a student who was having difficulty with understanding how to link claims to evidence. Mr. Davenport makes a planning sheet to assist Hector to compose graphically before formal writing. He leads Hector systematically through claims, and after discussion, he has the student write his claim in the center of the graphic organizer.

Hector's essay on sportsmanship begins with the claim that "There's lots of bad behavior on sports TV, and they just keep showing it over and over," he tells Mr. Davenport. "I hear your evidence in there," Mr. Davenport tells him, "but I'm not sure I follow. Can you tell me why that's meaningful?"

Hector lights up at the question, "Well, the announcers can talk about poor sportsmanship all they want, about how it's such a bad thing, and no one should do it, and it's a bad example for kids, and blah, blah, blah. But you still get to be on TV, and everyone knows your name, and so you get more famous."

"That's perfect, Hector! That's your link! Did you hear how you explained your reasoning to me? When I told you I didn't understand why that was important, you explained it. That's what you do when you write. You don't just give the evidence and move on, because maybe the reader doesn't interpret the evidence the same way you do. Your link spells out how *you* interpret it," says Mr. Davenport.

Over the next few minutes, Hector and Mr. Davenport complete the graphic organizer, and the student returns to his group to continue to write. Figure 5.4 shows Hector's completed graphic organizer for linking claims to evidence.

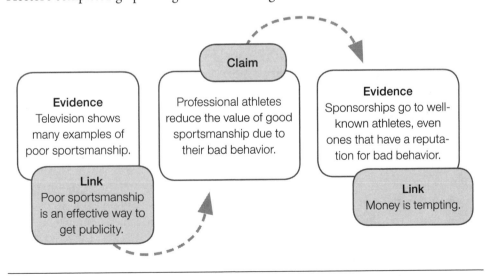

Figure 5.4: Sample graphic organizer for planning an argumentation essay.

Visit **go.solution-tree.com/commoncore** for a reproducible version of this figure.

As he works with Mr. Davenport, Hector is developing an increased understanding of the content such that he has sufficient background knowledge to write the essay. The other students in the classroom are also writing argumentation essays that they will share with the class, as will the other three students who participated in guided instruction with their teacher. If these four students do not make progress, Mr. Davenport will discuss them with his collaborative team and the team may recommend that the students receive Tier 2 and Tier 3 interventions. At this point, however, their learning needs are being exposed through formative assessments that provide Mr. Davenport with information about their learning needs.

Mistake Two: Relying on Prepackaged Curricula

While commercial programs labeled as being intervention friendly can provide some needed practice materials, they cannot replace well-designed and individualized lessons targeting the specific needs of students who require intervention. Robert Begaye, a sixth-grade English teacher at a tribal reservation school, comments to his team about the approach to using prepackaged materials: "We stress mutualism as a value, especially in the way that we learn and work together. Many of the conventional programs we reviewed required students to work alone. We knew that our children would learn best in an environment that was consistent with the other parts of the learning day," Mr. Begaye says.

He and the school's reading interventionist, Abey Johnson, work together to develop meaningful Tier 2 supplemental supports that can be delivered in the classroom in small-group settings. "This also meant that we had to reconfigure how we work together as adults," Ms. Johnson explains. "But the result was that these supplemental supports emanated directly from the content being taught, and within the classroom. We didn't just load up programs on computers and have all the struggling readers complete them, whether they needed it or not."

Through their collaboration, Mr. Begaye and Ms. Johnson ensure that the values of the classroom informed the way in which more specialized and individualized instruction could be delivered.

Mistake Three: Isolating Teachers and Interventionists

Coordinating learning across the school day is challenging under the best of circumstances, and adding intervention efforts to the mix can be difficult. It can be tempting to simply put one teacher in charge of an RTI program, give him or her a classroom, and turn attention to other matters. But isolating interventionists from classroom teachers severely limits the kind of collaboration between Ms. Johnson and Mr. Begaye. Instead, consider the team effort each student in an RTI[2] program will need to be successful. It is important to make sure that every student receiving supplemental or intensive interventions has an identified person coordinating instruction, and another coordinating intervention. Communication between these two educators can bridge the divide that can otherwise occur when interventions are disconnected from the core curriculum.

Mistake Four: Making Data Decisions Alone

Ms. Johnson, the reading interventionist, collects data each time she meets with a student so that she can track progress and determine what is working. Importantly, data collection and analysis also reveals when something is not working. Ms. Johnson comments about Taini, one student with whom she worked: "I initially started out using timed writing with Taini, but I quickly discovered that wasn't the best approach. I found that when I gave her a chance to discuss the reading with me for a few minutes first, her writing improved in length and content."

Both Mr. Begaye and Ms. Johnson serve on the school's RTI[2] subcommittee, an outgrowth of the Student Study Team formed to closely examine the circumstances surrounding specific students' behavioral or academic difficulties. The subcommittee meets regularly to discuss the progress of students receiving intervention supports. Ms. Johnson brings her data to the group for discussion and finds that others can sometimes spot a trend she has overlooked. In addition, she can share her insights about what she has found effective. For instance, she recommended that Mr. Begaye and Taini's other teachers collaborate in advance of extended writing assignments. Mr. Begaye observes, "I'm trying to do this more often, not just with Taini but with several others. I make sure that she gets a chance to talk with a small group of peers, and I'm beginning to see how she's organizing her thinking," he says. "It's showing up on her papers."

Mistake Five: Leaving the Family Out of the Planning

Family involvement is key when students who struggle are participating in RTI[2] efforts. In fact, family may possess quite a bit of information that can be helpful in determining ways to accelerate student learning. As keepers of their child's history, family members have firsthand knowledge about what has worked in the past. However, this information can come too late in the process when families are contacted only after a student's lack of RTI warrants a referral for special education testing. It is understandable that families can become justifiably frustrated when they learn that their child has been involved in an intervention for months without their knowledge.

At Taini's school, her mother and stepfather initially met with the administrator who oversees the RTI[2] program. She learned why their daughter was being recommended for supplemental intervention and gathered information from them about past efforts. Ms. Johnson speaks with them on the phone each month to share Taini's progress and ask them about their observations. While Taini's eventual progress meant that she didn't require a referral for special education testing, the school gains two important allies. "I thought the only time you heard from the school was when there was a problem," says Taini's mother. "But we were treated with much respect. It mattered what we knew."

Assessment, Intervention, and Instruction

Seventh-grade English teacher Charlie Brock routinely collects formative assessment information to plan instruction and design intervention as needed. These practices lie at the heart of teaching and learning and have been further strengthened through the ongoing work of his collaborative planning team. His formative assessments include recordkeeping of observational notes, especially the error-analysis tools he and his colleagues develop for each instructional unit. This practice alone has resulted in the team members being more alert to the first signs of academic struggle in students and in a marked change from past years when student failure was formally noted only after the unit of instruction.

One student who Mr. Brock has been concerned about lately is Micah, an English learner. Micah's first language is a Jamaican Patois, which is a nonstandard language with no official written component. He speaks and writes in English but in a limited way. Although he has been in U.S. schools since second grade, he has stalled at the intermediate stage of language acquisition. While his social language is quite good, and he communicates easily with friends, his academic language is at a much lower level. This is not uncommon among many long-term English learners: 59 percent of English learners in secondary schools in his home state of California have been in U.S. schools for more than six years (Olsen, 2010). Mr. Brock decides that the place to begin is with some individual assessments.

Assessment

Mr. Brock begins by revisiting the assessments he has already collected for Micah. For example, he administered an informal reading inventory at the beginning of the school year for students who the sixth-grade team identified as students to monitor closely. In addition, he had the results of the annual state language assessment for English learners. The results suggested that Micah needs to work on vocabulary and writing. Mr. Brock also collected a timed writing sample and used both holistic and analytic writing tools to gain a more detailed view of Micah's on-demand writing skills. From his analysis of the data, he notes that volume is a major concern, as Micah had only produced forty-eight words in five minutes. In addition, he appears to limit his writing to words he knew how to spell. When Mr. Brock interviewed Micah about his chosen topic, boxing, he found that Micah was much more expressive and knowledgeable than his written work suggested.

Mr. Brock collects data informally using the error-analysis tool he and his collaborative team developed for use during the first unit of the school year. Throughout this unit, students read, discuss, and write topical essays on a variety of subjects that present conflicting information. These point-counterpoint essays prove to be challenging for Micah. When Mr. Brock uses a retelling checklist, he notes that Micah uses few terms for comparing and contrasting ideas. Mr. Brock realizes that if they were not present in his oral language, they were not likely to appear in his written work. Micah is also unable to use evidence from the text, even when prompted.

Upon reviewing Micah's homework, Mr. Brock notices it is often incomplete. Mr. Brock is careful not to assign homework that draws on recently taught information.

Instead, he designs homework that relies on previously taught information from sixth grade that should serve as background knowledge for seventh-grade work. Over the course of the year, his homework will serve as a spiral review of content taught earlier in the school year, but at the start of the year he wants to be sure that students have retained previously taught content. Because Mr. Brock meets with sixth-grade colleagues regularly as a collaborative vertical team, he has a solid understanding of what they do. Mr. Brock knows they worked extensively last year on identifying an author's point of view in informational text, yet Micah struggled to do so when answering questions about short pieces of text.

Intervention

Based on his findings, Mr. Brock takes the data he had analyzed to his next collaborative planning team meeting. As part of their ongoing practice, the teachers discuss students of concern, then offer ideas for next steps instruction. This inquiry protocol has proven to be useful for identifying possible interventions. For example, Mr. Brock notes that Micah is inserting the word *it* into sentences, such as "The paper, *it* is ready for review." The team discusses why Micah might be making this mistake and then offers Mr. Brock some ideas about how to address this issue, including writing the error sentences down and then performing sentence surgery on them to create correct sentences.

The team examines Micah's work samples, and the student's former teacher supplies additional information about his past struggles and successes. After posing several questions for Mr. Brock to consider—such as how much vocabulary has Micah mastered, how much he reads on average each day, and whether he still receives daily small-group instruction—the team meets with the school's literacy specialist, Avril Aceves. In consultation with Ms. Aceves, the team designs a Tier 2 supplemental intervention, which includes additional small-group instruction for Micah and two other students. Several times a week, Mr. Brock meets with these students to preteach upcoming content, especially in the area of academic vocabulary. They make extensive use of open-concept sorts to strengthen general-academic and domain-specific words and phrases. The word cards used in these activities were then organized into binders. "Micah had a great idea early on," says Mr. Brock. "He's a big sports fan, and he suggested that we use the plastic sheets baseball card collectors use for his vocabulary cards." They group the vocabulary cards by concepts in the sleeves. "When it came time for Micah to write, he could quickly flip through the binder to find a category like *comparison words* and then shuffle through to locate the word he wanted to use," says Mr. Brock. Although Micah could locate similar words using a published thesaurus, Ms. Aceves advises that by taking the time to build his schema and see how word associations occur, he would be much more likely to retain the words in his personal vocabulary.

Instruction

Micah's writing steadily improves over the remainder of the year. Mr. Brock continues to monitor Micah's progress and uses assessments more frequently than for other students who are already making sufficient progress. He analyzes timed writing samples monthly and administers additional informal reading inventories two more times. He also provides his collaborative planning team with brief monthly updates on Micah's status.

As the seventh-grade year draws to a close, the team meets to share information about students with receiving teachers. Laura Henderson is already assigned as Micah's eighth-grade English teacher, and Mr. Brock is able to advise her about effective instructional approaches that would continue to build on his successes. He and Ms. Henderson make a plan to pair Micah with other students to continue preteaching content several times a week. In addition, he and Ms. Henderson plan to meet to review the results of the state language assessment to identify areas of progress and continued concern. Mr. Brock comments, "Although we all have new students each year, I like the fact that our professional learning community—this school—has made certain that students don't experience school as disconnected classes and grade levels. They know that if they attend this school, their new teachers will know a lot about them from their former teachers." Ms. Henderson adds, "After all, how can we expect students to be ready for college and career if we're not making certain that we're communicating regularly with one another?"

Conclusion

To really operationalize the information in this chapter, collaborative teams in professional learning communities must develop their assessment literacy (Boudett, City, & Murnane, 2005). In other words, they need to know which assessment tools work, for which tasks, and in which ways. Furthermore, teams—in collaboration with site leaders—should develop an assessment calendar so that all members of the school community know which assessments they should give and when. Once the more formal assessment system has been developed, then the team can turn its attention to monitoring student progress. This occurs on many levels, ranging from the analysis of state assessments to reviews of student work. Regardless of the level, the collaborative planning team should be on the lookout for students who are not responding to quality core instruction. In these cases, the team needs to discuss ways to ensure that students are supported, including through informal reteaching and formal RTI systems. Highly effective teams have data-management systems for keeping track of students as they progress through the year and early-warning systems that provide alerts when students are not making progress.

This chapter has focused on the many kinds of assessment instruments available to classroom teachers in order to plan instruction, monitor growth, and evaluate learning. However, as stated previously, no one assessment is ideal for every situation. As the teacher, you will need to determine what kinds of information you need about your students, which instruments can give you the information you are seeking, and how much time you have available to administer and analyze. Therefore, we believe that the assessments themselves need to be analyzed to see which best fit your purposes. Every time you consider a new assessment, we encourage you to ask yourself the following questions.

- **"What does this assessment really measure?"** Don't let the title of the assessment fool you. Look closely at the task demands to make sure that other skills like reading, writing, or using language ability don't confound results.

- **"What will the results tell me? What will the results *not* tell me?"** Make sure that the information an assessment yields is necessary and another assessment does not duplicate the data. Also, be clear about what other assessments you might administer in order to give a more complete picture of a learner.

- **"What expenditure of my time and effort will be required to administer and analyze the assessment?"** The time you have available is finite. Some assessments are time consuming to administer but yield rich results that make them worthwhile. Others are quick but may deliver little in the way of useable information. Plan your assessment calendar like you do your curricular one to ensure you are using your time (and that of your students) wisely.

- **"How will this assessment help my instruction?"** A New Zealand proverb says, "You don't fatten sheep by weighing them." We are concerned about the increase in the amount of testing that is occurring in schools in the name of accountability. Instructional time is increasingly being whittled away in order to do more testing. In this chapter, we have focused on classroom assessments that translate to instructional decisions. When chosen wisely and analyzed with care, these assessments ultimately save instructional time by allowing you to be more precise in choosing what to teach, what to reteach, and when the student can move on to new content.

- **"How can this assessment figure into my intervention efforts and reporting requirements?"** Not every assessment is suitable for such determinations, as some are diagnostic and others are used for accountability. However, the majority of assessments should provide information about next steps instruction and the possible need for intervention. In addition, these assessments should help inform the team about the effectiveness of the intervention efforts, known as *progress monitoring*, and can also be helpful in parent and student conferences as well as reporting successes and needs on report cards.

The Common Core State Standards for English language arts present an opportunity for teachers and their teams to collaborate in ways that result in improved student achievement. These standards represent a shift as well as an increase in expectations, and our students deserve nothing less than our very best effort to ensure that they meet these standards so they are prepared for the next stage in their life, high school, and beyond.

REFERENCES AND RESOURCES

Abbott, R. D., Berninger, V. M., & Fayol, M. (2010). Longitudinal relationships of levels of language in writing and between writing and reading in grades 1 and 7. *Journal of Educational Psychology, 102*(2), 281–298.

Adler, M. J., & Van Doren, C. (1940/1972). *How to read a book.* New York: Touchstone.

Afflerbach, P., Pearson, P. D., & Paris, S. G. (2008). Clarifying differences between reading skills and reading strategies. *The Reading Teacher, 61*(5), 364–373.

Alcott, L. M. (2012). *Little women.* New York: Simon & Brown.

Algren, N. (2011). *Chicago: City on the make* (60th anniversary ed.). Chicago: University of Chicago Press.

Allington, R. L. (2002). You can't learn much from books you can't read. *Educational Leadership, 60*(3), 16–19.

Alvermann, D. E. (1991). The discussion web: A graphic aid for learning across the curriculum. *The Reading Teacher, 45*(2), 92–99.

American Speech-Language-Hearing Association. (2012). *What is language? What is speech?* Accessed at www.asha.org/public/speech/development/language_speech.htm on June 4, 2012.

Baumann, J. (2009). Vocabulary and reading comprehension. In S. E. Israel & G. G. Duffy (Eds.), *Handbook of research on reading comprehension* (pp. 323–346). New York: Routledge.

Baumann, J. F., Font, G., Edwards, E. C., & Boland, E. (2005). Strategies for teaching middle-grade students to use word-part and context clues to expand reading vocabulary. In E. H. Hiebert & M. L. Kamil (Eds.), *Teaching and learning vocabulary: Bringing research to practice* (pp. 179–205). Mahwah, NJ: Erlbaum.

Bayliss, V. A. (1994). Fluency in children's writing. *Reading Horizons, 34*(3), 247–256.

Bayliss, V. A., & Walker, N. L. (1990). *Bayliss/Walker scales: Holistic writing evaluation, grades 1–6.* Springfield: Southwest Missouri State University.

Beck, I. L., McKeown, M. G., & Kucan, L. (2002). *Bringing words to life: Robust vocabulary instruction.* New York: Guilford Press.

Beck, I. L., McKeown, M. G., & Kucan, L. (2008). *Creating robust vocabulary: Frequently asked questions and extended examples.* New York: Guilford Press.

Beers, S. F., & Nagy, W. E. (2011). Writing development in four genres from grades three to seven: Syntactic complexity and genre differentiation. *Reading and Writing Quarterly, 24*(2), 183–202.

Bereiter, C., & Scardamalia, M. (1987). *The psychology of written composition.* Hillsdale, NJ: Erlbaum.

Berninger, V. M., & Abbott, R. D. (2010). Listening comprehension, oral expression, reading comprehension, and written expression: Related yet unique language systems in grades 1, 3, 5, and 7. *Journal of Educational Psychology, 102*(3), 635–651.

Bierce, A. (1891). *An occurrence at Owl Creek Bridge.* Seattle, WA: CreateSpace.

Bierce, A. (2011). *An occurrence at Owl Creek Bridge.* Mankato, MN: Creative Education.

Birenbaum, M., Kimron, H., & Shilton, H. (2011). Nested contexts that shape assessment for learning: School-based professional learning community and classroom culture. *Studies in Educational Evaluation, 37*(1), 35–48.

Blachowicz, C. L. Z., & Fisher, P. (2002). *Teaching vocabulary in all classrooms* (2nd ed.). Upper Saddle River, NJ: Merrill/Prentice Hall.

Bossert, T. S., & Schwantes, F. M. (1996). Children's comprehension monitoring: Training children to use rereading to aid comprehension. *Reading Research and Instruction, 35*(2), 109–121.

Boudett, K. P., City, E. A., & Murnane, R. J. (Eds.). (2005). *Data wise: A step-by-step guide to using assessment results to improve teaching and learning.* Cambridge, MA: Harvard University Press.

Bransford, J. D., Brown, A. L., & Cocking, R. R. (Eds.). (2000). *How people learn: Brain, mind, experience, and school.* Washington, DC: National Academies Press.

Britton, J. (1983). Writing and the story of the world. In B. Kroll & E. Wells (Eds.), *Explorations in the development of writing: Theory, research, and practice* (pp. 3–30). New York: Wiley.

Buffum, A., Mattos, M., & Weber, C. (2009). *Pyramid response to intervention: RTI, professional learning communities, and how to respond when kids don't learn.* Bloomington, IN: Solution Tree Press.

Bullough, R. V., Jr., & Baugh, S. C. (2008). Building professional learning communities within a university–public school partnership. *Theory Into Practice, 47*(4), 286–293.

California Department of Education. (n.d.). *Common Core State Standards: Frequently asked questions.* Sacramento, CA: Author. Accessed at www.cde.ca.gov/re/cc/ccssfaqs2010.asp on August 31, 2012.

California Newsreel. (2003). *Race—The power of an illusion discussion guide.* Accessed at www.pbs.org/race/000_About/002_04-discussion.htm on June 4, 2012.

Callison, D., & Preddy, L. (2006). *The blue book on Information Age inquiry, instruction, and literacy.* Santa Barbara, CA: Libraries Unlimited.

Carlson, C. (2000). Scientific literacy for all. *Science Teacher, 67*(3), 48–52.

Cassidy, J. (1989). Using graphic organizers to develop critical thinking. *Gifted Child Today, 12*(6), 34–36.

Cazden, C. B. (2001). *Classroom discourse: The language of teaching and learning* (2nd ed.). Portsmouth, NH: Heinemann.

Chall, J. S., Conard, S. S., & Harris, S. H. (1977). *An analysis of textbooks in relation to declining SAT scores.* Princeton, NJ: College Entrance Examination Board.

Chall, J. S., & Jacobs, V. A. (2003). Poor children's fourth-grade slump. *American Educator, 27*(1), 14–15, 44.

Churchill, W. (1940, May 13). *Blood, toil, tears and sweat.* Accessed at www.winstonchurchill .org/learn/speeches/speeches-of-winston-churchill/92-blood-toil-tears-and-sweat on October 29, 2012.

Cisneros, S. (1991). Salvador, late or early. In *Woman hollering creek, and other stories* (pp. 10–11). New York: Vintage Books.

Coker, D. (2007). Writing instruction for young children. In S. Graham, C. A. MacArthur, & J. Fitzgerald (Eds.), *Best practices in writing instruction* (pp. 101–118). New York: Guilford Press.

Cooper, S. (1973). *Dark is rising.* New York: Scholastic.

Council of Chief State School Officers. (2012). *The Common Core State Standards: Supporting districts and teachers with text complexity.* Washington, DC: Author. Accessed at https://ccsso.webex.com/mw0306ld/mywebex/default.do;jsessionid=KGRNPd6hnns hndyz9QLk5qthTtFvV6yPkQTTPg2XGvZ489Lm2pTQ!1006560109?nomenu=true &siteurl=ccsso&service=6&rnd=0.8424170944354614&main_url=https%3A %2F%2Fccsso.webex.com%2Fec0605ld%2Feventcenter%2Fprogram%2FprogramD etail.do%3FtheAction%3Ddetail%26siteurl%3Dccsso%26cProgViewID%3D22 on February 10, 2012.

Crain, W. C. (2000). *Theories of development: Concepts and applications* (4th ed.). Upper Saddle River, NJ: Prentice Hall.

Csikszentmihalyi, M. (1997). *Finding flow: The psychology of engagement with everyday life.* New York: Basic Books.

Csikszentmihalyi, M. (2000). *Beyond boredom and anxiety: Experiencing flow in work and play.* San Francisco: Jossey-Bass.

Darling-Hammond, L. (2010). *The flat world and education: How America's commitment to equity will determine our future.* New York: Teachers College Press.

Davidson, C. N. (2011). *Now you see it: How the brain science of attention will transform the way we live, work, and learn.* New York: Viking.

De La Paz, S., & Graham, S. (2002). Explicitly teaching strategies, skills, and knowledge: Writing instruction in middle school classrooms. *Journal of Educational Psychology, 94*(4), 687–698.

Dexter, D. D., & Hughes, C. A. (2011). Graphic organizers and students with learning disabilities: A meta-analysis. *Learning Disability Quarterly, 34*(1), 51–72.

Dickinson, E. (1997). The railway train. In T. H. Johnson (Ed.), *The complete poems of Emily Dickinson* (p. 585). Boston: Back Bay Books.

Donohoo, J. (2010). Learning how to learn: Cornell Notes as an example. *Journal of Adolescent & Adult Literacy, 54*(3), 224–227.

Dorn, L. J., & Soffos, C. (2001). *Scaffolding young writers: A writers' workshop approach.* Portland, ME: Stenhouse.

Douglass, F. (2005). *Narrative of the life of Frederick Douglass, an American slave.* New York: Barnes & Noble Classics.

DuFour, R., DuFour, R., & Eaker, R. (2008). *Revisiting professional learning communities at work: New insights for improving schools.* Bloomington, IN: Solution Tree Press.

DuFour, R., DuFour, R., Eaker, R., & Many, T. (2010). *Learning by doing: A handbook for professional learning communities at work* (2nd ed.). Bloomington, IN: Solution Tree Press.

DuFour, R., & Marzano, R. J. (2011). *Leaders of learning: How district, school, and classroom leaders improve student achievement.* Bloomington, IN: Solution Tree Press.

Duke, N. K., & Roberts, K. M. (2010). The genre-specific nature of reading comprehension. In D. Wyse, R. Andrews, & J. Hoffman (Eds.), *The Routledge international handbook of English, language and literacy teaching* (pp. 74–86). London: Routledge.

Eaker, R., DuFour, R., & DuFour, R. (2002). *Getting started: Reculturing schools to become professional learning communities.* Bloomington, IN: Solution Tree Press.

Elbow, P. (1981). *Writing with power: Techniques for mastering the writing process.* New York: Oxford University Press.

Faber, J. E., Morris, J. D., & Lieberman, M. G. (2000). The effect of note taking on ninth grade students' comprehension. *Reading Psychology, 21,* 257–270.

Fearn, L., & Farnan, N. (2001). *Interactions: Teaching writing and the language arts.* Boston: Houghton Mifflin.

Fisher, D., & Frey, N. (2007a). *Checking for understanding: Formative assessment techniques for your classroom.* Alexandria, VA: Association for Supervision and Curriculum Development.

Fisher, D., & Frey, N. (2007b). *Scaffolding writing instruction: A gradual release model.* New York: Scholastic.

Fisher, D., & Frey, N. (2010). *Enhancing RTI: How to ensure success with effective classroom instruction and intervention.* Alexandria, VA: Association for Supervision and Curriculum Development.

Fisher, D., & Frey, N. (2012). *Improving adolescent literacy: Content area strategies at work* (3rd ed.). Boston: Pearson.

Fisher, D., Frey, N., & Lapp, D. (2012). *Text complexity: Raising rigor in reading.* Newark, DE: International Reading Association.

Fisher, D., Frey, N., & Nelson, J. (2012). Literacy achievement through sustained professional development. *The Reading Teacher, 65*(8), 551–563.

Fleischman, J. (2002). *Phineas Gage: A gruesome but true story about brain science.* Boston: Houghton Mifflin.

Fletcher, L. (1948a). *Sorry, wrong number and the hitch-hiker.* New York: Dramatists Play Service.

Fletcher, L. (1948b). *Sorry, wrong number* [Radio broadcast]. Accessed at www.escape-suspense.com/2008/11/suspense---sorry-wrong-number.html on July 1, 2012.

Fletcher, L. (1980). *Sorry, wrong number and the hitch-hiker.* New York: Dramatists Play Service.

Frey, N., & Fisher, D. (2008). *Teaching visual literacy: Using comic books, graphic novels, anime, cartoons, and more to develop comprehension and thinking skills.* Thousand Oaks, CA: Corwin Press.

Frey, N., & Fisher, D. (2009). *Learning words inside & out: Vocabulary instruction that boosts achievement in all subject areas.* Portsmouth, NH: Heinemann.

Frey, N., & Fisher, D. (2010). Getting to quality: A meeting of the minds. *Principal Leadership, 11*(1), 68–70.

Frey, N., & Fisher, D. (2011). *The formative assessment action plan: Practical steps to more successful teaching and learning.* Alexandria, VA: Association for Supervision and Curriculum Development.

Frey, N., Fisher, D., & Berkin, A. (2008). *Good habits, great readers: Building the literacy community.* Upper Saddle River, NJ: Allyn & Bacon.

Frey, N., Fisher, D., & Everlove, S. (2009). *Productive group work: How to engage students, build teamwork, and promote understanding.* Alexandria, VA: Association for Supervision and Curriculum Development.

Frey, N., Fisher, D., & Gonzalez, A. (2010). *Literacy 2.0: Reading and writing in 21st century classrooms.* Bloomington, IN: Solution Tree Press.

Gaiman, N. (2008). *Stardust.* New York: HarperCollins.

Gamoran, A. (2007). *Standards-based reform and the poverty gap: Lessons from No Child Left Behind.* Washington, DC: Brookings Institution.

Ganske, L. (1981). Note-taking: A significant and integral part of learning environments. *Educational Communication and Technology: A Journal of Theory, Research, and Development, 29,* 155–175.

Gilbert, J., & Graham, S. (2010). Teaching writing to elementary students in grades 4–6: A national survey. *Elementary School Journal, 110*(4), 494–518.

Gladwell, M. (2010, October 4). Small change: Why the revolution will not be tweeted. *The New Yorker.* Accessed at www.newyorker.com/reporting/2010/10/04/101004fa_fact _gladwell?currentPage=all on June 4, 2012.

Goodrich, F., & Hackett, A. (2009). *The diary of Anne Frank.* New York: Dramatists Play Service.

Graham, S., & Perin, D. (2007). A meta-analysis of writing instruction for adolescents. *Journal of Educational Psychology, 99*(3), 445–476.

Graves, M. F., & Watts-Taffe, S. M. (2002). The place of word consciousness in a research-based vocabulary program. In A. E. Farstrup & S. J. Samuels (Eds.), *What research has to say about reading instruction* (3rd ed.; pp. 140–165). Newark, DE: International Reading Association.

Guillaume, A. M. (2004). *K–12 classroom teaching: A primer for new professionals* (2nd ed.). Upper Saddle River, NJ: Pearson/Merrill/Prentice Hall.

Haskins, J., Tate, E., Cox, C., & Wilkinson, B. (2002). *Black stars of the Harlem Renaissance.* New York: Wiley.

Hattie, J., & Timperley, H. (2007). The power of feedback. *Review of Educational Research, 77*(1), 81–112.

Hayes, D. P., Wolfer, L. T., & Wolfe, M. (1996). Sourcebook simplification and its relation to the decline in SAT-Verbal scores. *American Educational Research Journal, 33*(2), 489–508.

Hemingway, E. (1952). *The old man and the sea.* New York: Scribner.

Hemingway, E. (1996). *The old man and the sea.* New York: Scribner.

Hesse, K. (1997). *Out of the dust.* New York: Scholastic.

Hillocks, G. (2011). *Teaching argument writing grades 6–12: Supporting claims with relevant evidence and clear reasoning.* Portsmouth, NH: Heinemann.

Holland, J. (2011). *Unlikely friendships: 47 remarkable stories from the animal kingdom.* New York: Workman.

Horney, M. A., Anderson-Inman, L., Terrazas-Arellanes, F., Schulte, W., Mundorf, J., Wiseman, S., et al. (2009). Exploring the effects of digital note taking on student comprehension of science texts. *Journal of Special Education Technology, 24*(3), 45–61.

Howard, J. B. (1994). Addressing needs through strengths: Five instructional practices for use with gifted/learning disabled students. *Journal of Secondary Gifted Education, 5*(3), 23–34.

Hughes, L. (1990). *Selected poems of Langston Hughes.* New York: Vintage Books.

Individuals With Disabilities Education Act of 2004, 20 U.S.C. § 1400 (2004).

Individuals With Disabilities Education Improvement Act of 2004, Pub. L. No. 108-446, 118 Stat. 2647.

Jenkinson, E. B. (1988). Learning to write/writing to learn. *Phi Delta Kappan, 69,* 712–717.

Jeong, J., Gaffney, J. S., & Choi, J. (2010). Availability and use of informational texts in second-, third-, and fourth-grade classrooms. *Research in the Teaching of English, 44*(4), 435–456.

Joyce, B., & Showers, B. (1983). *Power in staff development through research on training.* Washington, DC: Association for Supervision and Curriculum Development.

Kanold, T., Briars, D., & Fennell, F. (2012). *What principals need to know about teaching and learning mathematics.* Bloomington, IN: Solution Tree Press.

Kirylo, J. D., & Millet, C. P. (2000). Graphic organizers: An integral component to facilitate comprehension during basal reading instruction. *Reading Improvement, 37*(4), 179–186.

Konigsberg, E. L. (2000). *Silent to the bone.* New York: Scholastic.

Kress, G. (1999). Genre and the changing contexts for English language arts. *Language Arts, 76*(6), 461–469.

Langer, J. (1986). *Children reading and writing: Structures and strategies.* Norwood, NJ: Ablex.

Lapp, D., Fisher, D., Flood, J., & Cabello, A. (2001). An integrated approach to the teaching and assessment of language arts. In S. R. Hurley & J. V. Tinajero (Eds.), *Literacy assessment of second language learners* (pp. 1–26). Boston: Allyn & Bacon.

Larson, K. (2006). *Hattie big sky.* New York: Delacorte Press.

Leithwood, K., McAdie, P., Bascia, N., & Rodrigue, A. (Eds.). (2006). *Teaching for deep understanding: What every educator should know.* Thousand Oaks, CA: Corwin Press.

Lennon, C., & Burdick, H. (2004). *The Lexile Framework as an approach for reading measurement and success: A white paper from the Lexile Framework for Reading.* Accessed at www.lexile.com/m/uploads/whitepapers/Lexile-Reading-Measurement -and-Success-0504_MetaMetricsWhitepaper.pdf on July 23, 2012.

Lezotte, L. W. (1991). *Correlates of effective schools: The first and second generation.* Okemos, MI: Effective Schools Products.

Longfellow, H. W. (2012). *Paul Revere's ride.* Accessed at www.theatlantic.com/magazine /archive/1861/01/paul-revere-s-ride/308349/# on October 29, 2012.

Lord, C. (2008). *Rules.* New York: Scholastic.

Malecki, C. K., & Jewell, J. (2003). Developmental, gender, and practical considerations in scoring curriculum-based measurement writing probes. *Psychology in the Schools, 40*(4), 379–390.

Manzo, A. (1969). ReQuest: A method for improving reading comprehension through reciprocal questioning. *Journal of Reading, 12*(3), 123–126.

McCutchen, D., Covill, A., Hoyne, S. H., & Mildes, K. (1994). Individual differences in writing: Implications of translating fluency. *Journal of Educational Psychology, 86*(2), 256–266.

McNeill, K. L. (2011). Elementary students' views of explanation, argumentation, and evidence, and their abilities to construct arguments over the school year. *Journal of Research in Science Teaching, 48*(7), 793–823.

Michaels, S., O'Connor, C., & Resnick, L. (2008). Deliberative discourse idealized and realized: Accountable talk in the classroom and in civic life. *Studies in Philosophy and Education, 27*(4), 283–297.

Miller, C. (1984). Genre as social action. *Quarterly Journal of Speech, 70*(2), 151–167.

Mitchell, D. (1996). Writing to learn across the curriculum and the English teacher. *English Journal, 85*(5), 93–97.

Moore, N., & MacArthur, C. (2012). The effects of being a reader and of observing readers on fifth-grade students' argumentative writing and revising. *Reading & Writing, 25*(6), 1449–1478.

Moss, B. (2003). *Exploring the literature of fact: Children's nonfiction trade books in the middle school classroom.* New York: Guilford Press.

Moss, B. (2004). Teaching expository text structures through informational trade book retellings. *The Reading Teacher, 57,* 710–718.

Moss, B. (2005). Making a case and a place for effective content area literacy instruction in the elementary grades. *The Reading Teacher, 59*(1), 46–55.

Moss, B., & Loh, V. (2010). *35 strategies for guiding readers through informational texts.* New York: Guilford Press.

Mueller, A., & Fleming, T. (2001). Cooperative learning: Listening to how children work at school. *Journal of Educational Research, 94,* 259–265.

Muschla, G. R. (1993). *Writing workshop survival kit.* West Nyack, NY: Center for Applied Research in Education.

Nagin, C. (2003). *Because writing matters: Improving student writing in our schools.* San Francisco: Jossey-Bass.

Nagy, N. E., & Anderson, R. C. (1984). How many words are there in printed school English? *Reading Research Quarterly, 19*(3), 304–330.

Nagy, W. E., & Scott, J. A. (2000). Vocabulary processes. In M. L. Kamil, P. B. Mosenthal, P. D. Pearson, & R. Barr (Eds.), *Handbook of reading research* (Vol. 3, pp. 269–284). Mahwah, NJ: Erlbaum.

National Education Goals Panel. (1998). *Ready schools.* Washington, DC: Author.

National Governors Association Center for Best Practices & Council of Chief State School Officers. (2010a). *Common Core State Standards for English language arts & literacy in history/social studies, science, and technical subjects.* Washington, DC: Authors. Accessed at www.corestandards.org/assets/CCSSI_ELA%20Standards.pdf on July 6, 2012.

National Governors Association Center for Best Practices & Council of Chief State School Officers. (2010b). *Common Core State Standards for English language arts & literacy in history/social studies, science, and technical subjects: Appendix A—Research supporting key elements of the standards.* Washington, DC: Authors. Accessed at www.corestandards.org/assets/Appendix_A.pdf on July 6, 2012.

National Governors Association Center for Best Practices & Council of Chief State School Officers. (2010c). *Common Core State Standards for English language arts & literacy in history/social studies, science, and technical subjects: Appendix B—Text exemplars and sample performance tasks.* Washington, DC: Authors. Accessed at www.corestandards .org/assets/Appendix_B.pdf on July 6, 2012.

National Governors Association Center for Best Practices & Council of Chief State School Officers. (2010d). *Common Core State Standards for English language arts & literacy in history/social studies, science, and technical subjects: Appendix C—Samples of student writing.* Washington, DC: Authors. Accessed at www.corestandards.org/assets /Appendix_C.pdf on July 6, 2012.

National Research Council. (1996). *National Science Education Standards.* Washington, DC: National Academies Press.

National Writing Project, & Nagin, C. (2003). *Because writing matters: Improving student writing in our schools.* San Francisco: Jossey-Bass.

Olsen, L. (2010). *Reparable harm: Fulfilling the unkept promise of educational opportunity for California's long term English learners.* Long Beach, CA: Californians Together. Accessed at www.californianstogether.org/docs/download.aspx?fileId=227 on July 6, 2012.

Padak, N., Bromley, K., Rasinski, T., & Newton, E. (2012). Vocabulary: Five common misconceptions. *Educational Leadership Online, 69.* Accessed at www.ascd.org /publications/educational-leadership/jun12/vol69/num09/Vocabulary@-Five -Common-Misconceptions.aspx on July 25, 2012.

Palincsar, A. S., & Brown, A. L. (1986). Interactive teaching to promote independent learning from text. *The Reading Teacher, 39*(8), 771–777.

Paris, S. G. (2005). Reinterpreting the development of reading skills. *Reading Research Quarterly, 40*(2), 184–202.

Pauk, W. (1974). *How to study in college.* Boston: Houghton Mifflin.

Pearson, P. D., & Gallagher, M. (1983). The instruction of reading comprehension. *Contemporary Educational Psychology, 8*(3), 317–344.

Petry, A. (1996). *Harriet Tubman: Conductor on the Underground Railroad.* New York: HarperCollins.

Pianta, R. C., Belsky, J., Houts, R., & Morrison, F. (2007). Opportunities to learn in America's elementary classrooms. *Science, 315,* 1795–1796.

Poe, E. A. (1844/1988). *Marginalia.* Charlottesville: University of Virginia Press.

Popham, W. J. (2008). *Transformative assessment.* Alexandria, VA: Association for Supervision and Curriculum Development.

Porter, A., McMaken, J., Hwang, J., & Yang, R. (2011). Common Core standards: The new U.S. intended curriculum. *Educational Researcher, 40*(3), 103–116.

Rasinski, T. (2011). The art and science of teaching reading fluency. In D. Lapp & D. Fisher (Eds.), *Handbook of research in teaching the English language arts* (3rd ed., pp. 238–246). New York: Routledge.

Richards, I. A. (1929). *Practical criticism.* London: Cambridge University Press.

Rudolph, J. (2010). *Whodunit.* Accessed at http://mysteryreadersinc.blogspot.com/2010/09 /whodunit.html on July 1, 2012.

Sacramento County Office of Education. (2012). *California's Common Core State Standards for English language arts, literacy in history/social studies, science, and technical subjects.* Sacramento, CA: Author. Accessed at www.scoe.net/castandards/agenda/2010 /ela_ccs_recommendations.pdf on August 31, 2012.

Salahu-Din, D., Persky, H., & Miller, J. (2008). *The nation's report card: Writing 2007.* Washington, DC: U.S. Department of Education, Institute of Education Sciences.

Sandburg, C. (1916/1994). *Chicago poems.* New York: Dover.

Santa, C. M, & Havens, L. T. (1995). *Project CRISS: Creating independence through student-owned strategies.* Dubuque, IA: Kendall/Hunt.

Schmar-Dobler, E. (2003). Reading on the Internet: The link between literacy and technology. *Journal of Adolescent and Adult Literacy, 47*(1), 80–85.

Short, K., Schroeder, J., Kauffman, G., & Kaser, S. (2004). Thoughts from the editors. *Language Arts, 81*(3), 183.

Simmons, J. (2003). Responders are taught, not born. *Journal of Adolescent and Adult Literacy, 46*(8), 684–693.

Soto, G. (1995). Oranges. In *Gary Soto: New and selected poems* (p. 42). San Francisco: Chronicle.

Steinbeck, J. (2002). *Travels with Charley: In search of America.* New York: Penguin Books.

Stevens, R. J., & Slavin, R. E. (1995). Effects of a cooperative learning approach in reading and writing on academically handicapped and nonhandicapped students. *Elementary School Journal, 95,* 241–262.

Sticht, T. G., & James, J. H. (1984). Listening and reading. In P. D. Pearson, R. Barr, M. L. Kamil, & P. Mosenthal (Eds.), *Handbook of reading research* (Vol. 1, pp. 293–317). White Plains, NY: Longman.

Stoll, L., Bolam, R., McMahon, A., Wallace, M., & Thomas, S. (2006). Professional learning communities: A review of the literature. *Journal of Educational Change, 7*(4), 221–258.

Taba, H. (1967). *Teacher's handbook for middle school social studies.* Reading, MA: Addison-Wesley.

Taylor, M. (1976). *Roll of thunder, hear my cry.* New York: Penguin Putnam.

Templeton, S., Johnston, F. R., Bear, D. R., & Invernizzi, M. R. (2008). *Words their way: Word sorts for derivational relations spellers* (2nd ed.). Upper Saddle River, NJ: Prentice Hall.

Templeton, S., Johnston, F. R., Bear, D. R., & Invernizzi, M. R. (2009). *Vocabulary their way: Word study for middle and secondary students.* Upper Saddle River, NJ: Prentice Hall.

Toulmin, S. (1958). *The uses of argument.* Cambridge, England: Cambridge University Press.

Troia, G. A., & Graham, S. (2002). The effectiveness of a highly explicit, teacher-directed strategy instruction routine: Changing the writing performance of students with learning disabilities. *Journal of Learning Disabilities, 35*(4), 290–305.

Turbill, J., & Bean, W. (2006). *Writing instruction K–6: Understanding process, purpose, audience.* Katonah, NY: Owen.

Vanneman, S. (2011). Note taking as easy as . . . ABC LOU. *School Library Monthly, 27*(4), 23–25.

Vasilyev, Y. (2003). The network of concepts and facts: Forming a system of conclusions through reflection. *Thinking Classroom, 4*(2), 29–33.

Vygotsky, L. S. (1978). *Mind in society: The development of higher psychological processes.* (M. Cole, V. John-Steiner, S. Scribner, & E. Souberman, Eds.). Cambridge, MA: Harvard University Press.

Weaver, C. (1996). *Teaching grammar in context.* Portsmouth, NH: Heinemann.

Wiliam, D. (2007). Content then process: Teacher learning communities in the service of formative assessment. In D. Reeves (Ed.), *Ahead of the curve: The power of assessment to transform teaching and learning* (pp. 183–204). Bloomington, IN: Solution Tree Press.

Wiliam, D. (2011). *Embedded formative assessment.* Bloomington, IN: Solution Tree Press.

Wilson, E. (2002). Literature and literacy in the social studies classroom: Strategies to enhance social studies instruction. *Southern Social Studies Journal, 28*(1), 45–57.

Wood, D. (1998). *How children think and learn* (2nd ed.). Oxford, England: Blackwell.

Wood, S. (Director). (1942). *The pride of the Yankees* [Motion picture]. United States: Goldwyn.

Yeh, S. S. (1998). Empowering education: Teaching argumentative writing to cultural minority middle-school students. *Research in the Teaching of English, 33*(1), 49–83.

Yep, L. (1975). *Dragonwings.* New York: HarperCollins.

Yovanoff, P., Duesbery, L., & Alonzo, J. (2005). Grade-level invariance of a theoretical causal structure predicting reading comprehension with vocabulary and oral language fluency. *Educational Measurement: Issues and Practices, 24*(3), 4–12.

INDEX

A

Abbott, R., 16
academic vocabulary and language, focus on, 18–20
Accelerated Reader, 31
action orientation, defined, 2
Adler, M., 84
anchor standards, defined, 20
anchor standards for Language strand, 111, 115
   Conventions of Standard English, 112, 116–121
   Knowledge of Language, 112–114, 121–122
   Vocabulary Acquisition and Use, 115, 122–128
   See also Speaking and Listening
anchor standards for Reading strand, 29
   Craft and Structure, 30
   Craft and Structure for informational texts, 49–52
   Craft and Structure for literature, 42–43
   Integration of Knowledge and Ideas, 30
   Integration of Knowledge and Ideas for informational texts, 52–54
   Integration of Knowledge and Ideas forliterature, 43–45
   Key Ideas and Details, 29–30
   Key Ideas and Details for informational texts, 47–49
   Key Ideas and Details for literature, 37–42
   Range of Reading and Level of Text Complexity, 30–36
   Range of Reading and Level of Text Complexity for informational texts, 54–57
   Range of Reading and Level of Text Complexity for literature, 46

anchor standards for Speaking and Listening strand, 99–102
   Comprehension and Collaboration, 99, 103, 105–108
   Presentation of Knowledge and Ideas, 99, 103–104, 108–111
anchor standards for Writing strand, 60–64
   Production and Distribution of Writing, 64, 78–81
   Range of Writing, 65–66, 87
   Research to Build and Present Knowledge, 65, 81–87
   Text Types and Purposes, 64, 70–78
anchor standards, role of, 20, 21
annotation marks, 84
argument, 70
argumentation, Toulmin's model of, 17
   argumentation skills, focus on, 17–18
assessments
   collaborative planning team, role of, 132
   example using, 149–152
   feed back (to build student agency), 140–141
   feed forward (inform instruction), 141
   feed up (establishing instructional purpose), 135–140
   formative and summative, 142–145
   mistakes made with struggling students, 146–149
   purpose of, 132–133
   relationship between instruction and, 133
   selecting, 142–145
   standards and role of, 132–135
ATOS, 31

B

Baugh, S., 3

Bayliss, V. A., 91
Beck, I., 19, 115
Beers, S., 17, 18
Berninger, V., 16
Bolam, R., 3
Britton, J., 129
Bullough, R., 3

C

Cabello, A., 132
Callison, D., 85
    CCSS (Common Core State Standards),
        assessments and, 132–135
CCSS ELA (Common Core State Standards
    for the English language arts)
    academic vocabulary and language, focus
        on, 18–20
    argumentation skills, focus on, 17–18
    development of, 12–13
    informational texts, focus on, 13–14
    purposes and organization of, 20–22
    for reading, 25–57
    reading and writing, focus on, 13–14
    speaking and listening, focus on, 15–17
    text complexity, focus on increasing, 14–15
    what is not covered by, 22–24
Choi, J.-O., 13
collaboration, role of, 1
collaborative reading, 105
collaborative teams
    assessment and use of, 132
    implementing Language standards and use
        of, 111–115
    implementing Reading standards and use
        of, 26–29
    implementing Speaking and Listening
        standards and use of, 98–99, 100–104
    implementing standards Writing standards
        and use of, 60
    meeting logistics/record tool, 10–12
    pacing guides and curricula, development
        of, 139–140
    protocol for determining text complexity,
        54–57
    questions for, 2, 10, 27, 37, 57, 60, 99, 105,
        116, 135
    role of, 3
collective inquiry, defined, 1
college and career readiness anchor stan-
    dards, 20, 21
Common Core State Standards. See CCSS
    (Common Core State Standards)

Common Core State Standards for the
    English language arts. See CCSS ELA
    (Common Core State Standards for
    the English language arts)
Comprehension and Collaboration, 99, 103,
    105–108
content
    not covered by CCSS ELA, 22
    purpose, 135
context clues, 52, 115, 125
continuous improvement, defined, 2
Conventions of Standard English, 112,
    116–121
Cornell note-taking system, 84–85
Council of Chief State School Officers
    (CCSSO), 4, 10, 12, 16, 23, 31, 70, 111
Craft and Structure, 30
    Informational Text standards, 49–52
    Literature standards, 42–43
Csikszentmihalyi, M., 89
curricula, problem with relying on prepack-
    aged, 148

D

Dale-Chall Readability Formula, 31
Darling-Hammond, L., 3
data decisions, problem with making, 149
Degrees of Reading Power, 31
De La Paz, S., 14
derivational constancy stage spelling, 120
discursive literacy, 17
discussions, 86
discussion web, 86
domains, defined, 21
Dorn, L. J., 116, 119
DuFour, R., 24

E

Eaker, R., 24
early writers, 67
Educational Testing Service, 31
Elbow, P., 93
emergent stage spelling, 120
emergent writers, 66–67
English learners, supports and expectations
    for, 23
error analysis, 143–145
essays, 76
evidence, use of, 18
experiences, creating, 88

F

Faber, J., 84
factual reports, 76
family involvement, 149
Farnan, N., 92, 119
Fearn, L., 92, 119
feedback
  actionable, 141
  forms of, 140–141
  peer, 80–81
  providing students with, 140–141
  specific, 141
  timely, 141
  understandable, 141
feed back (build student agency), 140–141
feed forward (inform instruction), 141
feed up (establishing instructional purpose),
    135–140
Fisher, D., 132
Flesch-Kincaid Grade-Level Index, 31
Flood, J., 132
flow, 89–90, 93
fluency
  power writing, 92–93
  writing, 90–92
formative assessments, 142–145
  See also assessments
fourth-grade slump, 13
freewriting, 93–94
Fry Readability Formula, 31

G

Gaffney, J., 13
generative writing, 116, 119
genre, type versus, 75
Gilbert, J., 65
goals, defined, 1
Graham, S., 14, 65–66
grammar, 67, 68, 77, 78, 111, 112, 116, 119
graphic organizers, 86–87
Graves, D., 88, 93
Guillaume, A. M., 142

H

Hattie, J., 135
Hillocks, G., 75
How to Read a Book (Adler and Van Doren),
    84
human captioning, 111

I

Individuals With Disabilities Education
    Improvement Act (2004), 23, 146
informational texts
  Craft and Structure, 49–52
  exemplars for, 47
  focus on, 13–14
  Integration of Knowledge and Ideas,
    52–54
  Key Ideas and Details, 47–49
  Range of Reading and Level of Text
    Complexity, 54–57
  Reading standards for, 46–57
informative and explanatory, 70, 76
initiate-respond-evaluate (IRE), 137
instruction
  feed back to build student agency, 140
  feed forward to inform, 141
  feed up by establishing instructional pur-
    pose, 135–140
  intervention versus, 146–148
  relationship between assessment and, 133
instructional purpose, establishing, 135–140
Integration of Knowledge and Ideas, 30
  informational texts standards, 52–54
  literature standards, 43–45
interactive writing, 88, 91
intervention, instruction versus, 146–148
interventionists, isolating teachers and, 148
intervention methods and materials, not cov-
    ered by CCSS ELA, 23

J

Jenkinson, E., 137–138
Jeong, J., 13
journal writing, 93
Joyce, B., 3

K

Key Ideas and Details, 29–30
  Informational Text standards, 47–49
  Literature standards, 37–42
Knowledge of Language, 112–114, 121–122
Kucan, L., 19

L

Language anchor standards, 111, 115
  Conventions of Standard English, 112,
    116–121
  Knowledge of Language, 112–114, 121–122
  Vocabulary Acquisition and Use, 115,
    122–128

See also Speaking and Listening
language purpose, 136
Lapp, D., 132
letter name stage spelling, 120
lexical dexterity, 19
Lexile, 31–32, 46
Lieberman, M., 84
linguistic literacy, 17
listening and speaking. *See* Speaking and
    Listening
list-group-label lesson, 126
literacy
    discursive, 17
    linguistic, 17
literacy teaching and learning, changes in
    focus on academic vocabulary and lan-
        guage, 18–20
    focus on increasing text complexity, 14–15
    focus on reading and writing to inform,
        persuade, and convey experiences,
        13–14
    focus on Speaking and Listening, 15–17
    focus on text-based evidence for argumen-
        tation, 17–18
literature
    Craft and Structure, 42–43
    exemplars for, 37
    Integration of Knowledge and Ideas,
        43–45
    Key Ideas and Details, 37–42
    Range of Reading and Level of Text
        Complexity, 46
    Reading standards for, 36–46
Loh, V., 126
looking inside a word (structure), 122, 125
looking outside a word (context and
    resources), 122, 125–128

M

Marzano, R., 3
McKeown, M., 19
McMahon, A., 3
MetaMetrics, 31, 46
mission, defined, 1
Morris, J., 84
Moss, B., 13, 126
Muschla, G. R., 91

N

Nagy, W., 17, 18
narratives, 14, 70, 76, 77–78
National Assessment of Educational Progress
    (NAEP), 13, 14

National Governors Association (NGA)
    Center for Best Practices, 4, 12, 16,
    23, 70, 111
NoteStar, 85
note taking, 81, 84–87

O

opinion, 70, 75–76
oral language activities, checking for under-
    standing using, 136

P

pacing guides and curricula, development of,
    139–140
paragraph frames, 110
partner reading, 105
Partnership for Assessment of Readiness for
    College and Careers (PARCC), 12,
    22, 134
Pearson Education, 31
Pearson Reading Maturity Scale, 31
peer feedback, 80–81
peer learning, power of, 104
Perin, D., 65–66
persuasive writing, 17–18, 70, 75–76
Pianta, R., 16
power writing, 92–93
Preddy, L., 85
Presentation of Knowledge and Ideas, 99,
    103–104, 108–111
Production and Distribution of Writing, 64,
    78–81
professional development, 3
professional learning communities (PLCs)
    characteristics of, 1–2
    common issues for, 2
    effectiveness of, 3
    questions, 2
projects and performances, checking for
    understanding using, 139

Q

Questar, 31
questioning
    checking for understanding using, 137
    reciprocal, 137
questions, types for students
    author's purpose, 40
    example of, 40–42
    general understanding, 39
    inferencing, 40
    key detail, 39

opinions, arguments, and intertextual connections, 40
  progression of text-dependent, 39
  vocabulary and text structure, 39–40

R

Race to the Top, 134
RAFT writing prompt, 139
Range of Reading and Level of Text Complexity, 30–36
  Informational Text standards, 54–57
  Literature standards, 46
Range of Writing, 65–66, 87
read-alouds, 36
reading
  close-reading approach, 50–51
  collaborative, 105
  informational texts, focus on, 13–14
  partner, 105
  speaking and listening, focus on, 15–17
  text complexity, focus on increasing, 14–15
reading, implementing standards for
  anchor standards, 29–36
  collaborative planning team, example of, 26–29
  for informational texts, 46–57
  for literature, 36–46
Reading anchor standards
  Craft and Structure, 30
  Craft and Structure for informational texts, 49–52
  Craft and Structure for literature, 42–43
  Integration of Knowledge and Ideas, 30
  Integration of Knowledge and Ideas for informational texts, 52–54
  Integration of Knowledge and Ideas for literature, 43–45
  Key Ideas and Details, 29–30
  Key Ideas and Details for informational texts, 47–49
  Key Ideas and Details for literature, 37–42
  Range of Reading and Level of Text Complexity, 30–36
  Range of Reading and Level of Text Complexity for informational texts, 54–57
  Range of Reading and Level of Text Complexity for literature, 46
reciprocal questioning, 137
reciprocal teaching, 48–49, 105
ReQuest, 137

Research to Build and Present Knowledge, 65, 81–87
resources
  dictionaries, 125
  glossaries, 125
  vocabulary words to teach, selecting, 125–126
response to intervention (RTI), 23, 146–149
results, defined, 2

S

self-extending writers, 67, 68–69
sentence combining, 121–122
Showers, B., 3
silo effect, 29
Smarter Balanced Assessment Consortium (SBAC), 12, 22, 134
social purpose, 136
Soffos, C., 116, 119
Source Rater, 31
Speaking and Listening
  focus on, 15–17
  peer learning, power of, 104
Speaking and Listening, implementing standards for
  anchor standards, 99–104
  collaborative planning team, example of, 98–99, 100–102
Speaking and Listening anchors, 99–102
  Comprehension and Collaboration, 99, 103, 105–108
  Presentation of Knowledge and Ideas, 99, 103–104, 108–111
spelling, 120–121
staircase effect, 15, 31
Stoll, L., 3
strands, 21, 29
students who struggle
  assessments and mistakes made with, 146–149
  supports and expectations for, 24
students with special needs, supports and expectations for, 23
summative assessments, 142–145
  See also assessments
syllable juncture stage spelling, 120

T

tests, checking for understanding using, 139
text, creating, 87–88
text complexity
  anchor standard, 30–36

collaborative team protocol for determining, 54–57
defined, 14
focus on increasing, 14–15
Informational Text standards, 54–57
Literature standards, 46
qualitative measures, 31, 32, 33–35
quantitative measures, 31–32
reader and task issues, 31, 36
Text Types and Purposes, 64, 70–78
Thomas, S., 3
Timperley, H., 135
Toulmin, S., 17
transitional writers, 67, 68
type, genre versus, 75

U

understanding, checking for, 136–139
U.S. Department of Education, 134

V

values, defined, 1
Van Doren, C., 84
Vanneman, S., 84
vision, defined, 1
Vocabulary Acquisition and Use, 115, 122–128
    looking inside a word (structure), 122, 125
    looking outside a word (context and resources), 122, 125–128
vocabulary and language, focus on academic, 18–20
vocabulary words to teach, selecting
    cognitive load, 128
    conceptual value, 127–128
    contextual analysis, 128
    repeatability, 128
    structural analysis, 128
    transportability, 128
Vygotsky, L., 104

W

Walker, N., 91
Wallace, M., 3
web pages, note-taking strategies for, 85
Wiliam, D., 134
within word pattern stage spelling, 120
words
    domain-specific (tier three), 19
    everyday (tier one), 19
    general academic (tier two), 19
    looking inside a word (structure), 122, 125

looking outside a word (context and resources), 122, 125–128
Vocabulary Acquisition and Use, 115, 122–128
    See also vocabulary words to teach, selecting
writers
    characteristics of, 66–67
    early, 67
    emergent, 66–67
    self-extending, 67, 68–69
    transitional, 67, 68
writing
    argumentation skills, focus on, 17–18
    checking for understanding using, 137–139
    dimensions, 88–89
    examples of student, 69–70
    flow, 89–90, 93
    fluency, 90–92
    free, 93–94
    generative, 116, 119
    informational texts, focus on, 13–14
    informative and explanatory, 70, 76
    journal, 93
    maturity signs, 91–92
    narratives, 14, 70, 76, 77–78
    persuasive, 17–18, 70, 75–76
    planning, 90
    power, 92–93
    process, 87–90
    reviewing, 91
    speaking and listening, focus on, 15–17
    translating, 90
writing, implementing standards for
    anchor standards, 60–66
    collaborative planning team, example of, 60
Writing anchor standards, 60–64
    Production and Distribution of Writing, 64, 78–81
    Range of Writing, 65–66, 87
    Research to Build and Present Knowledge, 65, 81–87
    Text Types and Purposes, 64, 70–78

Y

Yeh, S., 18

Z

zone of proximal development, 104

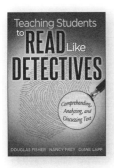

Teaching Students to Read Like Detectives
Douglas Fisher, Nancy Frey, and Diane Lapp
Prompt students to become the sophisticated readers, writers, and thinkers they need to be to achieve higher learning. Explore the important relationship between text, learner, and learning, and gain an array of methods to establish critical literacy in a discussion-based and reflective classroom.
BKF499

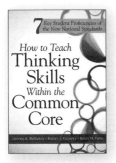

How to Teach Thinking Skills Within the Common Core
James A. Bellanca, Robin J. Fogarty, and Brian M. Pete
Empower your students to thrive across the curriculum. Packed with examples and tools, this practical guide prepares teachers across all grade levels and content areas to teach the most critical cognitive skills from the Common Core State Standards.
BKF576

20 Literacy Strategies to Meet the Common Core
Elaine K. McEwan-Adkins and Allyson J. Burnett
With the advent of the Common Core State Standards, some secondary teachers are scrambling for what to do and how to do it. This book provides twenty research-based strategies designed to help students meet those standards and become expert readers.
BKF588

Common Core Mathematics in a PLC at Work™ Series
Edited by Timothy D. Kanold
These teacher guides illustrate how to sustain successful implementation of the Common Core State Standards for Mathematics. Discover what students should learn and how they should learn it at each grade level. Comprehensive and research-affirmed analysis tools and strategies will help you and your collaborative team develop and assess student demonstrations of deep conceptual understanding *and* procedural fluency.
Joint Publications With the National Council of Teachers of Mathematics
BKF566, BKF568, BKF574, BKF561, BKF559

Solution Tree | Press
a division of
Solution Tree

Visit solution-tree.com or call 800.733.6786 to order.

Solution Tree

Solution Tree's mission is to advance the work of our authors. By working with the best researchers and educators worldwide, we strive to be the premier provider of innovative publishing, in-demand events, and inspired professional development designed to transform education to ensure that all students learn.

The mission of the International Reading Association is to promote reading by continuously advancing the quality of literacy instruction and research worldwide.